HOW TO COOK
WITHOUT
RECIPES

For my godson Merlin,
as a grateful mark of his miraculous escape
from death in Afghanistan.

First published in the United Kingdom in 2008 by
Portico Books
10 Southcombe Street
London
W14 0RA

An imprint of Anova Books Company Ltd

ISBN 9781906032234

A CIP catalogue record for this book is available from the British Library.

10 9 8 7 6 5 4 3 2 1

Illustrations by Lotte Oldfield (lotteoldfield.com)

Printed and bound by CPI Mackays, Chatham, Kent, ME5 8TD.

This book can be ordered direct from the publisher.
Contact the marketing department, but try your bookshop first.

www.anovabooks.com

GLYNN CHRISTIAN

HOW TO COOK WITHOUT RECIPES

CONTENTS

ACKNOWLEDGEMENTS

Ben Mason is owed any success this book has; he was the one who believed.

I was helped with tricky matters of taste by Ian Jarmarkier of Sainsbury's Food and Innovation Centre, by Professor Tim Jacob of the School of Biosciences, Cardiff University, and by my old schoolmate Professor Laurie Melton, now Director of Food Science at Auckland University. Books for Cooks were wonderfully helpful and my operatic neighbour Constance Novis produced a harmonious plot to keep me well fed for the entire run.

Otherwise, it's all my fault.

INTRODUCTION

Everyone who ever ate something they liked can cook.

This book tells you how you can create fabulous food without robotically following someone else's recipes. Just as authors should have done when they wrote all those cookbooks you never use, just like the TV chefs of *Ready Steady Cook* – just like me. All you have to do is to follow Flavour Trails.

Inspiration and guarantees are all around. If you enjoy the combinations in a sandwich you buy for lunch it's because there is a discernible Flavour Trail linking the ingredients together. That means the same combination can confidently be deconstructed and then served as a salad. The buttery, flaky pastry with strawberry mousse and chocolate sauce you scoffed at tea time is successful because chocolate and strawberries have an affinity with each other and with the pastry, making a reliably delicious Flavour Trail whichever way you journey between those ingredients. So you can reconstruct the ingredients in a different way to create a stunner of a pudding, perhaps fresh strawberries with a chocolate sauce and crisp squares of filo pastry. Or scoops of chocolate mousse and strawberry ice cream with butter-shortbread biscuits. Once your palate can identify Flavour Trails of ingredients that are complementary or have a natural affinity you are ready and able to create without using recipes. So, this is a cookbook for everyone who eats . . . and that must mean you.

If you are a hobby cook, a culinary star only at weekends and carefully chosen festivities, the book will fast-track you to greater success, demystifying the secrets of what goes with what, and why. The experienced cook will find greater kitchen power through greater appreciation of why and how to cook for the palate rather than the plate. And I fully expect the professional and those who already confidently cook without recipes to also find comfort and joy, for what is more gratifying than to read that what is mystique to another is what you've been doing right all along.

Good cookery, what Robert Carrier called 'giving people something nice to eat', is the practice of an art on a firm foundation of science; and like any artist or a composer, the firmer your feet are planted in science the wider will be the artistic horizons to which you can aspire. Painters need to understand the composition of their paints and canvases to get the right effects, and composers have to know all the instruments of an orchestra before they can pick exactly the right satisfying musical combination.

Sometimes, only the science of cookery has been learned laboriously by those who have no sense of its art; this is how we get bad home economists. Others have art that is only artifice because they don't know the science behind cookery, not even how the mouth tastes what; they are the ones who cook for the appearance of the plate rather than to gratify the palate.

The distinction between the art and the science of cookery is that one changes constantly but the other does not. The art of cookery is what enables the creation of something original – original to you anyway. But even the tiniest leap of imagination in cookery will only work if it is underpinned by scientific principles, an understanding of what happens when you do a certain thing, add that to this or this to that. These scientific principles used to be what was learned – albeit absorbed unconsciously – by watching mothers and others cook in the family kitchen, and by cooking a favourite dish again and again. Both arts and sciences come with aphorisms that express a general truth, and perhaps the best of these in cookery is:

You learn to cook by cooking the same thing a hundred times, not by cooking a hundred things once.

So, will you have to learn a lot of other stuff, too? Yep. Until you know something of the science of cookery – and of eating – you're hardly ready to be totally arty-farty; but relax, because you've got dozens of recipes stored in your mind already. That favourite sandwich, the salad you enjoy best, the fruit-and-ice-cream mixture you always choose – these are all recipes and can all be used in other ways. They each have a Flavour Trail between the ingredients you can follow again and again.

If you've ever eaten something you've liked, you can cook. In fact, you can cook without recipes.

THE INSULTS OF MODERN RECIPES

Following a recipe exactly, even one of your own, is a guarantee of bad food.

The modern recipe with exact amounts of ingredients is commonly held by Americans to have been invented early in the twentieth century, by one of their women's magazines; *Good Housekeeping* gets most votes. Well, they would say that, and maybe American writers were the first to be pernickety and start measuring by the eighth-teaspoon, and putting ingredients in an ordered, vertical list, but recipes gave proportions long before that; how detailed they were depended on the author and at whom their books were aimed.

Most early recipes, or receipts, were not for publication but were the personal notes of the cooks and chefs who passed through a particular kitchen. I have copies of books from a disappeared Cumbrian house called Netherhall, whence came Fletcher Christian's grandmother Mary Senhouse. The handwriting and early forms of shorthand show the books record recipes from a span of perhaps more than a hundred years, and because they were meant as an *aide-mémoire* rather than exhaustive instructions, the recipe 'To stue a chicken' takes but a few lines to tell you how to stuff a boned but not split chicken with sweetbreads, morels and bacon, to spice it with nutmeg and mace, to braise it with stock and then to serve with a cream sauce pointed with lemon; when I reproduced this reminder of my many-times-great-grandmother in a Sainsbury's book of *The Cookery of the British Isles*, it took me a couple of pages.

Few of today's cooks – or cookery editors – understand that a written recipe can be no more than a record of what happened with those ingredients in that kitchen, with that humidity and cooked by that person with that sort of palate. It's nothing more than a record; it's not an infallible list of instructions to be copied exactly. In fact, following a recipe exactly is perhaps the cause of more bad food than anything else. You should cook according to the ingredients you have, using a printed recipe as a guide if you must, but using your eyes, experience and palate to judge what leads to success. To suggest anything else is plain mischievous and not a little insulting to a reader's intelligence, and usually promoted by someone hoping to keep their job in cookery-book publishing.

Thus if your cinnamon is a month old you might need twice as much to get the same effect as the recipe writer experienced. But what if the recipe writer used stale cinnamon (Oh yes, they might have!)? In this case, using fresh in the recipe might take it over the top. You are *always* in charge, or should be, because you know your ingredients and what you like. Who made it a law you need cinnamon in that recipe anyway?

For instance, a baked apple is delicious cooked just with a little water in the dish for basting and a dab of butter, with or without sugar of some colour. Using cider instead of water, or choosing white wine, or honey and water, or quince jelly dissolved in water, all give different results, but not necessarily better ones. Success depends as much if not more on the apple variety you have chosen to bake, for each variety gives a different colour and texture when baked, regardless of what you might add. Equally, cinnamon might or might not be used; it could be ground or in whole or broken cinnamon quills, but it certainly isn't a necessity and if you leave it out you won't be baked in hell as punishment.

You can knock on the head the notion that spices were used in the past to hide the taste of rotten meat. Why should meat from the eighteenth, seventeenth or sixteenth century (or earlier) have been rotten? Even London had farms at its very walls and abattoirs within its milestones. Cows grazed in its parks if you wanted their milk or cream, in St James's Park you could milk directly into sweetened wine, so the force of the milk made a rich foaming syllabub. Geese were certainly raised rather more in, say, Norfolk than Kent, but they were then walked to market, with their feet protected by a coating of tar, and slaughtered only when and where they were wanted. Fish, too, was either salted and safe, or especially fresh, perhaps much fresher than today. There were great holding tanks for live fish at Billingsgate on the Thames and even laws allowing mackerel to be sold on Sunday, because like all oily fish they do not last well and might have gone off by Monday.

For many centuries the spicing of English cookery was based on the customs of the Eastern Mediterranean, and the kitchens of the Turkish Ottomans and the Persian court. Elegant, sensual, judged and delicious, you taste very much the same things when you eat the foods of Morocco today. It is thought the confusion about spicing and rotten meat arose because the first to look at these old dishes in modern times were historians and not cooks; they saw long lists of spices, without amounts always being specified, and immediately thought the result would be like bad curries. Dullards.

Collections of recipes in England date back to late fourteenth century, and in those times the cookery of the upper classes at least unashamedly still reflected the voluptuous enjoyment of the ingredients that had come back with the Crusaders: a whole baked fish stuffed with dates swollen with ground almonds, rice and cinnamon was a great favourite and, although disappeared from English tables, it is still a popular dish of Fez in Morocco, where many specialities are accurate echoes of what was once considered English cookery.

Perhaps the earliest cookery book with food rather more like we'd expect to eat is E. Smith's *Compleat Housewife* (1736). And as bread is one of the few foods common to all classes throughout history, I thought I might look to see what Smith and succeeding authors suggested for its use when stale. Here's a recipe from that book:

TO MAKE A BROWN-BREAD PUDDING

Take half-a-pound of brown bread, and double the weight of it in beef-suet; a quarter pint of cream, the blood of a fowl, a whole nutmeg, some cinnamon, a spoonful of sugar, six yolks of eggs, three whites; mix it all well together, and boil it in a wooden dish two hours. Serve it with sack and sugar, and butter melted.

Very nutritious, I'm sure, and it doesn't take long to work out how you would put it together: is anyone stupid enough to think you used the nutmeg whole and not grated? Sack was a sort of sherry, and heating it with sugar (very expensive at the time) and serving with melted butter was a very common finish to sweet dishes. It's only the cinnamon that is not specified exactly, because you need to know what your cinnamon is like, or how much you like it, before you add any, if at all.

It is a *canard* that American cookbooks are not relevant to the rest of the world. Once you find an inestimable copy of *The Best of Shaker Cooking* (Collier Books, New York, 1970) and perhaps track down *James Beard's American Cookery* (Little, Brown and Co, Boston, 1970), and safely ignore Julia Childs because she is so stubbornly Francophile, then you should head straight for *The Joy of Cooking*, by Irma Rombauer, first published by Bobbs-Merrill in

1975. It's a truly comprehensive book with fantastic technique and ingredient information, great clarity and every recipe imaginable plus many new to you, which will have you rushing to the kitchen – there are over 4,500! It's now available in the UK, too. Bread puddings of many kinds, seemingly so British, and just a mush of bread and milk and eggs, were a favourite of the thrifty Shaker communities of the United States, established in the 1790s based on the beliefs of Mother Ann Lee, who came from Manchester. *The Best of Shaker Cooking* is one of my most inspiring cookery books. It not only gives a basic bread pudding recipe from the Hancock Shaker village but also publishes variations from the kitchens of other communities; some include candied fruits and nuts, some revive recipes from The Old Country, others add tart red cherries and rose-water or diced apple with rose-water (both delicious new ways), or make chocolate-coffee bread pudding and maple-sugar bread pudding.

Today in Britain bread pudding has a rather down-market image, but when at its best and made with generous handfuls of raisins and spice and sugar it is superb – if you can find it.

So, let's continue with recipes for the more easily found bread and butter puddings, not slushy custards as is anything called a pudding in the US, but a baked dish of buttered bread in an egg custard and, whether visibly a-tremble and delicate, or robustly set and studded with currants or raisins or sultanas, perhaps the most fundamental comfort food of all.

BREAD AND BUTTER PUDDING

Slice bread spread with butter, and lay it in a dish with
currants between each layer; add sliced citron or lemon, if
to be very nice. Pour over an unboiled custard of milk,
two or three eggs, a few pimentos, and a very little
ratafia, two hours at least before it is baked and lade it
over to soak the bread. A paste around the edge makes all
puddings better, but is not necessary.

A New System of Domestic Cookery (John Murray, 1829, revised edition)

This requires a bit of effort to translate but any cook of the time would have known it takes four eggs to set a pint of milk nicely; it still does. But with so much bread to help the set, you can get away with perhaps only half that quantity; thus the milk suggested here is a pint to a pint and a half. The sliced citron or lemon would have meant candied peel. Pimento is the old name for allspice, which would have been ground, and ratafia is an alcohol made by mixing fresh grape juice with a brandy, which leavens the rawness of the spirit with a raisin-like succulence. Ratafia is still made and served in Champagne; Pineau de Charentes is another survivor, made with grape juice and lesser brandy distilled from grapes harvested in the same vineyards used for Cognac. Unboiled custard simply means a previously uncooked mix of milk and eggs. It is curious to find that although usually a writer of good straightforward recipes, TV cook Ainsley Harriot's recipe for bread and butter pudding goes through the complicated ritual of cooking and thickening the egg custard first, which can go seriously wrong; anyone for scrambled eggs? Anyway, it takes far longer for thickened custard to penetrate the bread and butter to make the correct texture, so it's counterproductive every which way. 'What *is* he like?' as Ainsley would ask.

Putting all the ingredients in together was the method suggested by Alexis Soyer, once chef of London's august Reform Club, but who also wrote extensively for the simpler household and invented the British army's portable field kitchen, first seen in the Crimean War. Soyer's genuine understanding of home kitchens makes this a simple practical recipe, but I can't believe it would work without first standing to soak and plump.

BREAD PUDDING

*An economical one when eggs are dear. Cut some bread
and butter very thin, place it in a pie dish as lightly as
possible, till three-parts full; break into a basin one egg,
add two teaspoonfuls of flour, three of brown sugar; mix*

all well together, add to it by degrees a pint of milk, a
little salt; pour over the bread; bake in oven; it will take
half an hour; this will make a nice size pudding for
four or five persons.

Alexis Soyer, *The Shilling Cookery for the People* (**Routledge, 1855**)

Note the elegant extra hint of filling the pie dish 'as lightly as possible'. Because such puddings were so ingrained in British cooks and those in many Commonwealth countries – until well after the Second World War, this recipe would have caused few problems of comprehension for at least a hundred years from the time it was published; everyone knew you baked anything like an egg custard at less than 180C/350F or it might split into curds and watery whey. It is galling to modern cookery writers, even those on television, that this 1855 edition took the book's print run to 120,000!

Mrs Beeton's contribution to recipe writing was to systemise recipes, by not only extracting the ingredients to start the recipe but also telling you how long it would take to prepare and cook, how much it might cost and how many it would serve, all edicts familiar to cookery editors today. In the edition that took her to over 401,000 books sold (!) she gives this:

BAKED BREAD AND BUTTER PUDDING

Ingredients – 9 thin slices of bread and butter, 1½ pints
of milk, 4 eggs, sugar to taste, ½lb currants, flavouring of
vanilla, grated lemon peel or nutmeg. Cut 9 slices of
bread and butter not very thick, and put them into a pie-
dish, with currants between each layer and on the top.
Sweeten and flavour the milk, either by infusing a little
lemon-peel in it, or by adding a few drops of essence of
vanilla; well whisk the eggs and stir these into the milk.
Strain this over the bread and butter and bake in a mod-
erate oven for 1 hour, or rather longer. The pudding may
be very much enriched by adding cream, candied peel or

more eggs than stated above. It should not be turned out,
but sent to the table in the pie-dish, and is better for being
made about 2 hours before it is baked.

Time: 1 hour or rather longer; Average cost, 9d; Sufficient for 6
or 7 persons; Seasonable at any time
Mrs Beeton, *Household Management* (**Ward Lock, 1861**)

If you look carefully, Mrs Beeton has only rewritten the 1829 recipe from *Domestic Cookery*, a 'refreshment' of someone else's work, still irritatingly familiar to food writers today.

In 1902 another of my most treasured cookery books was re-published. *The Complete Indian Housekeeper and Cook,* by Grace Gardiner and Flora Anne Steel (London: William Heinemann, 1902) was a guide for English women who went out to run a household in Raj India, their own or others. Gardiner and Steel had given a lot of thought to how different conditions were in India and, like women in the colonies of New Zealand, Australia and the rest, knew they would sometimes be without trustworthy British kitchen equipment: scales, for instance, and weights in avoirdupois increments and cooks who spoke the same language. Most colonials, including those of the US, resorted to measuring by the cup, no bad thing as long as you used the same cup throughout – a small cup was a teacup, the bigger one a breakfast cup. The problem we still have today is the English usually used the breakfast cup of an imperial half-pint or ten fluid ounces, but the US cup, based on the smaller teacup, was only eight fluid ounces, but still called a half-pint. The US bottle measure of a fifth is actually a quart in US measurement but a fifth of an imperial gallon of eight pints. No, I can't begin to imagine why they didn't call it a quart in their own country.

In Australia and New Zealand both cups were used and there is still some confusion when translating their recipes about which is meant, for many do not know there are two 'cups'. Gardiner and Steel hedged their bets and all their recipes are in 'units', a system easily transferred to whatever containers the resident Indian cooks generally used, something it was perhaps best not to know. Here's a recipe quite unsuitable for India, one would have thought, but which is eminently followable:

SCOTCH BROTH

Take 32 units of neck of mutton and joint. Parboil 2 units of pearl barley in 80 units of water. Add the meat, 6 units of turnips cut into dice, 2 units of onions sliced, a good handful of kale and some parsley. Season with salt and pepper and simmer gently for four hours. Etc.

It seems a very good system and you can easily work out how to make more, or less.

Mrs Beeton and her predecessors were writing for and about the management of large and small households with a cook, and that was pretty much the majority of everyone but the working class – who were the cooks. Then, and well into the twentieth century, there was quite another type of cooking, the lofty, complicated and indecently rich *haute cuisine*, based at first in restaurants opened by the desperate ex-chefs of guillotined aristocrats after France's 1789 revolution. Look carefully and much of it was essentially rather plain cooking masked with complex finishing sauces and, especially, with convoluted garnishes and ragouts or, if it came at the end of the meal, complicated with patterns and pipings that did little for flavour but much for the competitiveness of one's table.

Haute cuisine always came in French, required battalions of staff, a determined digestion, and troves of gilded porcelain for dining rooms as overdecorated as their guests. It belonged in hotel restaurants, in the greatest town and country houses, in palaces and wherever the roly-poly Prince of Wales and his Danish Princess Alexandra might be entertained. Buckingham Palace is thought to be the last kitchen in Britain where everything is still done in French.

Charles Francatelli was chef to Queen Victoria for many years and such *haute cuisine* books as *Francatelli's Modern Cook* (London: Richard Bentley, 1862, 14th edition) were very much for such kitchens only. I opened this book casually to page 107, to find a whole chapter devoted to Italian soups.

Semolina Soup a la Pisane – presumably a soup named for the city of Pisa – goes like this:

SEMOLINA SOUP A LA PISANE

Bone and braise two calf's feet and having pressed them
between two dishes, cut them into round pieces the size of
a shilling, with a tin cutter; place these in a stewpan
together with three dozen small quenelles a la Xavier
(pheasant, I think) and a glass of Madeira: allow them to
simmer on the fire for five minutes, and add them to . . .
soup . . . but omitting the fillets of larks.

Given previously, the soup is semolina boiled in game stock and finished with Madeira, Parmesan cheese, cream and egg yolks.

A most sustaining supper dish, you will agree, even without the fillets of larks, but at the time only one of seven or more dinner courses expected. The staff, *batterie* and skills needed just for this soup are unimaginable today. Such food was taken to its greatest heights by the finessing made possible by the introduction of controllable gas hobs and ovens in the latter part of the nineteenth century. Perhaps the brevity of the recipe was to protect the mystique of *haute cuisine*?

Marcel X Boulestin was an early twentieth-century French restaurateur in London who drew new boundaries by offering rather more bourgeois cooking in his establishment, and by writing books aimed at the home cook. In *What Shall We Have Today?* (Heinemann, 1931) he still gives every recipe a French name and lists very few quantities; his recipe for beetroot cooked in milk would today drive many a cook mad, but his books were huge bestsellers at the time.

BETTERAVES AU LAIT

Cook some beetroot in the oven in the ordinary way, peel
them, cut them in slices and put them into a saucepan
with a good piece of butter, salt and pepper, parsley and
chervil finely chopped. Cook slowly about a quarter of an
hour, add a pinch of flour, stir well, then add a glass of
milk, bring to the boil, cook another ten minutes, stirring
often, add a little piece of butter at the last minute. The
sauce should be well reduced and highly seasoned.

Elizabeth David is commonly said, far too often, never to give quantities in her many books, but this tired rehearsal is by people who haven't opened one for years. Her style fools the idle because she doesn't extract and list ingredients. All you need to know is there, in her inimitable neat, cursive way, this time including why you leave the beetroot in butter for a while:

BEETROOT WITH CREAM SAUCE

Boil some small young beetroots. Peel and put them into a
pan with a little butter. When they are thoroughly hot
pour over them a teaspoonful of vinegar and then 2oz
(for 1lb) of boiling cream.

Elizabeth David, *Summer Cooking* **(The Cookery Book Club, 1955)**

The cream would have to be double cream, thicker than any other liquid to which it was being added, or it would curdle. But what if this is the first time you have cooked beetroot and don't realise how long it will take? Or don't know what sort of vinegar is best or whether you need more or less of it? Better to learn from personal experience and remember than to rely on a book to re-create what happened when someone else, with a different palate from yours, was cooking somewhere else.

In 1954, when Elizabeth David was writing, *The Alice B. Toklas Cook Book* was published in the USA, by Doubleday-Anchor. The tiny partner of larger-than-life poet/author Gertrude Stein, Alice differs from other cookery writers largely by giving plenty of her own rather than collected recipes. Her book is luscious, immediate and gossipy, and especially delicious for being so acid and intimate. Of beetroot she says:

PUREE OF BEETROOT

As for beetroots, their excuse for being is the fine colour they add to pale dishes. As a vegetable this recipe combines the decorative with the tasty.

Bake beetroot in the oven until quite soft, peel and mash through a strainer with a potato masher, add one-third their volume of thick cream sauce. Place over low heat in a casserole, add salt and pepper. When about to boil, add 1 tablespoon butter cut in small pieces to a cup of puree. Do not allow to boil, do not stir but tip casserole in all directions, Serve in a mound on a preheated dish. Sprinkle with chopped parsley, or serve as a border around veal or pork roast.

That's quite enough information, without lists or numbered steps, for anyone to cook it. Well, I suppose you need to know how to make a thick cream sauce – but you have a microwave, don't you?

Today recipe writing is, well, it's whatever a cookery editor thinks will make his or her mark (not the writer's mark, note) and so being 'different' has a cachet within publishing. The emphasis is on brevity, perhaps because it's true that people buy cookery books and then use only one or two of the recipes. Or do they use only two or three because the recipes aren't helpful enough? I've even had photographers' assistants rewriting recipes so the photographs were closer to the 'concept' of the book; that's their concept, not mine, you'll note. Certainly much recipe writing has been designed for typographical effect rather than for practicality. And then there are recipes written by numbers, as though it were after all a science rather than something enjoyable to do, giving pleasure both to those who cook and to those who eat.

So should you use recipes at all?

Of course you should, and some Flavour Trail basics are included in this book, with more on www.glynnchristian.com. They are templates for you to use as reference, as is any other recipe. It is crazy to reinvent a recipe for carrot soup or a beef stew made with beer or a gooseberry and elderflower fool if you've never cooked such before. But treat recipes only as *aides-memoire* or as starting points and let your ingredients dictate the finer dictums, according to the state they are in, the flavour preferences of your palate or those of your guests. Following a recipe exactly – even one of your own – is a guarantee of bad food.

You knew what you were paying for when a restaurant served *haute cuisine,* not only for the often arcane ingredients but also for the monumental amounts of equipment, the porcelain, crystal, gold and silver, the décor and the effort and special skills that went into setting such food before the swollen bellies of gentlemen and the corset-heisted bosoms of their wives and mistresses.

When modern restaurants serve something differing very little from what might be achieved by the moderately experienced amateur in a kitchenette, one is right to wonder at its expense. With just a little thought, experience and a willingness to understand how ingredients work, you can do just as well, and then also cook without other people's recipes, becoming master/mistress in your own kitchen.

There was a time when every recipe ever published did not exist; it had first to be cooked without a real guide, constructed on a base of experience, instinct, available ingredients and personal preference. Cookery books should all start like that, unless they are recording socially relevant precedent, and so should the menu of every new restaurant – just like the chefs do before your eyes in *Ready Steady Cook*.

But first you must be certain you know the difference between a taste and a flavour.

CHAPTER ONE

HOW TO TASTE
PART ONE

TASTES AND FLAVOURS

Once you know the difference between a taste and a flavour you are well on the way to creating delicious Flavour Trails – to cooking without recipes

Taste means each of the five primary one-dimensional characteristics of what happens on the tongue and in the mouth. These are:

- Acid
- Salt
- Sweet
- Bitter
- Umami

The tongue has areas especially sensitive to each of these tastes and the sensitivity of each dictates quite what sort of palate you have. Knowing the different sensitivities of your tongue will go some way to explaining those times your experiences of food and drink have been different from others.

Although every taste bud has dedicated receptors for each of the five primary tastes, some seem to be more focused on one or the other, and are found around the outer fringes of the tongue. They all then segue into the centre, creating a bigger 'sweet spot' able to identify and deliver millions of complex tastes and flavours. Humans have up to 10,000 taste buds, which also register taste and flavour on the inside of your cheeks, the roof of your mouth and in your throat; even the lips have a few, especially sensitive to salt. But only if you are breathing, as you will learn.

Flavour means the multidimensional combinations of tastes and aromas that give each food or drink its ultimate individuality, thus enabling us to know the difference between lemons and limes; the *taste* of both is acidic but their aromas are what give them distinguishing *flavour*.

Although tastes and flavours appear largely to be identified by the tongue alone, the nose is an important partner in tasting full-flavour spectra. Both taste and flavour are delivered fully only by a combination of your tongue and your sense of smell, something else that maddeningly varies from person to person.

Note: although taste as a noun is used to mean only the perception of salt, sweet, acid, bitter or umami tastes, the verb 'to taste' is used properly to identify perceptions of flavour, to describe what is happening when you are eating and drinking.

THE FIVE PRIMARY TASTES

Each taste is essentially one-dimensional because none can be copied by combining other tastes

The five primary tastes are sweet, salt, acid, bitter and umami.
Each of these is essentially *one-dimensional* because none can be copied by combining other tastes, just as the primary colours of red, yellow and blue cannot be made by mixing other colours. These primary tastes can be combined in so many different proportions they make up the taste base of all food. Where there is an exaggerated balance of two or three tastes something quite new is created, like the sweet-and-sour sauces of Chinese cookery, a taste combination found naturally in such fruit as the pomegranate.

Think of each taste as a family name shared by a group of people; their first name is what makes them individual but their last name shows they belong to a particular family. Some members have double-barrelled family names because they are properly proud of their joint heritage; others have double-barrelled names because they are pretentious, doubly vulgar – like many sour-salty combinations.

Primary tastes are rarely experienced or eaten in isolation and are quite as identified by the sensation they leave in the mouth, their mouth-feel, as by their actual taste. These five primary tastes can be divided into three simpler groupings, which remind us we too were once uncivilised animals who had to hunt and forage to survive.

The Chasing-dragons Tastes

Sweet and salt tastes are primary indicators of a food's usefulness to the human body, so are harbingers of pleasure and sustainment. Yet both have vicious hooks with inverted barbs and once you start to take too much of either taste you damage yourself. Our taste receptors don't give a toss because all they know is you need sugar (carbohydrates) and you need salt to survive. If either is there they will accept it whether it's needed or not. Without awareness of this potential inner greed you are easily and dangerously hooked quite unconsciously, chasing dragons quite as deadly in the long term as those enslaving heroin victims.

Sweetness indicates the presence of carbohydrates, which we need for energy and resilience. It's a greedy-guts sensation not easily slaked and which promiscuously accepts far more carbohydrates than are good for us; but an innate sense of satiation is fighting other, stronger systems, whose sole aim is to build up stores against famine. Eventually you are no longer giggling because your underwear is tighter than it was – you are obese. You have allowed your tiny taste buds and their hunger for carbohydrates to vulgarise your body and shorten your life.

Salt is vital to the balance of the body's chemical structure and searching for sources of salt is one of every mammal's most basic instincts – life is impossible without it. Salt is also essential to the pleasure of eating, but the body can adjust to quite high levels, more than is needed for basic health. In the end salt, too, can be dangerous or fatal because it can hasten the hardening of arteries and thus make the heart work harder than it's designed to do.

The Spit-or-Swallow Tastes

Acid and bitter tastes are the primary protectors of the human body. Food that is 'off' or well on its way is often unpleasantly acidic, so identifying the presence of acids warns the brain quickly to decide if the food is safe or dangerous.

Bitterness commonly flags poisons in nature, so its detection, too, incites the brain to life-critical decisions in nanoseconds.

Mercifully, both acid and bitter tastes are also princely contributors to many of our most noble foods. You just have to learn which is safe and which is not when your taste buds warn you.

The Full-on-Pleasure Taste

Umami receptors hunt for and recognise proteins, which we need to build and sustain muscle, to drive the machine in its hunt for sugars and salt. Umami is the taste that makes being human better than being bovine or ovine or leonine; it rewards us by making roasted meats more delicious than raw, and that's the taste marker that draws the most distinct of lines between us and the rest of the animal kingdom. Remember that next time you or someone else has a go at monosodium glutamate or foods containing glutamates, for it's those that make them taste so delicious. Many of our most popular foods contain glutamates naturally, and that's why we love them. Without its inherent glutamates a tomato would be just another squishy red fruit.

Now for a closer look at each of those tastes . . .

THE SWEET TASTE

The tongue's most sensitive area for detecting sweetness is a relatively small, almost circular area at the tip of the tongue.

Sweetness essentially means sugars – all kinds of sugars. As well as sucrose, i.e. refined white table sugar, sweetness comes as natural sugars, in fruit, vegetables and honey. And inherent sweetness is an important part of our attraction to fats and oils. It's worth noting that *every* ingredient you find on a food label that ends in -ose is a sugar.

The first tastes we like as newborns are sweet and comforting, and only slowly do our physiology and experiences help us to appreciate salty, acidic, bitter and umami tastes. The mouth needs training and developing just as much as our legs, arms and brains. Depending on how a mouth is constructed and the opportunities for education it is given when quite young, it may never appreciate a great deal of what is put into it except for sugary-sweet foods.

Thus, a sweetness-fixated mouth is essentially an infantile mouth, and this is what so easily leads to obesity, caused by eating too much of too many sugars and sweet fats and oils in search of satisfaction. A sweetness-fixated tongue is often a slow or insensitive tongue too, and what satisfaction it gains from eating can be based more on a heightened appreciation of mouth-feel than of flavour or taste. Once identified as such, most immature tongues can be retrained to sensitise other taste areas.

Before sugar became widely grown and available, sweetness came most easily from honey, which is essentially only sucrose in simpler forms. Although eaten gratefully, honey and naturally sweet vegetables and summer fruits always brought with them the mixed pleasures of a spectrum of other flavours. In winter a snow-chilled parsnip is sweet because the temperature has converted its starch into sugar. It was relied upon to add sweetness to all manner of dishes – and might even have been fried and served as a sweetmeat. Mature main-crop carrots, too, added important sweetness in both sweet and savoury dishes. But neither parsnip, carrot nor honey could be added to other food without changing its essential flavour.

The introduction of sugar, refined to be white and tasting of nothing much but sweetness, meant cooks might at last sweeten and heighten flavours without radically changing the foods by adding other flavours. Less refined sugars, the 'brown' sugars, had as much sweetness plus new darker undertones, giving cooks new tools and giving diners new experiences; they are flavoured variations of sweetness but without vegetable or honey flavours.

As it became more and more available, white sugar changed sweet cooking dramatically, and also added new texture. This possibility of adding sugar's silken mouth-feel to syrups, sauces, cakes, ice creams and more has always been as important as sugar's contribution to flavour (see Mouth-Feel – page 158–9).

Today, choosing the right sugar to vary the style of sweetness even in simple recipes is an excellent place for a cook to begin their journey towards a greater knowledge of ingredients and the ideal of using fewer ingredients but creating better flavours. Raw or molasses sugars, demerara sugars, other brown or golden sugars, or the less well-known palm sugar and maple sugar each give a unique twist that might be all a recipe needs to make it memorable.

Equally, the careful choice of the correct honey made from a single type of flower can change food marvellously: the light, scented honey from orange blossoms is entirely different from the rich, dark, herbal honey from New Zealand's native pohutukawa tree or the unique deeply tropical honey of Pitcairn Island, made from the nectar of mango trees, passion fruit, rose apples and more.

Caramelised flavours are the result of sugars being browned, important not only in sweet dishes but in savoury ones, too. The wonderful satin-sweetness of a baked whole onion and the succulent skin of a long-baked joint both owe their heightened flavour to the changed chemistry of natural sugars. As the roast browns, the natural sugars in the skin and fat develop a complementary acidity at first and then a light, caramelised bitterness without destroying their essential sweetness. Discovering how quickly a gorgeous balanced syrup of caramelised sugar turns from acid-sweetness into inedible bitterness is the most unforgettable kitchen experience; but a small degree of bitterness only enhances the mouth's pleasures when sweetness and acidity are also there.

Nature caught on to our inherent sweet tooth, and most fruits and vegetables are noticeably sweet when ripe. The most enjoyable fruits or vegetables you might eat raw also finish with a clean acidic taste: if they didn't their unalloyed sweetness would seem cloying. Vegetables tend to develop sweetness only when lightly cooked. Just as often, their inherent sweetness is lost by bad cooking. For maximum sweetness in vegetables they should be cooked in a microwave, and with no added water.

A Fruit or a Sweetie?

One of the most difficult differences to learn is between sweetness and fruitiness, particularly in wines. It's a matter of which parts of your mouth are sparked off and in what order and, ultimately, of knowing the difference between a taste and a flavour.

A fruity wine, one that essentially presents a heightened sense of the grapes' ripe flavour, will initially be tasted all over the palate and then finish with a clean acidity and flavour that fills the mouth and lingers. There will be little or none of the full, velvety mouth feel associated with sugar and what there might be is experienced only in the first seconds. That's why you should shut up and not pronounce a wine as sweet on your first impression – it's what happens next that counts.

A full-flavoured fruity wine can be absolutely dry yet easily dismissed as sweet: the big fruit flavour is confused with the simple taste of sweetness. This is a common mistake when assessing the wines made in countries with a lot of sun, like New Zealand and Australia. A quick sip and a dismissal of a wine being too sweet is a common and unsophisticated mistaking of fruitiness for sweetness.

A good sweet wine, a pudding or dessert wine, will finish the same way, but that first satin-smooth mouth-feel taste of sweetness will continue as the flavours of fruitiness build. They will combine to give a markedly round fullness that only slowly changes to acidity, sometimes only after you have swallowed. The slower speed of change in mouth-feel from a definite sensation of sweetness to acidity is an important key to recognising a sweet rather than a fruity wine.

But even a sweet wine is not only sweet. Without balancing acidity a sweet wine is flabby and floppy in the mouth, as ungratifying as a cheap boiled sweet. The great sweet wines combine superb, big mouth-feel and aristocratic acidic finishes with extraordinary heightened flavours. That's why they are served in small glasses . . . they are too flavoursome for an educated palate to swig.

Balancing Sweetness

Sweetness is tamed by two things: by the acid taste, or by simple dilution, which will also lessen flavour. Sweetness and acidity have such a liking for one another you can barely go wrong, for whatever pleases your palate is what you should do. You might have eye-watering sweetness with a hint of acidity right down to eye-watering acidity with just a hint of sweetness. Halfway along this very long Flavour Trail you'll have an equal balance, the sweet-sour flavour taste that sits so happily in any course of a meal. The fun begins when you think more carefully about which acid taste you'll use. Lemon or lime juice are what most people reach for first. But think about the flavour change you might get from using another type of citrus, or from using zest rather than juice. Then there is the wide wonderful world of vinegar: from the fruitiness of raspberry vinegar through cider and herb vinegars, and from single-grape vinegars such as chardonnay or muscatel vinegar to the dark, fantastic realms of balsamic vinegar, aged sherry vinegar and the thick dark rice vinegars of China, which can also come sweetened and deliciously spiced.

Next time you want to tame sweetness, look at the Flavour Trail lists and perhaps you'll go off on an unexpected journey of greater pleasure than you'd imagined. That's their point.

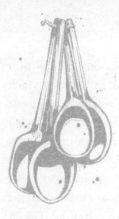

THE SALT TASTE

There are two sensitive areas that particularly detect the taste of salt.

Salt is not a food; in fact, eat too much of it and it can kill you. Yet without salt most food would be bland to most diners, because salt is the on–off switch to our taste buds.

The ideal use of salt is to sensitise our tongues to the tastes and flavours of food without imposing much or any of its own flavour; but most salt comes with the baggage of other natural or added chemicals, each of which adds flavour and thus will change the characteristics of other foods.

Nobody sane chooses to eat salt on its own but, because salt is a great preservative, highly salted foods are commonly encountered. It has ever been this way. Tracks made to and from salt sources are believed to be the oldest surviving marks humans made on Earth.

Does the type of salt you use make a difference? Not really, and certainly not in cooking. Using expensive single-source foam-born salt crystals or man-created flakes in cooking water is pointless for most people, because the dilution makes their special and costly characteristics indistinguishable. Superior flaked salts are best used at table, crushed directly onto your food, where individuality and texture can be appreciated.

The failure to consider the dilution of salt in cooking is why professional and domestic cooks commonly shy away from using iodised salt, for it does smell and taste different when dry. Yet in a country with no iodine in its soil like New Zealand, iodised salt protects against goitre, a nasty ailment that is increasingly being seen again as good-sense iodised salt is replaced by designer salts. Using iodised salt diluted in cooking water, but natural salt everywhere else, is a very good choice in most countries.

And now, the most challenging concept in this book and one that will be difficult for many to accept:

It is impossible, absolutely impossible, to tell another person how much salt they do or do not need to get their tongue into full working order.

It is quite wrong to believe or to say that salt brings out the flavour in food. It doesn't directly interact with the flavour of food in any way. Instead, salt stimulates your taste buds into action, so they taste the food as well as they can. It's their on–off switch, but just because your buds are switched on doesn't mean they work the same way as any other person's buds, because each mouth works differently and needs more salt or less salt or no salt to taste the same as one another. Sometimes it's because a tongue is badly furnished with taste buds, sometimes it's because what are there are ageing – or aged.

Thus, it is incorrect to call food tasteless just because it has no salt. It is only tasteless to you, and to many others it could well be very tasty. When food is tasteless to an individual, it's simply because there is not enough salt to switch on their taste buds, or, even if there is, those buds might be numerically insufficient or physically incapable of working to detect and pass on the tastes and flavours another mouth might detect.

You will find ignorance of the true nature of salt and how it works at every turn. I have known a student threatened with failure at a chic and expensive UK cookery school because he was judged never to use enough salt. He finally and successfully argued he was using enough salt for his tongue. He then went on to cook for three duchesses and had huge success. None of his august clients ever asked for more salt – his palate was entirely in accord with those for whom he cooked.

Any food writer who specifies exact amounts of salt for anything but a brine simply doesn't know what they are talking about. They should be telling their reader to season to taste, but even that can be challenging if you've never been taught to do it properly. Chefs who refuse to put salt on the table of their restaurants are like Grand Prix teams who refuse to put fuel in their racing cars. Disqualification is all they deserve.

Seasoning to Taste

There is a simple way to season to your taste. Take a good tablespoon or dessertspoon or so of the dish at the temperature it should be eaten – cold, cool, warm or hot. Taste it with your eyes closed and see where the flavour ends; how far back on the tongue do you taste it? If the flavour doesn't go back very far, add more salt to the dish (not to the spoon) until all your tongue is tasting. When the mouth is full of flavour, stop adding salt.

If, however, you start to taste only more salt and/or the flavours of the dish resolutely stop halfway along the tongue, this means the dish is under-flavoured and unbalanced and needs some help. That's it. Frustratingly, whatever you taste will also differ according to the food's temperature and everyone else will taste something different anyway.

Balancing Salt

Compensating for too much salt is very difficult. In something like a stew or soup it's said that you can add potatoes and they will absorb the excess: I've never found this effective, or have found it takes too long before you get it right. Adding the extra acidity of good vinegar can work, but by heightening this other taste, both it and the saltiness can blind the tongue to the essential flavours of the dish. Adding sweetness does much the same thing. Always under-salt is the rule, especially when cooking for a mixed bag of people. If they are polite they will taste the food and add extra salt if they need it. This is never a slur on your palate or briny judgement, but a mark of the sort of palate they were born with or which has disintegrated with advancing age.

When assessing other people's recipes, ignore dogmatic specifications of silly amounts like one eighth of a teaspoon. These are often not what the writer specified but the requirement of a bad cookery editor, the literary equivalent of a kitchen neatnik, the type who prizes neatness over flavour.

You *will* have to use more appropriate and accurate measures if the salt is making a brine to preserve lemons, or if you want to salt fish or duck before smoking it. The use of salt here is a culinary technique and needs certain proportions to work and to keep the food safe.

THE ACID/SOUR/SHARP TASTE

The most sensitive areas for acidity are thin strips on the edge of both sides of the tongue.

It is not abusive to call a food acid or acidic. Acidity, also called sourness or sharpness, is essential to constructing balanced and gratifying food. Once you begin exploring flavours on your tongue you will recognise that almost anything you thought deliciously sweet also comes with acidity. The acidity is what balances and expands the flavours, giving a greater, more satisfying experience. The same is true of fruit, sourdough breads and old-fashioned acid drops. In fact, just about every worthwhile food or drink includes acidity to expand the flavour experience further and further into and around the mouth.

Unlike the sweetness of sugar, acidity is rarely available just by itself: it would be nasty. The easiest way to understand the taste of acidity is to think of the sharpness behind a simple vinegar or fresh lemon juice. The mouth-feel of acidity is of dryness and perhaps we will pucker if something is too acidic. This is the meaning of a dry finish when speaking of wines that are patently wet – the flavour finishes with an acidic effect, a thin and rather cleansing effect rather than a sugary sensation.

Most of us like vinegars because although initially chosen for their acidity they also offer a raft of flavours complementing that acidity. The addition of a little excellent sherry vinegar or balsamic vinegar to a casserole of white or red meat just before serving will reward the palate with marvellously complicated sweet/sour flavours: it seems to fill in the missing parts, creating Flavour Trails between sweet fattiness and its own sharp acidity. Indeed, a very small amount of good vinegar will save and invigorate many a flabby dish and, although it might also have sweet or balsamic or herby flavours, acidity is the magic ingredient.

Our most popular fruits rely on a cargo of acidity to balance their sweetness. Although such sweetness is immediately appealing, the enjoyment is heightened by an acidic finish, leaving the mouth refreshed and waiting for more. This is why fruit is successful whether made sweeter by preserving in a sugar syrup, or more acidic by making into chutney: both sweetness and acidity build on what is already present.

Equally, orange, lemon and lime juice make most other fruits sing: thickly cut strawberries in a little fresh orange juice ascend heavenwards, passionfruit pulp mixed into a syrup of caramelised sugar and orange juice is good enough to eat by itself, and lime juice on fresh pineapple takes acidity to its sharper edge – but both lime and pineapple have far greater sweetness and flavour profiles than expected and so perform wondrously in spite of all that acidity.

Like zillions of other flavourings, cumin and coriander seeds and the leaves of basil and mint have citric-flavoured acidity as an important part of their make-up. It's worth slowly chewing on such ingredients to focus on identifying these citric/acid base notes. We generally think of them just as fragrant, but when isolated on your palate you'll recognise each is so good at extending other flavours because of the acidity.

Balancing Acidity

A food that is too acidic can be brought back into line by adding sweetness. At its most basic this can mean combining the tastes of sweet and sour, but of course both those tastes usually come with flavours and thus make something very complex. Adding sugar only might be the best way to save a dish with otherwise interesting flavours to offer. But adding sweetness is also an opportunity to be truly creative and to add an unexpected edge, as you'll quickly see in the Flavour Trail list of sweet-tasting ingredients on page 68.

THE BITTER TASTE

The area most sensitive to bitterness crosses the back of the tongue and can extend quite a way down the throat, too – it is the final barrier food must pass.

Bitterness is perhaps our least-liked taste and the one we experience far less often than others. This is why many people find difficulty in recognising and distinguishing bitterness from acidity, often through slack use of descriptions they've been given. It's easier to distinguish the two once you know bitterness is registered most strongly at the back of the tongue.

Bitterness pulls and puckers the mouth, particularly towards the back – it's commonly experienced when you drink red wines high in tannin because they have not aged enough. So why do we even contemplate eating bitter-tasting food? It could be instinctive, because it's long been believed bitter ingredients stimulate our digestion in a special way, which is to release a full range of digestive juices not only in the stomach but in other areas of the digestive tract. It follows that drinking or eating something bitter at the start of a meal is thought to make eating and digestion more enjoyable, explaining why so many apéritifs are made to taste so bitter.

Those who commonly register their first sensation of, say, a dark marmalade as bitter are quite wrong – this first taste is of high, forward acidity, and the bitterness – if there is any – will not come until later, as the flavour travels to the back of the tongue. One of the joys of a true Seville orange marmalade is that the acidity of the flesh and juice perfectly balance the undoubted original bitterness of the rind; bitter orange is another name for Seville oranges.

Balancing Bitterness

Bitterness is encountered in overcaramelised sugar, in smoked foods, overbrewed tea and badly made coffee, and it can be very hard to balance and to make palatable. Sugar is not the answer, because bitterness cannot be balanced by sweetness: all you are doing here is dramatising sweetness to the same level as the bitterness and then tasting both to the max. To ameliorate bitterness only acidity works.

After the misunderstanding of how salt works, the use of acidity to soothe away bitterness is perhaps the least known of all food facts. This is what we are doing when we squirt lemon juice onto smoked salmon and other smoked fish. It is not to 'flavour' the fish, which should have plenty anyway. The citrus is to tone down the bitterness of the preservative process, which once had to rely on heavy salting and smoking to keep food palatable and safe. Now salmon, herrings, eel and other fish are pre-sliced and put into long-life vacuum packs, so smoking is no longer needed as a preservative but is used only as flavouring (and precious little of it even then). Without the bitterness of a high smoking, today's smoked fish thus needs little or no added acidity. Soaking a plate of modern smoked salmon with lemon juice is publicly declaring you can't stand the taste of smoked salmon, or have so little sensitivity you can't taste it at all.

Because sugar does nothing to ameliorate bitterness in a black coffee, many countries prefer to drink indifferent and thus overly bitter espresso coffees diluted with lots of milk – the combination of dilution and the way the fat in the milk coats the tongue and inhibits what your taste buds can recognise makes the coffee more palatable but does not actually change the bitterness.

The Roman way of adding a slice of lemon to bitter coffee works and leaves the coffee flavour largely intact, as lemon also does when added to strong tea, a Russian custom that compensated for the poor quality and bitterness of their usual teas. Adding lemon to weak but good-quality tea or to any decent tea – especially to Earl Grey, already flavoured with lemon's equally acidic cousin bergamot – is affectation of the worst kind.

The acid/bitter solution is why holidaymakers like Spain's sangria so much. The savage rawness of very young wine is largely because it is very tannic, puckeringly so. Yet add oranges and lemons and it miraculously becomes something we quaff with great pleasure. The same improving effect is why true Hungarian *paprikas*, a wet stew of white meat and potatoes flavoured with paprika, has soured cream dolloped on the top to balance the bitterness of that spice.

A more bucolic example of how acidity rescues bitterness is that quintessentially English summer treasure, elderflower syrup. Once the blooms have been steeped in water, you can sweeten this as highly as your fillings and temples can stand, but the bitterness will still make it unpalatable. Yet squeeze in some lemon juice and it is suddenly as though the sun has burst through golden clouds. To the sound of trumpets.

THE UMAMI TASTE

Umami, the twentieth-century addition to the family of taste, has not yet had its palate profile fully identified...

Umami is the savoury taste of roasted meats and long-cooked stocks, and also explains why tomatoes and potatoes are so universally enjoyed.

Like the four other primary tastes, umami cannot be made up of other tastes, yet isolating it is one of the hardest of all culinary quests. A good place to start is with dashi, the seaweed-based stock of Japanese cuisine, not least because it was this that first stimulated the detection of the fifth taste.

The umami taste is unquestionably associated with naturally occurring glutamates, a family of food enhancers – MSG (monosodium glutamate) is only one of these. It is wrong to say umami is the taste of a glutamate: the chemistry of glutamates help us taste umami – they hunt the proteins in food and make them taste especially good to us, even adding body and comforting mouth-feel to the experience.

Generally, umami is considered as having a 'broth' taste, like the meaty extract of long-cooked flesh and bones. In the West umami is most often encountered as the predominant taste of roasted meats, closely followed by tomatoes and potatoes.

Umami is a taste that works a little like salt to energise your taste buds and thus get greater pleasure from other foods on the plate. The crusty outside of a nicely browned roast naturally offers each of the primary tastes except for salt (unless it has been added) but the lack of salt is compensated for by umami. Even the smallest piece will simultaneously switch on all the taste buds you have, giving huge pleasure and stimulation not only of flavour, but of taste, mouth-feel and of a long finish. The heightened flavour of the browned crusts of roasted, baked or grilled meat is called the Maillard effect. But call it what you will, its appeal is based on simple, effective chemistry. It turns you on, because it turns on all your taste buds.

Tomatoes, especially cooked ones, have a definite umami advantage. This is the unconscious reason we like to add tomato sauce to so many other foods – it adds more than taste, it enhances the enjoyment of other proteins on the plate. Meat is one thing; meat and tomato sauce a world of taste away. The umami advantage is also why concentrated tomato, as purée or paste, goes into almost every Italian meat sauce, and why tomato is so popular in cooked dishes. It's the largely unrecognised pleasure of its umami taste that made it conquer the world. Not the colour, not the flavour, but the almost ineffable comfort of tomato's umami taste.

Adding the umami taste is also the role of the fish sauces of Southeast Asia, too. Unquestionably, the most readily available taste they offer is salt, and we know that will enhance anything savoury to which it might be added. But there is also umami, which greatly builds up our enjoyment of any protein – thus stocks and soups are much tastier and satisfying than we might expect them to be. Sneakily, umami makes a small amount of protein seem bigger and tastier too, so fish sauce is a kind of prestidigitation, magically transforming a small portion into something that seems a lot bigger. Soy sauces and misos also come with the umami effect.

Although it's seen largely as an Eastern phenomenon the West is just discovering, the umami taste was almost single-handedly responsible for two major changes of eating in the West – the adoption of the potato and the development of *haute cuisine* in Western Europe in the nineteenth century. It's only very recently the umami taste has been identified in potatoes. This explains its (eventual) meteoric rise in popularity – the umami content made any meal more savoury and tasty, and because the palate was being gratified, the stomach was more easily satisfied.

Super-chef Escoffier – and others – discovered that if they used rich meat-based stocks to make sauces, enjoyment was increased massively more than this simple ruse would suggest. They weren't able to explain what happened, but we now understand they were serving much greater and more concentrated servings of the umami taste. Not only did food seem bigger in flavour, the umami effect also enhanced its mouth-feel and the general enjoyment of other savoury flavours on the plate.

The MSG Message

If you haven't moved on from being frightened of MSG, you'd better get going. Monosodium glutamate is not a demon and you are not allergic to it. Well, no more so than millions and millions of Chinese, Japanese, Thais, Laotians, etc. MSG helps our tongue find flavour and pleasure from protein and does so without adding much of its own. Those whiners who say they can taste MSG can do no such thing – they are tasting the effect of it, i.e. greater savoury flavour than they might have tasted before, perhaps even tasting their food the way others taste it. Exactly like salt, MSG is just another on-off switch for the taste buds, but it is more focused on where it works – it doesn't care about and won't change the perception of sweetness at all.

The only baggage MSG carries is that of every other food – used incorrectly it causes side effects. Chug down a bowl of soup as a first course in a Chinese restaurant and you might well get dizzy and fall down, or suffer a dozen other effects. But so would most Chinese. They don't because they sip soup throughout a meal, and MSG is only dicey if you eat a great deal of it on an empty stomach. It's not the MSG but the way people eat it that causes the undoubted problems.

The great and largely unexploited use of MSG is to make food tastier for those who must reduce their salt. If they've a slow tongue this means every meal is the bland leading the bland into an abyss of overeating in the hope of finding some satisfaction of their mouth hunger. Tiny amounts of MSG will make savoury food sing in their mouth – and there will be no salt/sodium problem.

The US Food and Drug Administration, one of the few of that country's organisations that can be believed, has stated quite categorically that monosodium glutamate used properly is safe for humans of all ages and, yes, that does include babies. It's only problematic if used improperly, just as water or carrots might be.

THE HOT, PEPPERY
SENSATIONS

*. . . commonly used by underpowered
chefs as instant food-bling, and just
as cheap and vulgar . . .*

Somewhere between tastes and flavours there is another
world, a world of mouth sensation. Sometimes this brings
elements of taste, sometimes there is distinct flavour. Often it is
just sensation, like astringency or the heat of very hot food served
directly from the pot or pan, or the dramatic coldness of frozen
food. A great cook will utilise both temperature sensations,
knowing that as heat dissipates and frozen foods thaw, the
flavours and tastes of the foods involved will also be changing.

And then there is the sensation of fizzing, or of foaming,
a sensation for the eyes as well as for the palate. It's a shame
foam is currently becoming so debased in restaurants – it seems
everything that once grew can be served as a foam or
'cappuccino' on top of something that was once alive. Still, foams
do give some advantage to restaurants over home cooks and
that's a boon. You could compete by pouring a shot of
champagne or sparkling wine over ice cream or into, say, a

chilled pea soup, when the green fizz will break all conversation barriers there might have been.

But neither taste nor flavour is the objective of the most common use of sensation on the palate: that is to sting the tongue, in fact to damage it until there is discernible pain. Why do we do this? Because when the body is hurt our brain compensates by releasing serotonins, the natural feel-good opiates that are the real pursuit of all those who can't eat food without covering it with pepper or chilli, wasabi, mustard or horseradish, rocket, watercress or mizuna or whatever.

A small degree of hot pepperiness is a good thing, and is often the final anchoring or weaving together of separate flavours and tastes. This is what we do when black pepper is ground over a plate, and suddenly disparate tastes and flavours seem to belong to one another. Sometimes we also do this with rocket or with watercress leaves. Ginger, too, munches down on the tongue, but its bite generously brings along a sumptuous flavour, even when dried, as when it is cooked with butter and cumin and paprika in Moroccan tagines.

Hot peppery sensations are commonly used by under-powered chefs as instant food-bling, and are just as cheap and vulgar as flashy jewels and amulet-sized watches. Ultimately all fashion becomes boring and thus we will move on. Fashion will replace stings with some other trend and their bling will leave little or no trace behind. At least I hope so. In the meantime thousands of palates are being ill-educated or scarred and becoming habituated more and more to hot, peppery one-dimensional eating. It's flavour the mouth wants, not pain.

The pursuit of sensation over flavour is why I remain unconvinced by sushi and sashimi with soy and wasabi. In both styles of eating, the fresher the fish, the less flavour it will have. So why pursue such perfection only to waylay it with lacerations of wasabi? Even when man-made from horseradish and colouring, it's hotter than most mustards. If you think about it, all you have in your mouth is largely flavourless texture plus a hot peppery sensation with some saltiness. It's hard to see the appeal, isn't it other than getting something to happen in your mouth to justify the expense?

Putting the Heat on Pepper

For all that I rail against the misuse of chilli there is an important place in many recipes for a bit of a bite-back that's more than mere taste and flavour. Add lettuce to a cheese sandwich and you add sweetness, a new texture, acidity and, in some, a touch of bitterness – it completes the spectrum of tastes and adds extra flavour and your mouth is going to be much happier. If you then add pepper in some form you really wake up the mouth.

The bite of black pepper is one of mankind's oldest pleasures, and together with ginger made up the major source of heat in the diet before chilli crossed the Atlantic from South America. When I made my BBC-TV series in Sri Lanka I found cooks there still use pepper the old way, in a hot curry-style dish using startling amounts of black pepper as a source of heat. These dishes are robustly hot, searingly so, but have, to me anyway, the salvation of being highly flavoured in a way most chilli dishes can't begin to approach. In Thailand, too, I found an old royal recipe that bakes pork under a layer of black pepper covered with pineapple skins and serves the raw pineapple flesh chopped and absolutely smothered with black pepper. The heat-oxidised, less-fragrant flavour of the cooked peppercorns on the pork was refreshed and revitalised by the sharper fresh pepper on the pineapple.

The masterful way pepper appears to weave together and dramatise lesser flavours and tastes is why rocket, watercress and the like are so universally used in modern styles of cookery. Serve a green salad with chicken, grilled red pepper and shards of Parmesan and most tastes will be ticked off. But add rocket with restraint and the biting sensation makes a lively and welcome addition, just as watercress once did traditionally.

And then there are chillies . . .

TASTE TWOSOMES

Although it is more usual to create recipes based on *flavour* and *flavour families,* there are certain styles relying for effect on the heightened blending of underlying *tastes.* Best known of these are the sweet-and-sour mixtures so associated with Chinese cookery. Here the effect is a dominating combination of the two tastes with the comforting recognition of both of them; success comes when the two are both pleasant, both recognisable. Pomegranates offer this twin taste naturally.

Sweet-and-sour pickles are another example likely to be familiar; some of the best use fruit, like sweet pickled strawberries, which can be so good they are just as much at home with cold meats as they are on vanilla ice cream – especially so if the sour/acidic content is a balsamic vinegar.

There aren't many others. Salt/sweet combinations can be surprisingly good, as in salt-water caramels. Or try salty feta cheese with sweet melon. Totally delicious.

Sour/salt combinations, found in some versions of pickled cucumbers, are less common and less likely to be good or of mainstream acceptance.

Hot and sour is an unusual combination, relying on acidity plus the heat of hot, peppery sensations. It's often found in Chinese soups, particularly from the colder northern regions, and thus in Peking/Beijing cuisine.

CHILLIES – THE HOT BLOT

'I found a lot . . . bury the flavour of everything else. A really strong habanero flattens your taste buds. It's like listening to really loud music all the time. You don't hear any of the nuance anymore.'

Joe Perry (of rock group Aerosmith), *Bon Appetit* **magazine**

'Encore, Joe! Encore!' That's what I say. Most people, perhaps everyone, reading this book, should have no need to rely on drug-induced euphoria to get pleasure from food and eating.

Chillies are not so much a flavour or taste as they are mouth trauma. Some deliver flavour, of course, yet it is not taste buds that most potently register chillies on our palate, but pain receptors, which ultimately reward us with doses of the inner pleasures of opiates. That's why chillies are the refuge and culinary saviour of the poorest geographical areas of the world: Notting Hill Gate does not qualify.

Any feeling of pleasure after eating chilli-hot food is that of the brain compensating for the pain on your palate by releasing endorphins, the natural feel-good equivalent of morphine and opiates. As with any drug, well-fed, affluent Westerners become addicted too. In fact, there is no dietary need for Westerners to eat more than a pleasurable suggestion of chilli, but a physiological one can be found. For those with tongues that taste little of what passes their way, even with lashings of salt, the powerful physical high felt after eating chillies is the closest they get to the satisfaction others enjoy just by eating well.

Check out the geographical areas where chillies are most used and you'll find these universally ill-furnished with good ingredients. All of Thailand uses chilli, but in dramatically different proportions. Royal Thai food based in the verdant gardens and rich seas close to Bangkok uses almost none: those living on the scant soils of the poor northeastern provinces are renowned for the heat of their food. It's easy to understand. A bowl of rice and a scatter of vegetables or meat don't do a lot to make peasant families feel they have eaten. Yet add chilli and they will be all smiles, thinking they have dined well: they are victims, grateful victims, of one of the world's most common drug addictions – an addiction to the physical effects of chilli peppers. Royal Thai food uses better ingredients and more of such delicious flavourings as lemon grass and lime leaf and galangal to create equally gratifying dishes, dishes that satisfy because of flavour, not cheap sensation and pain. You should do the same.

Men and women who publicly seek hotter and hotter chillies are not always braver or tougher; they are often thicker and slower of tongue and too insensitive to taste other food. The more they eat chillies the more they need, until the tongue is so scarred and battle-worn even the hottest heat won't penetrate to satisfy them. But there is no going back. Chilli is an evil and unforgiving master.

If you go abroad and eat local chilli-scorched food, and think this is how it must be to be authentic, you are wrong: very hot food does not register like that to people who eat it every day and have a chilli-scarred tongue. It is incorrect to come back from India or Thailand insisting authentic food must have a high chilli-count. The heat-scarred local tongues in your holiday resort don't experience anything like the heat your apprentice tongue does. So, it is more authentic to cook with fewer chillies or to ask for very mild or mild-to-medium heat in a restaurant – a mild or mild-to-medium sensation is what people who eat chillies all their life generally *experience*.

With few exceptions, the smaller the chilli, the fiercer their heat. If you slice raw chillies across into rings they are hotter towards the stem end, for there is more inner membrane there and it is the membranes and not the seeds that are the major repositories of stinging capsicain, or chilli oil. It's generally true that a dark hue to the otherwise whitish membranes is usually a signal of more intense heat. The seeds of dried chillies are utterly useless as anything but bowel roughage. It's usually best to halve fresh chillies lengthwise and then to scrape away the membranes, lessening the heat content dramatically. Scraping away the seeds is just good housekeeping, to keep the dish looking good.

A Burning Question

What can I do to cool my tongue when it is burning with chillies?

Asian and Oriental food is cooked and flavoured to be eaten with rice in at least equal proportions with every mouthful. When we greedily dig into a helping of curry, finish that, have some rice and then gorge ourselves on another dish it all goes wrong. The chilli content is hot to us because we have twice as much meat, poultry, fish or vegetables in our mouth as the cook intended – every mouthful should be half rice, half something else, diluting any heat and ensuring chilli remnants are well mixed with other food. This kinder mixture is less assaulting to the palate and much nicer to the sensitive lining of our bowels.

The sting is contained in capsicain oil, and oils won't be diluted or moved on by water or saliva. Just waiting for the pain to subside does work but can take ages, and anyway you look awful with streaming eyes, drooling mouth and scarlet face, like any lager lout fighting to keep down a Friday-night vindaloo.

Gulping beer, water or fruit juices cannot possibly cool a palate burning with chillies – the chilli oil repels such liquids. Something fatty – yoghurt or milk – will do the best job, which is why they are served with curries. Actually, it is best not to drink at all when eating chilli-hot food, or only to sip throughout a meal, the way soups are used in Thailand and China. When cold beer is skulled back it gathers up the largely indigestible chilli and rushes it directly onto the sensitive intestinal walls, where it burns badly. It is the beer or whatever else you drank upsetting your system next day, not the food. Eat the same food with yoghurt instead of drinking anything during the meal and all will be calmer, because the chilli will be passed with the other residue.

What's the Difference between Chilli, Chili, Chille and Chile?

Is there any difference?

There certainly is, and ignorance of the facts explains the horrid grey but fiery messes served as a bowl of chili in pubs worldwide. If the word has two helpings of an 'l', as in chilli, it should mean the thing itself, fresh, dried or ground. If there is but one 'l', it should mean a cooked dish or the mixed-spice seasoning/compound with which you make such a dish.

Chilli is rarely used without other spices or herbs, so chucking chilli powder (i.e. simply ground chillies) into undercooked onion, cheap mince and tinned tomatoes does no good at all. What you should be using is chili compound or chili seasoning – look at the label and it will be a mixed spice with a predominance of cumin and some garlic, perhaps oregano too; yes, I do know the companies who pack such flavourings don't seem to know either. Check what is in the ingredients list on the pack rather than rely on what the front label says. The extra spices of true chili seasoning add flavour to the chillies and flavour to the dish, and makes something into a chili, with or without beans. If you are cooking for others who bear chillies better than you, cook to your own palate and serve Tabasco of several colours on the table. Avert your eyes.

Another cavalry charge that rescues or strengthens almost anything, including chili compound, is a square or two of chocolate or some cocoa powder, thus creating a captivating but minor version of *mole*, the major impious achievement of Portuguese nuns in South America, who combined the best flavours of both the Old and the New World to make something so sensual it must have been a celebration of past and present pleasure rather than a sublimation of ungratified yearnings, which is the usual explanation.

If you have digestive problems with Asian food, eat equal amounts of rice with every mouthful, eat yoghurt dishes and don't drink anything. That way you'll enjoy tonight and tomorrow. Your bum will thank you.

Is there a Proper Use of Chilli?

Of course there is. Use it sparingly and give pleasure not pain. It's becoming a cliché, but a touch of chilli with almost anything chocolate will extend the flavour and taste with its sensations. Indeed, wherever there is a degree of fattiness or creaminess, a little chilli makes an excellent final gesture. Look back at books only fifty years old and almost everything with a sauce was finished with a sprinkle of hot cayenne pepper. It was as elegant as the dishes, a final flourish to fascinate the tongue. Would that it were still the same, because the pleasure of a little bite accompanied by a lot of flavour is universally appreciated – and respects the ingredients of the dish.

For many years I have added a little Tabasco to coffee ice cream, and just as the cream and coffee tastes and flavours are subsiding up pops a tingle of chilli; I think the effect is even better with a Chocolate or Coffee Rocky Road Ice Cream – the chilli seems to clear the palate of all the previous flavours and sets it up for more. The same restrained and, you will be astonished to hear me say, *elegant* sensation can be used in butters, sauces and baking.

Over thirty years ago my friends Viv and Richard Furlong reckoned I changed their enjoyment of life, simply by saying I wouldn't eat with them again unless they reduced the amount of chilli in the curries they served. They did, and almost at once realised for years they had never really tasted any of the other ingredients they had used. Their cooking – and their palates – recovered and became wondrously fragrant and exciting. That's the promise I make to anyone else who thinks hotter is better. Hotter is dumber.

For a table comparing the heat of various chillies see page 76.

CHAPTER TWO

FLAVOUR TRAILS

THE THREE FLAVOUR TRAILS

Everyone who has ever cooked successfully without another person's recipe has based their creation on one of only three Flavour Trails.

When I was presenting recipes on BBC-TV's Pebble Mill at One and then three mornings a week on *Breakfast Time*, most of them were original, created to illustrate a seasonal ingredient, a new ingredient – or a new technique. It was a sensation when I also demonstrated the first nonstick frying pan, introduced the astonishing idea of wine from New Zealand, yellow water-melons from Israel and the golden sugars of Mauritius – and told my audience in 1982 they could expect as much as 1 tonne of farmed salmon to be harvested that year. Today the annual harvest is over 130,000 tonnes. But nothing stopped traffic quite as much as my broadcast on LBC radio about pink peppercorns – when even London taxi drivers stopped to write down the details and my recipes. The news just weeks later that the pink peppercorns sold then were from Florida Holly, a close relative of poison ivy, and that they could cause major haemorrhoids, heart problems and breathing difficulties was received with rather less enthusiasm. Today's pink peppercorns are a different thing altogether, no longer the berries of Florida Holly but of the gorgeous weeping *Schinus*, the pepper tree, so called for the distinctive black-pepper tang of its leaves and its berries.

At a time when interest in food was new and intense – and there was virtually no competition on television –whatever I did had to be virtually foolproof. At the same time I was judging cookery competitions all over the country so, being untrained as a chef, I felt it only fair I worked out a basis for judging dishes, whether traditional or new. That's when I began to formulate what has become this book.

I realised that under all the mystique, behind the bubbling and the chopping and calling things by foreign names, there are just three basic ways to construct a combination of ingredients and then put 'something nice to eat' on a table. I called these Flavour Trails and they are based on ingredient knowledge, or, at least, some capacity to remember what you have eaten and liked.

Add an understanding of Flavour Trails to knowing how your tongue works to distinguish taste from flavour and you will have put an end to slavishly following other people's recipes – and to discovering they often didn't know what they were doing either.

Instead you'll know what goes with what and why, and be able to work it out in your head or on paper. Indeed, when you have really mastered these techniques you can confidently create new flavours as you shop, think, walk or . . . well, whatever. Good-tasting food is always based on one or more of my three Flavour Trails, and this is true for everything from sandwiches to banqueting food.

Following Flavour Trails means you can always trace why and how each ingredient is working with the others in a combination – and then know how to dramatise that combination, substitute another ingredient, or leave one out altogether. The three trails are:

Solo Flavour Trails – variations on a single ingredient
Affinity Flavour Trails – the magic of one plus one making three or more
Bridging Flavour Trails – bridging two ingredients with a third ingredient or technique

The Solo Flavour Trail

Before you look for a new ingredient to enhance something, think first about using a different version of one already in the dish.

This is the safest but least used trail towards creative cooking, relying on the absolute affinity an ingredient will have for itself, even in different forms.

Rather than choosing to flavour an apple pie with orange or nuts or quinces, the Solo Flavour Trail technique predicates choosing only other ingredients made from apples.

When I baked deep-dish apple pies for Mr Christian's Deli in London I would chunk or thickly segment apple and then combine these with apple sauce or purée. Other times I mixed them with cooked sliced apples, or with raw apple, sliced, chopped or grated. If one of the apples were acidic I'd choose a naturally sweeter one for the other – say Gravenstein apples in slices combined with sweeter Braeburns as the purée. I could also have added spiced apple butter, apple honey or apple cheese, apple leather or crab apple jelly, or Calvados (apple brandy) or concentrated fresh varietal apple juice or cider or apple wine. Each would give a different end-flavour: each is guaranteed to work because each is made from apple.

Follow a Flavour Trail of flavour, texture and colour with the same ingredient and you really can't go wrong – unless you use too many at a time. Even then it will be more of a muddle than a disaster, which is why the Solo Flavour Trail is so reliable when you are in a hurry. But if you added something that didn't taste of apple but which merely has an affinity with it – cinnamon say, demerara or maple sugar, or grated orange zest or rose-water – and if you added too much of any of these, it could be disastrous. Adding more or less sugar to your apple pie will heighten rather than change the flavours that are there.

If you use only such sweet apples as Braeburns or Cox's Orange Pippins for an apple crumble or apple sponge or apple pie you don't even need sugar. That's an excellent example of letting an ingredient do the work for you, and you only have to take notice when you eat the raw apple to know such things.

But Solo Flavour Trails don't have to stick to variations of an ingredient against such simple backgrounds as a creamy cheesecake or tomato sauce. Whatever else is sitting sullenly before you in need of a flavour or taste boost, you'll always be better thinking about dramatising one of the ingredients already in the dish than adding something new.

Sometimes it is as simple as stirring in fresh herbs or spices, the same herbs or spices that have been cooking for some time. The tang of their freshness now complementing the mellowness of the long-cooked ones is probably all the sulky pot needed.

Taste Trails, Too

Trails can be a flight of taste rather than of flavour, a progression of something salt, sweet, acid, bitter or umami.

When a slice of sweet fresh white bread is spread thickly with butter (essentially sweet with a salt undertone) and then with a fruit jam, the sweet taste is actually your essential building block, and it is onto variations of sweetness that you have added flavour – a little from the bread, something from the butter and loads from the jam. It's something we have unconsciously done for pleasure from the moment we were first allowed to help ourselves at table. And when delicious flavours are also present – the starchiness of the bread, the creaminess of the butter and the fruitiness of the jam – it's easy to see why something so simple can be so satisfying. It's hitting all the buttons of taste *and* flavour.

The Affinity Flavour Trail

Affinity means putting two ingredients together and getting a result tasting like three or more.

When two simple ingredients go together extra-harmoniously it is called an affinity, and every good cook exploits these mercilessly. It's not always lazy or uncreative to serve just two ingredients on a plate. Nature's bountiful generosity effortlessly does the work when you combine just two ingredients that work wizardry together, many of which you have been enjoying all your life – bread and butter, bacon and eggs, strawberries and cream . . .

An Affinity Flavour Trail zooms your senses off into unexpected realms and so is a secret of getting good food onto the table quickly. It's dear Dame Nature doing the work for you, and I shouldn't give a single guilty thought. It's what she does.

You know dozens of Affinity Flavour Trails, but what you think makes them work together isn't always the first flavour you taste in your mouth but sometimes the more subtle flavour lurking beneath, like the citric acidity beneath basil, or the spiciness behind Valrhona's single-estate Gran Couva chocolate.

Some flavour affinities are more powerful than others. Some are mere complements, where two ingredients just play particularly nicely together, like butter with peas or carrots. Others send urgent sensual messages, and the playing about becomes adult and edgy, like chocolate and raspberries, or raspberries and rose-water. As well, personal preferences and individual palates come into play; one man's mere complement might be another's sublime affinity.

As you look through the Affinity lists on page 63–88 you will – or should – suddenly see recipe ideas flash into your mind. Trust them, for when your recipe whims are based on classic affinities, you can follow Flavour Trails confidently and always have the basis of something delicious.

The Affinity Trail Quick Fix

If you are stuck for ideas, start with the partners of a familiar and trusted affinity and take one or both of them to a new place.

Sometimes you'll find a new flavour just by playing with the proportions of an affinity couple, perhaps even turning the affinity on its head. Instead of serving bacon with a little maple syrup, think of maple syrup as the main flavour with bacon as the backup, in a quick-bread perhaps, or scones or pancakes.

With tomato and basil, where tomato usually dominates, a basil pesto might become the main ingredient and then, studded with chunks of sun-dried tomato, double up as a quick dressing for a plate of pasta. Different proportions and textures and flavours, but the rock-solid Affinity Flavour Trail between tomato and basil means it can't help being a triumph.

Anything really worth eating will always be able to be broken down to find reliable affinities somewhere in its construction: a recipe with no identifiable affinities is not a recipe to be trusted. It's amazing how quickly you can learn to deconstruct any recipe into its important primary and secondary affinities. If you can't understand the structure of a recipe based on affinities, turn the page, order something else or start again. Combine this with reading recipes for affinities as a hobby. Each time you recognise whether there is or is not a basic affinity at work by looking for Flavour Trails you have learned a new lesson, and have taught yourself a little more about cooking without other people's recipes.

Longer Affinity Trails

You don't have to stop at one affinity. If you follow trusted Affinity Flavour Trails you can build a chain of affinities. A fruit salad is a good example, because each fruit goes with each of the other fruits, some better than others. But nonetheless you are usually on solid ground when you are combining fruits.

One affinity I know I can always trust is bacon and potato, a real winner. To that I know I can happily add well-cooked onion, because that has an affinity with both bacon and potato. Where next with bacon, potato and onion? Something to do with tomato would work, and so would cumin seeds, building a chain of related flavours. But this won't make something nice to eat unless you sort out in your mind the proportions you want, and thus which *taste* should dominate (salt, sweet, etc.), and then which aspect of which *flavour* of each of the ingredients should be the focus. It could be the inherent sweetness of the onion and potato, dramatised by chopped tomato, or bound with tomato sauce and given a salty tang by the bacon. It could be the sweetness of long-cooked onion that has then been caramelised and used as the base for chunks of the other ingredients, in a sauce on a pizza . . . and so on.

Next time you are in a fix and want to add a flavour or taste or ingredient, run your eyes back and forth over the invaluable affinity lists later in the book and pick out something from there. You'll have to think about how much you should use, but you'll have a fair chance of it being both right and somewhat flexible because it will be at home with other affinities of the same ingredient.

You will instinctively know many two-ingredient affinities are even better if a third ingredient is added, the Bridging Flavour Trail technique. New worlds are created when you add butter to carrots and dill, or cream to chicken and tarragon. Chocolate and raspberry are powerful partners that need no one and nothing else. Yet if you interfere and bully them up to greater heights by daring to introduce them to cream or orange or strawberries or rum . . .

The Bridging Flavour Trail

In most good things you eat you will be able to identify three major components.

Here's where you really start to strike out and become original. For here the Flavour Trail is based on complementary ingredients rather than affinity ingredients. Affinity ingredients rarely need much else with them to be satisfying to eat together –

although the pleasure is often increased when you do this. Complementary ingredients go together but . . . somehow there is a hole in the middle of the palate, there's not total satisfaction with the combination, and what you add to fill the missing gap is what makes you a culinary genius or a tasteless drone.

The three major components of a Bridging Flavour Trail are:

1 The **MAIN INGREDIENT**
   plus
2 The **MAJOR COMPLEMENTARY INGREDIENT**
   plus
3 The **FLAVOUR BRIDGE**, which is the **INGREDIENT** or **TECHNIQUE** blending the first two into something bigger and better

The key to the most exciting cookery ideas is how you identify and construct that vital third component, the Flavour Bridge, the special something that solves a problem and then allows your Flavour Trail to travel further afield.

Constructing such Flavour Bridges is the major technique used in creating new recipes, and the major reason for the success of old ones. The best way to illustrate this is a simple formula:

> *If* **a** *goes with* **b,** *and* **b** *goes with* **c,** *and* **c** *goes with* **d,**
> *then* **a** *will go with* **d:** *but you must build a Flavour*
> *Bridge between* **a** *and* **d** *and this must be built on*
> *affinities and complements from* **a** *to* **b** *to* **c** *to* **d**.

Following Flavour Trails from ingredient to ingredient, based on each one's affinities and flavour family lets you check if a combination that veered into your mind from a side track will or won't work. You generally find your trail has been discovered after tracking up several byways where you found no true affinity awaiting. But generally you are looking to be able to see and say what the flavour links are between any two ingredients.

Sometimes the bridging component of a recipe might actually be a combination of ingredients, like a mint-raspberry gravy or a complicated curry paste. However, even within the paste's ingredients you will recognise a single dominant spice or spice affinity (usually cumin and coriander) supported and expanded by subsidiaries following lesser Affinity Flavour Trails. Often you'll find several of the spice combinations do this and then create a wondrous Bridging Flavour Trail between a couple of spices you'd think didn't belong. The addition of salt, sugar or lemon juice is not included in this book as a major ingredient or as a major complement and this is its own warning: it is pointless to prepare and cook anything if its appeal is then smothered by sugar, salt or lemon juice. To which sins must be added the mindless scattering of chopped chives, as though they had no discernible flavour to impinge on what has been created.

The drench of lemon juice and shower of chive are commonly seen on television. And although the acid of lemon juice is indeed a terrific way *finally* to season and bind flavours, lemon juice is more than acidity. It has flavour of its own and thus can also be used to hide faults in flavours of the dish (and it often is). Added profusely it becomes the major flavour and this is just as bad as thoughtlessly adding raw onion or chives or chillies; I sometimes watch and wonder if there was any point having other ingredients present for anything but to soak up the juices – you can't taste much of them with so much lemon juice suffocating them. Ditto the use of chilli and other strong herbs and spices, cheese and other last-minute camouflage. If you want to finish something with chives, particularly, remember they have an onion flavour, and that should have been factored in from the start. Too often the chives are there 'for colour': using that phrase to explain any ingredient on a plate is the most damning condemnation of a cook or chef's inability really to understand flavours, in cooking or eating – unless we are all to revert to a previous custom, and never eat what was meant to be a garnish.

In virtually all great eating the Bridging Flavour Trail is the major technique underpinning its success. It's how both the simplest and the most creative dishes work and if that structure can't be found at once, and you can't find good affinities, perhaps you should choose something else.

INTENSITY OF FLAVOUR

The final flourish of a successful ingredient combination will all depend on the intensity of each taste and flavour. It's all very well adding a drop or two of lemon juice to an oyster to add a piquant acidic edge to the salt-sweetness. But add too much and the intensity of the lemon juice will over-balance the natural sweetness of the oyster – and what's the point of that?

The coldness of ice cream will blast up the intensity of any acid taste but mask the full effect of sweetness; it doesn't matter how carefully you made your ice cream, if the strawberries don't have a big enough flavour or natural sweetness (even if from an added ingredient) the ice cream can't possibly taste balanced or as good as you hoped. Mean-flavoured strawberries should only be eaten at ambient temperature when whatever virtue they have will be at its maximum.

Thus when you are looking for Flavour Trail helpers or for substitutes, think as much about each ingredient's intensity level. If you wanted to add an elderflower scent to cream you'd have to let blossoms soak in it for ages to pick up any scent and might also have to compensate for their inherent bitterness by adding lemon juice – and suddenly the recipe wouldn't be at all what you had in mind. A muscat grape or elderflower cordial offers the same flavour in much greater concentration and intensity, and so a very little would flavour the cream at once – and you could experiment to get the intensity just as you want, from a tantalising whiff to a really strident presence. You can work out such things in your head, but your tongue will tell you more confidently. And next time you might do it the other way round.

FLAVOUR TRAIL LISTS

These invaluable lists are the start of personal Flavour Trails and also suggest substitute ingredients.

LIST ONE

CLASSIC AFFINITIES

Here is a checklist of just a few of the most important classic affinities you might – should, even – have eaten and enjoyed. All are the basis of delicious, reliable dishes. The list is not intended to be exhaustive, and the affinity ingredients in each listing are in no special order. More than anything it's a checklist to set your mind racing – and as you recognise more of what goes well with what, you'll grow in confidence as you strike out on your own Flavour Trails.

Note: Depending on an individual's palate profile, one man's affinity will be another's mere complement, in which case they'll need the benefit of a Bridging Flavour Trail, so don't expect fireworks with every combination suggested by this list.

Almonds with sugar, sweet spices, cream, butter, rose-water or orange-flower water, praline, rum, cognac, beans, broccoli, potato, pumpkin, sweet potato, oranges, plums, pears, apricots, dried fruits

Apple with Cheddar cheese, blue cheeses, pears, quince, all citrus (orange particularly), cream, butter, most herbs and spices, rose-water, orange-flower water, pork, duck, goose, bacon, onion, potato, pumpkin, sweet potato, root vegetables, red cabbage

Bacon with eggs, maple syrup, fresh green and red cabbage, pickled cabbage, onion, garlic, potato, all beans and pulses, green beans, capsicums, apples, pears, peaches, dried apples and pears, pineapple, chicken, turkey, game birds, juniper, cumin, coriander

Basil with tomato, pumpkin and squash, fish, shellfish, pork, lamb, orange, lime leaf, lemon grass, garlic, pasta, pine nuts, almonds, Parmesan, Grana Padano, vodka

Black pepper with dill, strawberries, butter, hot lightly caramelised pineapple, vodka, mixed spice (for baking)

Blue cheese with red or white sweet wines, apples, pears, butter, cream, celery, walnuts, almonds

Brie with fresh pears, butter, oatmeal

Cabbage with bacon, black pepper, pickling spices, butter, garlic, caraway, juniper berries, cumin, coriander, mustard, salt beef, potato, onion, apples, dried apples, dried pears

Cardamom with Danish pastry, sugar, coffee, chocolate, butter, raisins, cinnamon, cumin, coriander, saffron, rose-water

Carrot with dill, parsley, coriander leaf and seed, chervil, ground coriander, cumin, ginger, cinnamon, butter, cream, garlic, orange, lemon, apple, pineapple, raisins, currants

Chicken with tarragon and . . . everything!

Chocolate with coffee (mocha), orange (Jaffa), lemon grass, raspberry, rose-water, mint, vanilla, violet, thyme, rosemary, lime, black pepper, cream, milk, cinnamon, allspice, nuts (especially toasted), fish, and many more including a touch of chilli or chili compound

Coffee with cinnamon, walnut, orange, allspice, cardamom, rum, vanilla, butter, cream, chocolate, chili compound

Coriander leaf with . . . everywhere you would use parsley but note the root, usually discarded in the West has by far the biggest and most virile flavour

Coriander seed with most vegetables (especially pumpkin), oranges, fruit salad, pork dishes, chicken dishes, such oily fish as salmon, bay leaves, most fruits, especially red plums

Corned beef with cabbage, parsley, carrots, potato (mashed)

Courgettes with chicken or tarragon (celestial when all three are served together), summer vegetables (especially tomato, aubergine, capsicums, garlic, onion), cheeses (especially cream, Gruyère, Parmesan, Grana Padano)

Duck with orange, pear, apple, cherries, mango, pineapple, lychees, caramel, peas, poached cucumber, cumin seeds, black pepper, cinnamon, bacon, rhubarb, mint, dried apples and pears, pickled cherries

Fish, flat with butter, citrus, grapes, poached cucumber, dill, parsley

Fish, oily with cider vinegar, onion, pickling spices, bay, garlic, horseradish, beetroot, parsley

Fish, round with butter, parsley, tomato, olives, olive oil, garlic

Gin with tonic and cucumber (a Potteresque transformation), fresh pineapple (ditto)

Green beans with nutmeg or summer savoury, dill, toasted hazelnuts or almonds, butter, bacon, peas, broad beans, peas

Lamb with mint (*not* mint sauce, which is for hogget and mutton), thyme, garlic, fresh not dried rosemary, Kaffir lime leaf, medlars, rowan, redcurrants, quince, honey, dried apricot and mint, sweet spices, saffron, dried apricot or armadine, oranges

Mint with apricot (especially dried or as armadine), strawberry, raspberries, rhubarb, orange, lamb, duck, cold salmon, mackerel, salad ingredients (especially tomato), tomato sauces, sweet spices, chocolate, black tea, green tea, lemon grass

Mutton with mint sauce, garlic, curry spice mixtures, sweet spices and dried fruits, laver bread (some say!)

Pecans with butter, caramel, cinnamon, allspice, nutmeg, sweet potato, yams, pumpkins and squashes

Pineapple with gin (with no heat – amazing!), orange, lime, mango, passion fruit, rum, brown sugars, butter, black pepper (with pineapple cooked and caramelised in butter), mint, coconut, fresh ginger, chocolate

Pine nuts with currants, rice, sweet spices, butter, quince, apples, dried apricots, caramel, lamb, fish, almonds, rose-water, orange-flower water

Pork with bay leaf, brown sugars, ground coriander, five-spice, cloves, pineapple, apples, dried pears, stone fruits (including prunes), oranges, raisins, currants, rum

Prawns with butter, olive oil, garlic, dill, mint, tomato, basil, orange, saffron, cumin (especially roasted seeds)

Quince with apples, pears, almonds, bacon, lamb, pork, chicken, duck, goose, game birds, vine fruits, cinnamon, bay, cardamom, butter, olive oil, saffron, vanilla

Raspberries with rose-water, chocolate, strawberries, cream, orange juice, orange-flower water, orange spirits and liqueurs, butter (shortbread), mint, rhubarb

Rhubarb with orange, lemon, brown sugars, cinnamon, cardamom, allspice, mint, strawberries, raspberries

Root vegetables with other root vegetables butter, cream, sherry (especially with swedes)

Rum with vanilla, butter, sweet spices (especially nutmeg), chocolate, coconut, pineapple, mango, raspberries, coffee

Saffron with rice, potato, fish, seafood, seafood soups, pears, apples, quince, chicken, butter, cream, milk, vanilla, rosewater, orange-flower water, ground almonds, honey, sugar, lamb

Salmon with butter, vanilla, poached cucumber, dill, tarragon, celery, green tea, lemon grass, Kaffir lime leaf, citrus juices, bacon, pancetta, chorizo

Smoked fish with horseradish cream, mustards, citrus juice, beetroot, green or smoked bacon, vinegars, sauerkraut, soured cream

Strawberries with orange juice, mint, raspberries, orange-flower water, black pepper, green peppercorns, nuts (especially toasted), cream

Tarragon with courgettes/zucchini, especially with cream and/or chicken, fish, black pepper

Tomato with walnut, hazelnut, orange, basil, garlic, olive oil, sherry vinegar, balsamic vinegar, bay leaf, oregano, mint, thyme, or almost anything

Vanilla with rum, cream, butter, milk, black tea, coffee, chocolate, caramel, sweet spices, fish and seafood, almonds, walnuts, pistachios, dried fruits (especially apricots, prunes and plums), rose-water, orange-flower water, berry fruits, carrots

Walnuts with honey, cinnamon, tomatoes, dark sugars, caramel, almonds, butter, sweet potatoes, yams, pumpkins and squashes, butter – and a substitute for pecans

SWEET-TASTING INGREDIENTS

Here are groups of (usually) multi-flavoured ingredients sweet enough to fit into the 'sweet primary taste' family. Add extras as you encounter them, whether or not they also belong to any other grouping. Note as you do how the sweetness is almost always balanced by a cleansing, finishing acidity (except for such as marshmallows, candyfloss, cordial drinks, cakes, muffins and fizzy drinks, but they don't really count as ingredients).

Use the list to find substitutes for Flavour Trail necessities when your cupboard is unexpectedly bare.

Alcohols: sweet dessert wines (such as Sauternes, Tokays and muscats), botrytised wines, *vin santo*, ice wine, amontillado, cream and Pedro Ximinez sherries, Malmsey and Bual Madeira wines, Malaga wine, port wines, Mirin and Shaoxing rice wines, demi-sec and doux champagnes, and most fortified wines. Liqueurs are always sweet, sugar being added to flavoured white spirits: if a liqueur is not sweet it is not a liqueur. Unsweetened spirits are rum, vodka, gin, and fruit brandies like Calvados or an eau-de-vie distilled from grapes or fruit, or Cognac, Armagnac and grape brandies made anywhere other than those two French districts

Butters, creams and milk products: these all have a marked natural sweetness largely from lactose, the major milk sugar, and from milk fat. Cream contains no lactose and its sweetness thus comes solely from milk fat. Many cuisines deliberately use butters and creams as sweeteners, particularly with fish. Mascarpone (a soured cream and not a cheese), cream cheeses, such soft cheeses as Camembert and Brie when in perfect condition, and true mozzarellas – bufala made from buffalo milk and fior de latte made from cows' milk – all contain natural sweetness

Fruits: most ripe fruits have inherent sweetness; the exceptions are the quince, sloes and medlars and old varieties of persimmon, all noted for bitterness. Note the last two eventually ripen or blet (over-ripen) to delicious sweetness

Dried fruits: currants, raisins, apricots, pears, peaches, apples, prunes; cranberries are not naturally sweet so dried cranberries come with added sugar

Fish: very fresh squid/calamari, monkfish, cod, grouper, sole, halibut and turbot all have a sweet element. This is because of their glycol content – yes, that's right, an antifreeze

Fruit juices and fruit purées: many need added sweetness or acidity to make them finally palatable but are fundamentally sweet

Herb: stevia

Seafood: lobster, crayfish, scallops, white crabmeat, small mussels

Sweeteners: honey, palm sugar, maple sugar and maple syrup, golden syrup, molasses, corn syrup, maltose, glucose, glucose syrup, sugars (white, golden and brown), coconut milk, coconut cream, barley-malt syrup, date sugar (dried ground dates), natural/concentrated cane-sugar syrup

Vegetables: parsnip, yams, carrots, sweet potatoes, sweet corn, pumpkin, fresh green peas and beans

SALTY-TASTING INGREDIENTS

Here are groups of (usually) multi-flavoured ingredients salty enough to fit into the 'salt primary taste' family. Add extras as you experience them, whether or not they also belong to any other grouping. And use the list to find substitutes for Flavour Trail necessities when your cupboard is unexpectedly bare.

Cheese: feta cheeses – kept in brine: such blue cheeses as Roquefort, many other sheep's milk cheeses

Condiments: anchovy paste (including Gentleman's Relish), Asian fish sauces (nam pla, etc.), soy sauces (but see umami, too), miso, Asian dried shrimps, shrimp paste (*kapi*)

Fish: anchovies (dry-salted or brined), salt cod/stockfish, many smoked fish, botargo (salted roe), smoked roe, salted herrings (many variations)

Fruit: olives*, salt-preserved lemons, umeboshi (Japanese salted plums)

Meat: hams, gammons, bacon, lardons, pancetta, salt/corned beef, pickled pork, other brined/corned cuts, other smoked flesh (such as chicken breast, duck, turkey, etc.), mutton birds

Seafood: oysters, raw clams, cockles, winkles, etc. – the natural saltiness from the sea is diluted when they are steamed or boiled.

Vegetables: samphire (naturally salted), sea vegetables/seaweed, capers, cornichons, gherkins, salt cucumbers (many variations), canned vegetables in brine

Olives can be drained of brine and then stored in olive oil, which makes them more palatable to many and more amenable to having other flavourings added; the possibilities seem endless.

ACID/SOUR/SHARP-TASTING INGREDIENTS

Here are groups of (usually) multi-flavoured ingredients acid enough to fit into the 'acid primary taste' family. Add extras as you experience them, whether or not they also belong to any other grouping. And use the list to find substitutes for Flavour Trail necessities when your cupboard is unexpectedly bare.

Condiments: vinegars of all kinds, balsamic vinegars, Italian *sapa* and *vin cotto* (which are pretty much the same thing), sumac, citric acid, verjuice (sometimes only marginally acid)

Dairy: all fermented milk products from yoghurts to soured cream to kumiss, true buttermilk, cultured buttermilk

Fruit: citrus of all kinds (flesh, zest and juice), unripened orchard fruits especially apples, barely ripe grapes), cranberries, tamarind, gooseberries, rhubarb, some cherries, pomegranate pulp, passion fruit, tamarillo

Herbs: sorrel, lemon grass, Kaffir lime leaf, lemon balm, lemon thyme

BITTER-TASTING INGREDIENTS

Here are groups of (usually) multi-flavoured ingredients bitter enough to fit into the 'bitter primary taste' family. There are very few foods where bitterness is the major taste; it is something more often found as an aftertaste. Add extras as you experience them, whether or not they also belong to any other grouping. Use the list to find substitutes for Flavour Trail necessities when your cupboard is unexpectedly bare.

Alcoholic drinks: many traditional 'medicinal' drinks made with herbs or roots are distinctly bitter even though also rather sweet – Fernet Branca is one. Campari and other alcoholic bitters served as aperitifs are less confrontational in bitterness, but that's what they are. Any beer, lager or stout that is hopped will have a greater or lesser bitter element; so will young red wines with a high tannin content

Condiments: angostura and other culinary bitters

Citrus: some rinds (usually ameliorated by cooking). concentrated citric oils

Drinks: tonic water, bitter lemon, over-roasted or over-brewed black coffee, over-brewed black tea, some tannic green teas

Flavouring/ingredient: unsweetened chocolate, high-cocoa-solid/low-sugar chocolate bars, cocoa powder, quinine, smoke/smoked coating on smoked foods, tobacco

Flowers: elderflowers, hops (see drinks), lavender flowers (don't do it!)

Fruits: aloes, sloes, persimmons (old varieties), quince.

Herbs: rue, yarrow, wormwood, chamomile, tansy, gentian, horehound

Spice: paprika (especially smoked paprika)

Vegetables: green-leaf chicory and relatives, mizuna, cavolo nero, dandelion leaf, endive/witloof, kale, Treviso, radicchio, overcooked spring greens, ditto brussel sprouts, silver beet/chard, romaine lettuce, iceberg lettuce

UMAMI-TASTING INGREDIENTS

Here are groups of (usually) multi-flavoured ingredients umami enough to fit into the 'umami primary taste' family. Add extras as you think of them, whether or not they also belong to any other grouping. Use the list to find substitutes for Flavour Trail necessities when your cupboard is unexpectedly bare.

Condiments: tomato sauces, ketchups (including Worcestershire sauce), soy sauces, fish sauces (nam pla), Marmite/Vegemite, miso

Drinks: green tea

Fish/Seafood: *katsuobushi* –dried tuna flakes

Flavouring/ingredient: Bovril, aged cheeses (especially Parmesan, Grana Padano and other aged hard cheeses); seaweeds (especially kombu) and dashi (the stock made from it); meat, poultry and fish stocks (especially beef and veal)

Meat: pork (including ham and other processed products), beef, veal, poultry

Vegetables: cooked mushrooms, cooked and some raw tomatoes, potatoes

LIST SEVEN

HOT, PEPPERY INGREDIENTS

Most of these are condiments, and some like horseradish and mustards will extinguish much of their power when heat is applied, leaving aromatic flavours behind: that's why mustard makes a surprisingly good coating for oily fish that is to be roasted or grilled. The bite will be tamed, the flavour enhanced. Good.

Condiments: horseradish, mustard (English, Dijon, etc.), wasabi, some olive oils (particularly Tuscan oils made with the *frantoio* or *moraiolo* olive), Tabasco, chilli sauces (including sweet chilli sauces)

Spices: ginger, peppercorns (black, white, green and red), Australian native pepperbark, horopito and kawa kawa from New Zealand, Szechuan peppercorns, chillies (green and red), cayenne pepper, *quatre épices* and other pepper mixtures, hot paprika

Vegetables: rocket, watercress, mustard greens, mizuna, raw garlic

CHILLI HEAT TABLE

Chillies change their heat quotient and flavour as well as their names when they are dried – mild jalapenos become the much hotter habaneros when they are dried and lightly smoked – and are perhaps the most intriguing challenge of all for the creative cook

Until the 21st century, the hottest chilli pepper recorded was a habanero with a Scoville reading of 577,000 units. This has been unequivocally eclipsed by the Dorset Naga, sourced from Bangladesh but grown in the UK, and which has been rated at over 900,000 Scoville heat units. Interesting but, to my mind and palate, food only for thought.

Classically, chillies were measured on the Scoville chart, but this has been simplified into the Official Chilli /Chille Pepper Heat Scale of 0–10; you'll find both here.

OFFICIAL CHILLI /CHILLE PEPPER HEAT SCALE

Rating	Scoville units	Varieties
10	100–300,000	Habanero, Scotch Bonnet
9	50–100,000	Bahamian, African Birdseye, Santaka, Chiltepin, Aji
8	30–50,000	Thai (prik khee noo), kwangsi, Piri piri, Piquin, Cayenne, Tabasco
7	15–30,000	de Arbol, Habanero Hot Sauce
6	5–15,000	Serrano, Hot Yellow Wax,
5	2,500–5,000	Tabasco Sauce, Jalapeno, Mirasol, Amarillo
4	1,500–2,500	Large thick Cayenne, Louisiana Hot Sauce, Cascabel, Sandia
3	1–1,500	Yellow Wax Hot, Ancho, Pasilla, Espanola
2	500–1,000	Old Bay seasoning, Big Jim
1	100–500	Cherry, pickled pepperoncini, Hungarian hot paprika
0	0–100	Sweet Banana, Bell, Capsicum, Sweet Peppers

THE BACKGROUNDS

These are the ingredients drawn on singly and in different combinations to provide bulk and background to the more important ingredients of a meal. Some are bland, some (like buckwheat) have a definite flavour, others (like polenta) have a sweetness to add. Their differences are what makes them appealing, and most can be substituted one for another to advantage.

Baked: breads, pastry
Dairy: eggs, milk, cream
Grains: rice and rice noodles, wheat, pasta and couscous, polenta, amaranth, quinoa, buckwheat
Pulses: soybeans and products (noodles, tofu, mung bean noodles), kidney beans, chick peas
Vegetables: potatoes, taro, yucca/manioc

THE FLAVOUR FAMILIES

Flavours are the aromas and sensations that provocatively swirl about on top of the five tastes in your mouth. It is flavour that kick-starts you into creating your own recipes to swiftly solve the problem of not having a specified ingredient in your store cupboard. By recognising the Flavour Family to which the fugitive belongs you can safely move to a substitute – which could be even better.

You might find I have identified rather more Flavour Families than you expect or that you will disagree with my groupings. No matter. These are what work for me. Feel free to rename groups or to develop groupings of your own, a sure sign your unique palate is developing.

It's worth taking some time to go through the Flavour Trail lists. Mentally taste some of the ingredients in each group to discover what they might have in common. This is not always easy – I can't always put into words the relationship of one to another, but I know if I think of them as, say, earthy or sappy or floral I will use them in the right way. It's worth going a bit further, and also to work back to assign each of the ingredients to one of the Taste Families.

Remember, too, my Flavour Families are based on the most immediate flavour that each ingredient has. With few exceptions, flavours are made up of lots of components, and sometimes it is a lesser contributor that is actually the key to opening the way to a new Flavour Trail. For instance, it is thought chocolate is a mixture of up to 400 different flavours and aromas. Identifying the rock-bottom characteristics of each flavour is a sure way to turn off the motorways of banal flavour to explore the country lanes of seductive Flavour Trails, which then lead to gratification by providing something new. Life should be so simple . . .

These lists are perhaps the most important resources of all for the creative cook who likes to blaze their own Flavour Trail. When considering substitute ingredients think not only of their taste and flavour characteristics but also about the intensity of each.

Recognising an individual ingredient's intensity of flavour is vital to understanding Flavour Families and how they can help along Flavour Trails to quite new destinations. Adding a mild ingredient might mean adding so much to get the right flavour you also change the texture of the dish unacceptably: choosing a very strong one means the slightest slip-up can mean instant disaster.

I don't suggest these lists are final or exhaustive. They are meant to get your mind racing, not to inhibit it by doing all the work for you.

So, here's the final list.

Aniseed/Liquorice

This flavour is anathema to some people, something most dramatised when you serve fennel, raw or cooked. It's probably my favourite vegetable but there are others in my family who can barely be at the same table. An equal surprise to many is that aniseed is one of the major flavours of basil, which they all love.

Drinks: absinthe, the anisados of Ecuador, anisette, arak, Kummel, ouzo, pastis, raki, Pernod, Sambucca
Flavourings: liquorice powder or paste, Tahitian vanilla
Fruit: Ellisons Orange apple – develops after picking; some russets have a notable fennel flavour (Brownlee's Russet and Reinette Grise de St-Ogne are very strong) and the French *fenouillets* family of apples all have this characteristic
Herbs: aniseed myrtle (an Australian native herb), anise vert, basil (especially Thai or Holy basil varieties *O. basilicum*

'Horapha', and *O. x citriodorum* 'Siam Queen'), chervil, colts-foot, dill weed, Durban-poison (a very strong locally bred South African marijuana), fennel leaves or stems of green fennel, sweet cicely, tarragon (the French variety only and never grassy Russian tarragon)

Spices: celery seeds, dill seed, fennel seeds, five-spice powder, liquorice root, Spice of Angels (a Californian, fennel-based pollen), star anise (the flavour of pastis)

Vegetable: basil sprouts in salads, sweet fennel bulb (raw or cooked)

Buttery

Buttery flavours are often, perhaps always, accompanied by a texture that reminds you of butter; they are essentially sweet but, like butter, have a little acidity too. They seem to like salt and sometimes it's hard to distinguish buttery from creamy.

Drinks: true buttermilk
Flavourings: butterscotch, of course
Fruit: avocado, ripe bananas
Nuts: Brazil nuts
Vegetables: butternut squash

Citric

Here I mean the flavours of citrus fruits, all of them identified as having an acidic taste to a greater or lesser measure. Members of the citric family aren't quite as interchangeable as many chefs think. Orange juice often needs plenty of lemon juice in it to work in cooking – and lemon but not orange juice has the property of keeping such as sliced apples from turning brown. Grapefruit is often a disaster in cooking and is very difficult to make seem anything more than feral or an outsider. It's the sort of ingredient that looks good on paper but generally disappoints; anyway, grapefruit interferes with some very important commonly taken drugs and who knows who is on what these days? I'd never choose grapefruit if anything else citric were available, not even the pink ones . . . except the top award at the 2005 Great Taste awards went to the pink grapefruit and gin sorbet from Minghellas of the Isle of Wight. (If your breakfast grapefruit seems a bit boring tomorrow, you know now how to add the liveliness you crave.)

But when you think citric, think of more than just their juice, think of freshly grated zest, aged zest, poached segments . . . and think how many fruits have citric overtones and undertones. Have you explored Australia's native produce, especially lemon myrtle? It's a revelation.

Drinks: Curacao and Cointreau are the best-known liqueurs (many countries have such specialities – Corfu makes one with bergamot, the citrus that flavours Earl Grey tea), Earl Grey tea, Lady Grey tea (which is orangey), real lemonade

Flavourings: orange-flower water, Boyajian oils (lime, lemon and orange), dried tangerine and other peels, Iranian dried limes, Iranian sumac

Fruit: bergamot, calamondin, clementines, grapefruit, kumquats, lemons, limes, mandarins, minneolas, oranges

Herbs: Kaffir lime leaves, lemon balm, lemon grass, fresh bay, lemon thyme, Australia's lemon myrtle, coriander leaf

Spices: coriander seeds (orange-like), cumin seeds (lemon-like)

Creamy

Creaminess in food and drink is as much about mouth-feel as taste and flavour. That's because creaminess is much associated with fat and oils and these are the greatest givers of comforting mouth-feel. Most foods we think of as creamy taste that way because they contain cream.

Cheeses: cream and full-milk cheeses

Drinks: full milk, horchata from tiger nuts, coconut water and milk, coconut cream, almond and other nut milks, cream liqueurs (Baileys and such)

Flavourings: butter (especially unsalted), cream, such cultured
products as sour cream, crème fraîche, etc
Nuts: almonds, Brazil, cashew, macadamias
Vegetables: mashed potatoes with butter and milk don't count!
Some potato varieties do

Earthy

Others might call these flavours woody or a combination of woody
and earthy. Just thinking about them one by one will show the
connection, however you choose to describe them.

Herbs: saffron
Vegetables: raw beetroot, raw or lightly blanched beet leaves,
swede, turnip, the best black truffles, and some dried mushrooms (cep/porcini, morels and fairy-ring particularly)
Other: snails without garlic butter, some starchy potatoes,
squid ink

Floral

Just think how many fruits have floral flavours, especially
the more fragrant lychees, mangoes, strawberries and raspberries. That's why fruity and floral flavours generally have
excellent affinities. Rose-water blends seamlessly with lychee,
and makes raspberries taste even more of themselves. Orange-
flower water inches even the best strawberries closer to celestial
perfection; strawberries dipped into undiluted elderflower
cordial jostle them.

Drinks: elderflower cordial, rose syrup
Flavourings: vanilla, orange-flower water and rose-water, jasmine
essence, screw pine (pandanus) essence, edible lavender oil
(use only the English *augustifolia* varieties and not the French
stoechas, the varieties with those tarty butterfly tops)
Flowers: edible flower petals (elderflower, pansies, violets, heart-
sease, violas, day lilies, roses, marigolds – *officinalis* only –

nasturtiums and many more), and lavender (but use the flowers only as decoration, never as an ingredient, for they are always chewy or bitter or both)

Fruit: mango, white peaches and nectarines, passionfruit pulp with or without the seeds and ideally never cooked

Fruity

Sometimes there's an affinity between fruits of quite differing flavours because they are from the same botanical family: hence apples, pears and quinces always make friends in a dish because they are all members of the *Rosaceae* family, the rose family. That's why rose-water is so good with each of them – American Shakers baked an apple and rose-water pie, the Middle East knows how good orange-flower water or rose-water (or a mixture of both) are with dried fruits. But be careful to know what is fruity and what is merely sweet – see above.

Flavourings: some floral honey, especially orange-blossom honey and the tropical bloom honey from Pitcairn Island

Fruit: Muscat/muscatel from elderflower or from grapes

Herbal

The flavour of herbs, which are almost universally green leaves, is more complicated than people imagine, and most have an extraordinary ability to bring together other flavours in an entirely new way yet still retain individual virtues. That's why we love them and why they have been loved for so many centuries. But use them to stitch, to complement, to underpin and not to dominate; that's not their role. Now do the single most important thing you can to improve your cooking. Throw away your packets of mixed dried herbs. Start to use each herb individually and ally them to individual flavour families, like citric for thyme and chervil, aniseed for basil or tarragon. Your food will croon rather than cackle like a lunatic.

Lactic

It's common to think this means something tasting sharp because of lactic acid, but it doesn't, it means milky. Unsalted butter is called lactic butter, a term that means the pasteurised cream has had a bacterial culture put back to replace that killed in the pasteurising process; when it develops it adds a particular flavour most encountered in unsalted/lactic butters of Germany and Denmark. The lightly acidic milk made from almonds might also be called lactic, as is the milk made from tiger nuts, horchata.

Nutty

This is related to the sweet taste and it commonly gives an especially rich, round mouth-feel because of nuts' integral oils. Yet a nutty flavour is normally a sort of aftertaste, a comforting aspect of the way some fruits end up in the mouth.

Fruit and vegetables: All the nuts in the world, of course, plus coconut and chestnut. The Blenheim family of apples, Orleans Reinette, Egremont Russet, with Woodstock Pippin and the Ballinora. It's also present in some vegetables – some varieties of potato and squash, for instance – and that's clue to what you might add to them: pecan nuts with squash and pumpkins, with or without a further underpinning of maple syrup/brown sugar/rum and butter; mashed potatoes finished with walnut oil and a sprinkle of toasted walnuts . . . you get the picture.

Sappy

These resinous, pine and other sap-related flavours are not always appreciated, but careful addition of gum mastic (*mastika*) to such creamy dishes as a rice pudding, or to the sweetness of Turkish Delight, show the possibilities. Such flavours are most commonly encountered when exploring Australian native produce, which often include eucalypt nuances.

Drinks: Greek retsina wines
Flavourings: gum mastic (*mastika*)
Nuts; green cobnuts, green almonds
Spices: green cardamom

Smoky

Always an added flavour through a direct smoking process, or by the transference of charring-based flavours, as in barbecued vegetables or meat, and now available as liquid smoke, an artificial liquid additive. Originally smoking was a preservative technique, not a flavouring: it was not something done by choice. Even with refrigerators and freezers smoking is still taken way past what is needed for flavour, sometimes to a point where only bitter smoke residue is tasted.

If you want to balance smoky or charred flavours in food, blanching is the usual starting point, so some of the smoke flavour is dissolved out by heating in a liquid. Otherwise you need equally strong flavours with more than a little sweetness and acidity. So, a fresh horseradish sauce made with sweet cream and/or butter will help over-smoked salmon and does the same for an over-smoked ham, mussels or oysters. Balancing bitter smokiness with acidity and then balancing the acidity with sweetness is why a dark caramelised marmalade made with Seville oranges is a winner with smoked hams and birds. Eggs are so good with bacon because the viscous yolk coats the tongue, preventing its buds getting the full effects of the salt and/or smoke. Wines and beers to go with smoked food must be full-bodied and big-flavoured and have both high acidity and a degree of residual sweetness.

Spicy

Spices are usually seeds, husks or bark and thus are invariably brown – cinnamon and nutmeg, mace or cloves and so on. Usage is changing – indeed may have changed in the USA – but properly spiciness should not indicate chillies or heat in food. Spiciness should mean spices, those intense and aromatic flavours, sometimes with an important degree of sweetness, often with useful acidity but always reflecting their woody bark, seed or flower-bud origins.

It's good to divide spices mentally into gentle sweet ones and the more aggressive ones, like cloves, cardamom, star anise or Chinese five-spice, which might also be grouped as an aniseed family. Make sub-groups of your own taste.

It's important, so I'll repeat it. The effects of chillies are not 'spicy'. A chilli is *hot*, chillies are *hot* and so are chilis, the dishes made with them. It is not proper to describe a chilli as spicy. This might already be a lost battle.

Spirituous

This means the powerful effects on your tongue and in your mouth *after* you swallow a distilled spirit: it does not mean the taste of the whisky, the gin or the rum. Another example is the smell when you cook away the alcohol from wine, or heat and ignite, say, a brandy. If you put a lot of brandy in a chocolate icing, and use so much chocolate you only experience the bite of the brandy, the effect is only spirituous and comes with none of the brandy aromas and flavours – hardly worth the trouble.

With a little restraint, a spirituous presence – even with some flavour of the rum, whisky, etc. – does add a spine, a robustness, to anything heavy with fat, cream or butter, as long as little or no heat is applied after the addition.

From a flavouring point of view, flaming spirits is usually a complete waste of time. Quite moderate heat will drive off the alcohol anyway. If the flaming is done at the start of cooking you might caramelise something in the pan, but this could equally have been done by turning up the heat. Flaming when serving also means you might caramelise appropriate surfaces: it usually burns them instead, adding vulgarity where there might have been subtlety.

However, shamelessly flaming a shish kebab carried on a sword or a processional Christmas pudding are both ceremonial flourish rather than flavouring, and should be ruthlessly encouraged. If the flames go out early enough there will not only be a bit more flavoursome liquid to eat with the meat or pudding, but some of the spirit might have survived, making your pudding experience both spirituous and spiritual.

Starchy

Floury, and usually associated with a degree of sweetness: the essential appeal of grains and such root vegetables as potatoes. Starchiness is enhanced by creaminess and sweetness, which could be a component of added oils and fats. Cooked pasta and wheat noodles taste starchy before other flavours are added. Sauces made with flour or with cornflour taste starchy if they have not been cooked long enough for some of the starch to turn to sugars. The following are the world's most popular starchy backgrounds to other foods; substituting one for the other might be all you need to do to make your own Flavour Trail.

Beans: white, red, black, etc., as well as glass/cellophane noodles made from mung beans, soybean curd, etc. (but these are bland rather than truly starchy)

Grains: corn – cornflour, polenta, hominy, grits; millet; wheat – bread, pasta (long or short, smooth or textured), couscous, ramen (Japanese wheat noodles)

Rice: white, brown, red, green or black, short or long grain, sticky; also rice noodles, rice sheets

Nuts: chestnuts, chestnut flour

Vegetables: potatoes, taro, yams, yucca

Vinous

The aromatic, sometimes intense flavour and fragrance that comes from adding wine to a dish. Generally wine is used to meld into the background, so food should only be notably vinous for a short time after the wine is added. If you make a jelly or aspic using wine with its alcohol intact, you will get a sharper and more savoury flavour – good to remember if planning bite-back food for outdoors.

It's a great plan always to splash a little of the original wine into a dish or sauce just a few minutes before serving; it's a version of the tempering technique – see page 233–4.

UNIFYING BACKGROUNDS

Substituting one background ingredient for another will immediately give a different look and flavour to the plate.

In almost every culture there are ingredients used to add bulk as a unifying background to more flavourful ingredients. More often than not they are starchy but all have a relatively bland flavour that underpins yet does not intrude on other flavours. Sometimes, like pasta, they identify a particular national culture, other times they are a personal point of recognition, like bread, potatoes or rice, or a point of difference, like millet.

The use of bland backgrounds in Flavour Trails is enormous. Because simply substituting one for another will immediately give a different look and flavour to the plate. The most common background is bread. Whatever can be dredged up to put on a plate, accompanying it with bread of some sort not only makes it more filling, but more interesting and texturally different, too. Some people have little choice but to eat only simple wholemeal breads or breads with rye or other grains in them, and these have much more flavour than a white bread. That's not always a good thing because it's easier somehow to tire of a big rather than a small flavour. Hence the attraction of good white bread; starchy and with background sweetness, or sweetness and sourness, it's like a well-mannered escort, noticed but not focused upon unless there's a specific task to perform.

The other most useful such ingredient internationally is the egg. Its unique, comforting flavour, whichever bird it comes from, makes friends with every taste, every flavour, from artichoke to apples, salmon to salt cod or saffron, from apricot to gooseberry, cinnamon to tarragon, coffee, chocolate and tea. To eggs you must also add the creamiest and most mild of cheeses, milk and cream. Put together they make more complicated but still mild-flavoured backgrounds that nobly stand back to let other tastes and flavours excel.

Although each of these background ingredients has a flavour, few are very strong. Thus, when you have a superb affinity of just two ingredients, say of courgette and tarragon, or of courgettes and chicken, and want to present them with no further complication but also need to bulk up the amount, eggs are the ideal choice. The simplicity of a custard of eggs and cream makes a superb background for a tart of courgette and tarragon. Indeed one of the world's greatest treats is a true quiche Lorraine, a lightly set custard only of cream and egg baked in pastry, tipped towards savouriness with a little leek and bacon.

Just as simple is the addition of butter or oil. It takes courage first to serve a vegetable with only a little butter or olive oil as a first course, yet little is ever better. So although butter and olive oil can both have mouth-filling flavour, I very much include them among the best of the best background ingredients, and explorations of their many flavours and tastes is a lifelong pleasure. And then there is that sublime combination of butter or oil and flour: Pastry.

Essentially only a cooked version of other background ingredients – white flour and butter or oil – pastry is one of the very best ways to support, to bridge or simply to complement. Apple, cinnamon and sugar make a great combination. The same combination baked in pastry is greater. Spinach, feta cheese, fresh dill and nutmeg is a terrific blend of affinities, but set the mixture with egg and bake that in filo pastry as *spanokopitta* and a Flavour Trail to eating nirvana has been set before you. Even more simply, strawberries or raspberries with cream are summer's gifts made edible, but accompany them with a buttery shortbread or a crisp *tuile* and the pleasure is enormously enhanced. Of course, if your Flavour Trails explorations lead you to heighten the pastry with chocolate, or with orange-flower water, with almonds or hazelnuts . . .

These relatively bland background ingredients and man-made foods give us far more than their individual components suggest they might, proving great food does not need great expense or many ingredients. They are also your greatest key to presenting uncomplicated flavour combinations with the sort of support everyone enjoys.

And there is one more, which divides people as much if not more than any other. That is tofu, or soybean curd. Its importance is far greater than its use as a background. Soybeans are the only vegetable (actually a pulse) offering the same complete protein spectrum as meat; indeed, you need to eat far less to get an equivalent dose of top protein and at the same time avoid problems of fat and cholesterol.

There is one problem with tofu. It's not always bland. Depending on the variety of soybean used, tofu can come with an intrusive, bullying raw-bean flavour I find quite unpalatable. If this has happened to you, keep trying different brands and sources, because not all of them taste as horrid as that. And also introduce it slowly into your diet, so your system has time to adjust, otherwise tofu can initially do more harm than good to your comfort.

CHAPTER THREE

HOW TO CREATE
FLAVOUR TRAILS

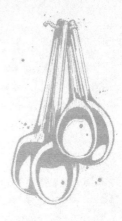

HOW TO CREATE FLAVOUR TRAILS

*Creating Flavour Trails is
cooking with your tongue.*

The requirements and perfectly reasonable expectations of
making something nice to eat are few, and each is simple and
achievable.

- Flavour Trails can be followed between the ingredients
- It will taste good
- It does not contain pointless ingredients
- It does not require useless, time-wasting techniques

When you eat something that comes to you self-contained, like an
apple or a piece of cheese, you rather have to accept what it gives
to your palate. But when you are constructing even a simple
sandwich or salad, it's an opportunity to give the tongue and
palate maximum pleasure. To do that you start by rapidly
assessing which *tastes* are present, which *flavours* are there, and
which of either or both are missing but would be advantageous

to include. You are ultimately cooking *for* your tongue, so you might as well cook *with* your tongue.

Thus the way to start even the simplest putting together of ingredients is to allow your palate to identify what you can about the tastes and flavours of your main ingredient. Is there some sweetness, what is acidic or bitter, what about saltiness? What might happen if you were to add sweetness or saltiness or acidity? Then identify what makes up the flavour spectrum, both those which are immediate and those concealed at first, like the underlying aniseed and citric flavours in basil, or the orange of coriander seed. It's very much easier than you might first think, especially if you've been assiduous about testing your tongue. Once you can sort out what is there and what is not, you are in charge, at the start of yet another successful Flavour Trail.

With your starting base clearly defined, then think about ingredients that will perform the cleverness you expect. Here's where the Flavour Trails lists of tastes, flavours, sensations and background ingredients become your best friends, helping you see connections you'd forgotten or overlooked, affinities new to you or substitutions you might not have realised were relevant.

Composing a Tomato Salad

When you taste a high-quality, fully ripened tomato you hope to recognise sweetness, nicely balanced by acidity. Too often it is the other way around. The gratification level from these tastes is a reflection of their individual intensity plus the savouriness of umami, but that is usually minimal until the tomato is cooked. Only saltiness and bitterness are absent. But those are tastes, and what a tomato is often lacking is deep flavour, so this is what to think about first. You can add all manner of flavours, each of which will affect the basic sweet/acid platform of the tomato.

Let's say you were composing a salad. One ideal addition to any tomato is real (as opposed to plastic pizza-style) mozzarella, either a cows' milk *fiore di latte* or *bufala*, the buffalo milk mozzarella. This is a classic background ingredient and its milky sweetness will both nicely partner that of the tomato and tame the tomato's acidity. You could just as well have added bland chicken, or cubes of properly ripe avocado, or you could go fruity and add mango . . . all of which have a good but different degree of sweetness as part of their taste structure. Let's stick with the mozzarella option.

You have to think about salt both as a taste and as an enhancer of every other flavour. Rather than adding just salt for saltiness, this is the time to think of adding a tasty ingredient that comes with plenty of salt, so it makes more than one contribution. I'd think about adding a vegetable in brine, say grilled capsicum from a can, or some olives or capers – you might even make a mixture of them, knowing their accentuated saltiness also makes them into a salt Taste Trail of their own. Capsicums in brine have usually been grilled and the resultant charring will add some welcome bitterness, completing the taste profile. But you might have added a salty ham, or some smoked fish, perhaps even anchovies. You might even decide on salty cubes of feta or of blue, sheep milk Roquefort.

Let's review what's there:

- Tomato – high acid, low sweetness, low-medium flavour (too often)
- Mozzarella – medium-sweet with a little lactic acidity, low to medium creamy flavour
- Grilled capsicum in brine – saltiness, some sweetness and some acid, plus bitterness from the grilling, and medium to strong flavour

That's actually a good Bridging Flavour Trail; tomato is the major component, mozzarella the major accompaniment and capsicum the bridging ingredient.

This combination of tomato and mozzarella with something salty is now a strong combination, ready to be eaten with a good olive oil for texture and savoury sweetness, perhaps some flat-leaf parsley to add fresh acidity and a balancing cleanness. But because it is a strong trio it is equally able to accept other additions. You can pick up and run with any of the tastes or flavours there. The lift of refreshing added acidity with compensating sweetness and big flavours could come from pith-free orange segments, which have affinity with tomatoes; you could add sweetness and acidity plus gratifying umami with aged Parmesan or Grana Padano cheese, perhaps even some vintage Cheddar, but do it in chunks rather than grating it, so it is meant. Nuts would add sweetness with welcome texture, a little creaminess and a little starchiness, plus some welcome bitterness if you had first roasted them. That final touch of freshness given by flat-leaf parsley could also come from coriander leaf, taking you off in another direction and perhaps suggesting a dressing made with lime juice rather than vinegar.

And finally you stand back and season. Does it need salt? It may not with the brined vegetable and the cheeses. Is the sweetness of the tomato and the mozzarella subtle and mysterious or weak? Whatever it is doesn't matter if you like it and it neither dominates nor overpowers.

Black pepper will knit everything together in a magical way – but perhaps you might want to add the peppery sensation in a way that adds colour, with watercress leaves or rocket, or dandelion...

Then you have to think about the dressing, and I do mean think. Here is where you can really get the plate and the palate singing or ruin the dish totally. If there's enough sweetness in the dish you might not want to use a sweetish olive oil, like those from the elegant *arbequinas* olives of Catalonia of northeast Spain, but to go instead for a Tuscan oil with the powerful pepper-bite of the *frantoio* olive. The one thing feeling neglected in the balance of this dish now could well be the acidity with which you started. Why do we add oil and vinegar to salads? Because without these the acid/sweet spectrum is not strong enough to be satisfying. So choose a vinegar or other acid and an oil that will help underpin and dramatise what is there. But perhaps all this needs is a swirl or two of hazelnut oil or walnut oil? You don't always have to have both oil and vinegar.

WHEN IT'S NOT A RECIPE

Innovative association of ingredients is not enough to make a recipe. If what is on the plate has had no time or technique used to present an ingredient differently, or no time taken to allow flavours to conjugate consensually and then to create a new experience, it's not really a dish at all, and certainly not a recipe. It's an arrangement.

Someone must do something more than merely arrange ingredients for food on the plate to be worthwhile. It is not enough that interesting things happen when you combine the ingredients in your mouth. This might not be quite so true with a simple sandwich or a salad, but even so a special choice of bread or spread or of dressing might have sewn the ingredients together in a new way. When you have ingredients sitting independently on a plate they are still just that, an arrangement. If the heaps are leftovers, each a memorial to a previous meal, you have only a culinary graveyard, something to further chip away any residual belief you might have in the virtues of recycling – or of resurrection.

Analysing a bad combination will reveal ingredients there just for swagger or sensation or, worse, added in a last-minute panic because the essential mixture doesn't perform. Chillies, mixed herbs, raw onion, and cheese sprinkled on top and put 'under the grill until bubbling and golden-brown' are primary examples of ingredients used like foam on a chemical fire, to smother absolutely the noisome horror beneath. But if the blaze is you creating Flavour Trails, you'll never make these mistakes again.

Deconstruction

Deconstructing something you have eaten and enjoyed, and then serving it in a different way, is a deceptively easy way to begin your creative cooking. Here's a really simple example from Kate McGhie, Melbourne's super-foodie and food writer, which will have even the least experienced cook talked about for weeks.

Deconstructed Rhubarb Crumble

Bake long pieces of rhubarb with very little brown sugar and some orange zest at 180C/350F until they are tender but not squishy – 20 minutes at the most. Meanwhile find any crumble recipe, make it up, perhaps adding some chopped macadamia nuts or other nuts, and then put that into a flat baking tray in an uneven scatter and cook that until brown and crisp, tumbling it about from time to time to ensure even cooking and browning. Serve the hot crumble mixture in a bowl, the cooling rhubarb in the dish it was baked in and bridge the tastes and flavours with clotted or whipped cream.

The benefit of this deconstruction is not just the visual fun of serving the ingredients of rhubarb crumble separately. It creates the opportunity for greater individual pleasure as guests serve themselves in whatever proportion they want, and also ensures the crumble is crisp and cooked through rather than the common sticky gum with random crunchy elements.

Feeling confident? Then use the Affinity Trail Lists to ring some serious changes. Check out the possibilities and you'll see rhubarb has an affinity with raspberries and strawberries, and that both those have one for preserved ginger, which will also add the new dimension of a hot sensation. Use syrup from a jar of ginger instead of sugar and chop some of the ginger finely and add it to the crumble mixture. Or make a deconstructed apple crumble or a peach-and-blackberry one. Or, joyfully, a summer-berry crumble that is not mush on mush, but with berries barely frightened by heat, still individually shapely and immodestly starting their seductive oozing striptease of juices.

Recommended Detours

- Almost any chopped nut can be used instead of macadamias – almonds, pecans, hazelnuts, even greenery-yallery pistachios.
- Use orange rather than lemon juice.
- Bake the rhubarb on a layer of peeled sliced apple, with or

without orange zest.

- Sprinkle halved strawberries over the rhubarb and bake together.
- Bake thick slices of apple or pear, dotted with butter, sprinkled with Calvados, Cointreau, rum or brandy.
- Solid-pack pie-filling apple works very well if you are in a hurry. It can be heated in a microwave but the crumble must cook in an oven.
- Use any other solid pie filling, usually bought in cans – the cherry one is always excellent when served hot. If you use one of these, simply heat in the microwave and then put into a pretty bowl and serve with hot or cold crumble.
- Serve the hot crumble over a can or bottle of fruit from your store cupboard – like Victoria plums or luscious quinces dusted with chopped pistachios.
- Cut ripe firm bananas into chunks at least 5cm (2 inches) long and bake with dark rum or brown sugar, lime juice and lime zest.
- Bake any mixture of apple and berries.
- Bake peach or nectarine halves or quarters, with or without berries.
- Bake scoops of feijoa with chunks of apple.
- Bake scoops of tamarillo, with or without apple.
- For extra-luscious juices, spoon on some honey or dilute a good berry jam with a little red or white wine and spoon that on before baking.

Now start thinking about other favourite recipes you might deconstruct, like a lemon tart.

Deconstructed Lemon Tart

Worried about baking a lemon tart? Well, yes, it is tricky to keep the pastry thin enough to be really crisp but thick enough to hang around for some hours before you can serve it. Instead, make a sharp lemon custard to serve chilled in tall glasses with chunky butter shortbread, or to spoon between fly-away squares of see-through filo pastry as you serve. You might even bake a classic lemon tart filling in individual ramekins and serve each with rolled cigarettes of filo or with an almond and ginger shortbread.

Constructing differences

Of course, you can do the reverse of deconstruction, and put together ingredients usually served separately. Making a sandwich of a favourite meal or snack is blindingly obvious but always a serious hit. What's better than bacon and fried eggs between bread? But why not go the whole hog?

Roast beef sandwiches can't possibly compete with a roast beef sandwich in which is also found roast potatoes, gravy, leftover Yorkshires (if there is such a thing) and a few green beans or peas, plus the usual condiments, of course. That's a cooking-without-recipes idea that can run for ever.

Ice cream is great for deconstructing – and for constructing. Cookies 'n' Cream give you the idea; whatever you serve together as a pudding can go into an ice cream. Those deconstructed ingredients from a crumble make a terrific ice cream, as does deconstructed lemon tart, or the components of a strudel or fruit salad with meringue. Take apart a Black Forest cake and mix the components into ice cream, or do the same with a steamed syrup pudding, an upside-down pineapple cake, a chocolate-iced banana cake, a strawberry and passion-fruit crowned pavlova . . . Or you can buy an ice cream, work out the contents and serve the ice cream with its deconstructed ingredients scattered about it. It's hard not to shudder with pleasure.

Variations

Frankly, variations are the best way quickly to gather confidence in using Flavour Trails to improve your creative abilities. Choose a recipe you know works and then use the Flavour Trail lists to tweak it, or add your own 'twist' (as so many chefs say when actually all they have done is to mangle). But don't be afraid to put your mind to work even on such classics as Tarte Tatin.

This upside-down French tart is hugely popular because its in-built taste and flavour affinities are as powerful and as simple as they can be: cooked apples enriched by butter and caramelised sugar on a base of butter-loaded pastry; sweetness, acidity and a touch of bitterness plus huge flavour whichever way you turn. Even the look is encouraging – billows of plumped apple segments are about the most viscerally enticing thing known to man, and when glistened with golden caramel, and dribbling the last buttery juices into the interstices of golden pastry . . . then there is the aroma, even when cold.

Of course, such apparent simplicity is not simple at all. You need the right sort of apple, one which will keep its bosomy swell – and Golden Delicious really are the originals and the best by far. You need to judge the caramelisation of the sugar perfectly; be weak and you'll hardly see or taste it, be too bold and the dark colour and bitterness will interfere with your ultimate enjoyment. Many recipes tell you to caramelise the sugar with the apples already in the cooking pan but I couldn't take such a risk. There's nothing wrong with making the caramel separately, pouring that into the cookery pan if you are happy with it and then arranging the apple segments upside down on that. Pack them in, because they lose bulk in the cooking. And then you need to judge the cooking time so the pastry is cooked through, all through, before it is overcooked and becomes bitter. You can do all that? Time to move on.

Rethinking Tarte Tatin

Once you can get a Tarte Tatin right you are ready to hit new Flavour Trails. Thinking about the affinities of apple and of caramelised sugar are the places to start. You could be British and add the spice affinities of apple (and butter) – sweet cinnamon or a heftier old-fashioned mix that includes ginger and black pepper. You might think further afield and alight on star anise, which is most anxious to please when caramel is about. Even cloves, which can be tricky, would work, again because a judicious powdering of them would be skipping about atop a huge sweetish depth of flavour and cloves need serious flavour competition if they are not to scream everyone else off the stage.

My first thought when fruit is around is always orange. Here it would be because I have just remembered images of the great pleasures of caramelised oranges in the *locantas*, bistros and *ristorantes* of the 60s and 70s. Such worldly evidence proves oranges like caramel and that's all you need to know to go to work on your version of a Tarte Tatin.

You might simply toss the apple segments in plenty of freshly zested orange peel – plenty of it because it has to fight to survive the length of the cooking and the huge taste of the caramel –the affinities are so strong you can hardly go wrong with putting in too much. Or, having made the caramelised sugar, you could 'let it down' by adding orange juice and then reducing the combination back to the proper sticky consistency. Or you might do both.

You could also alternate the apple segments with quince or pear, all members of the same botanical family, at which point you'd have to think about orange-flower water, too (particularly if you used quinces poached to a delectable blush and fragrance). That combination of quinces and orange-flower water is aeons old but still weaves spells.

The gorgeously flavoured acidity of passion-fruit pulp is extraordinary with caramel, doubly so with an orange caramel. I have used lime oil with quinces and with apples, I have used melted chocolate with pears (which I find often need extra acidity and flavour boost, so I've included lime, too). Berry fruits, especially blackberry, as a top or bottom layer work extremely well if you are generous enough with them. Try purple plum tartes tatin, golden peach and rose geranium tarts, or red ones of *peches des vignes*. And of course you could deconstruct any of these and serve fruit in a caramelised-sugar sauce with pastry somethings on the side. Then there are vegetable versions.

Vegetable Tartes Tatin

These are not strictly Tartes Tatin, but vegetable versions have been appearing for some time. Onions roasted until seriously sweet and tender make exceptional replacements for the apples. You might think you'd have no real need of added caramel, but you do for its acidity and bitterness not its sweetness. You could generously smother the sweet onions with the high-flavour acidity of a spiced black-rice vinegar from China, with balsamic vinegar, or with caramelised sugar let down with soy sauce, one of the many flavouring twists I learned from master-chef Mark Gregory. It's one of the best flavour/taste combinations I know, bright with salt, sweetness, umami and altogether fantastic mouth appeal.

You could make such a tart of parsnips with a simple orange or spiced caramel; or one of sweet potatoes, pecan nuts and honey with the same choice of caramels; or of plump oven-roasted tomatoes stuffed with basil pesto and completed with a soy caramel. Endive and beetroot versions have their supporters too, but I usually end up making only a fennel version. First braised in chunky quarters in the microwave with butter, garlic, lemon and a little stock, the tender fennel is arranged on a sharp caramel pointed with rich sherry vinegar or a cheap balsamic, with their fat bottoms snuggled tight around the edge of the pan and their pointy bits inwards; each piece might overlap rather than lie flat if you like. The reduced juices from the braising are poured onto the fennel pieces, on goes the pastry top, which will become the bottom, and then into the oven it goes. It's then I think I should also have included oven-roasted tomatoes, too. I will one day. In the meantime a slice of this is a fabulous first course, an intriguing accompaniment or a terrific main course when there's plenty else to eat. A fennel upside-down tart is also outstanding for eating warm or cold outside.

But don't forget the pastry also offers easily achieved variations. It doesn't have to be a shortcrust. The most spectacular upside-down tarts I have made all used filo pastry, some twelve individually buttered sheets of it, which lifted and crinkled as they cooked. Turned out and inverted, the tart looked as though it was floating on waves of the wispy pastry.

If you try this you have to cut and serve quickly because the opportunistic juices will now turn tail and try to dissolve the pastry. In the meantime you have made a very grand *coup d'oeil*. And all you did was to use a different pastry. With time and further thought you might have layered the pastry with herbs or spices or zests, with fruit chunks or nuts or have used flavoured butters, flavoured oils, etc.

Study the Flavour Trail lists, free up your mind and then play the variations game – it will keep you enchanted and serving great food for as long as you like. You are, of course, using other people's recipes to start you off. What do you think everyone else does?

Solo Flavour Trail Routes

Orange-Orange Cheesecake

A Solo Flavour Trail to flavour a cheesecake is simple to achieve because almost anything sweet or savoury will go with a creamy cheesecake mixture; it is one of the most important backgrounds upon which flavours may perform. But your solo ingredient must be capable of more than a few guises. How about an orange-orange cheesecake?

At first the mind will race to affinities and complements: orange goes with strawberries or chocolate or raspberries, in fact with all fruits. But I like to use such affinities more dramatically when serving, rather than making, a cheesecake. Let's imagine a basic cheesecake, flavoured only with a Solo Flavour Trail of variations on orange.

Some of the orange-flavoured ingredients you might use are:

- orange juice, fresh or bought, concentrated or not
- orange oil
- such orange liqueurs as Cointreau or Curacao
- fresh orange segments

- orange segments poached in a sweet red or white wine
- orange segments poached in orange juice
- fresh or poached blood-orange segments
- fresh or poached orange segments marinated in liqueur
- roasted orange segments
- roasted orange segments marinated in liqueur
- orange zest finely grated or in long strands
- aged orange zest
- orange-flower water
- candied orange peel
- chopped orange jelly
- chopped orange jelly with liqueur
- orange wine
- coriander seeds

These provide quite different flavours and textures, but all orange and altogether yummy, especially in a creamy cheesecake. The creaminess of the cheesecake will coat the taste buds, making flavours harder to detect, so it's very important to ensure whatever you use has a fairly high intensity. Thus I'd use orange segments only whole or halved, or in quite big informal pieces anyway, so they were neither lost nor smothered. Orange juice probably works best if concentrated, such as frozen concentrate, or it will affect the consistency of the cake, so the exact intensity of highly concentrated genuine orange oil is ideal for this sort of task. Zest or peel would make great textured additions, orange-flower water would take the cheesecake into more exotic parts of your mouth, while orange liqueurs would add an adult element. Roasted orange segments would come about because you cooked the cheesecake with them on the top. An uncooked cheesecake? – then roast them separately and arrange at your pleasure.

I tend to use orange-flower water and candied orange with a roasted segment topping, to which I can never resist adding the richness of ground almonds, a subtle affinity combination with orange made in super-heaven. Which combination would you use? Remember odd numbers work best and three ingredients are better than five or seven. You can always make another version next time. Perhaps with those coriander seeds, which have an orange flavour in their background.

And you still have the option of then serving the multi-layered orange flavours of the cheesecake with those strawberries, raspberries or chocolate, adding both visual and flavour drama to a cheesecake which has journeyed far on only the advantage of orange's Solo Flavour Affinities. If you had made the cheesecake with, say, raspberry and orange, or chocolate and raspberry, you wouldn't have the same serving freedoms without risking a blurring or confusion or imbalance of flavours. Not that it would matter that much when all those flavours are such great mates, but sometimes you have to force yourself into restraint.

Next time, the confident cook might add just one affinity ingredient to the orange mix – perhaps ground nutmeg or grated chocolate or chopped toasted hazelnuts. Or choose an ingredient already combined with an orange affinity by, say, chopping up dark, orange-centred chocolates; Kiwis might crunch up Jaffa lollies, which come in this combination. That sounds so good I might have to leave you and make one right now.

But beware of overconfidence. How you cook is quite as important as what you cook.

Cumin and Cumin Seeds

For a savoury Solo Flavour Trail, let's imagine I had used ground cumin in a simple tomato sauce made by boiling down a can of chopped tomatoes with some olive oil or butter to make a rich emulsion – itself an affinity blend of tomatoes and olive oil or butter, of course. By adding cumin, the oil or butter then becomes a Flavour Bridge between the tomato and cumin.

Instead of going off into other realms of ingredients and flavours to add drama, I will safely sprinkle roasted whole cumin seed onto the finished dish – that's a different flavour and different texture of cumin, but absolutely reliable because it is only a variation of the spice already in the dish. There is also a lift in acidity and, in high-roasted seeds, a touch of bitterness. Roasted cumin seeds always contribute sudden textural difference and fascinating explosions of intense taste and flavour when encountered, knowingly or not, in almost anything you care to imagine, including salads, sandwiches and pasta, as a strewing garnish for fish and seafood dishes including prawn cocktails, or a tempering for curries which already include ground cumin.

Between roasted and unroasted, dark-roasted and light-roasted, and ground or whole, there are dozens of fascinating and safe combinations at your fingertips all with cumin alone, with little physical work and no mental strain. You know it will work because you have used a Solo Flavour Trail and the result will be so much more interesting than stirring in a spoonful of dubious curry paste.

Affinity Flavour Trail Routes

Basil and tomato make a classic Affinity Flavour Trail because together they make something bigger and better than you might expect. But there's more to basil than you first think.

Basil and Citrus

Chew some basil slowly and you will realise basil is not just one flavour. Try to identify the flavours accompanying the clean acid taste as basil finishes on your palate. An important part of the flavours in your mouth is curiously aniseed or even liquorice-like and thus might be used in a Chinese or Thai pork or seafood dish, dishes you might expect to find with a little star anise or five-spice powder, which have the same dominating flavour. Indeed Thai Holy Basil, with smaller leaves and more pungent flavour, is used just like that, but only at the last moment so its intensity is not frittered away.

Think again and you'll realise basil also offers lemony-citric flavours in partnership with its acid taste spectrum. That means you might create a salad of intensely flavoured roasted tomatoes and then add fresh basil, only to discover its citric characteristics are there but rather overpowered because the tomatoes are so concentrated. That might not matter, but if so I'd then look to increase basil's citric characteristics. I'd go for the tangy salt-preserved lemon of Morocco rather than knee-jerk lemon juice, and thus make a powerful Flavour and Taste Trail with both high-profile saltiness and citric flavour. With raw or lightly grilled tomatoes this combination might tip against the tomato, but combined with the tightly focused sweetness of roasted tomatoes they will stand just as proudly and your mouth will be vastly entertained.

Or I could leave the salt level as it is and add the fascinating but less common lemony-citric flavours of lemon grass and Kaffir lime leaf, and again realise why basil combined with both of those works so well in Thai dishes – it's not the liquorice flavour of basil that cobbles with the lemon grass and lime leaf, but its underlying citric flavours.

Basil and Lime Leaf

Chef de cuisine John Williams MBE at London's Ritz hotel serves a dessert course of vivid basil jelly that's stunning in both colour and flavour, teamed with a granita of Kaffir lime leaf, a combination clearly based on the lemony-citric flavour trail between these ingredients. He adds to the combination with finely chopped fresh pineapple and wafer-thin air-dried pineapple, both further extending the refreshing acidity of the dish but adding a sweet fruity flavour, which first perfectly builds on the acid affinity between the main ingredients and then on affinity flavours, intensifying what is there and adding a further bridging sweetness and flavour.

Oysters with Basil

The greatest triumph I had using basil's lemony-citric flavours was in Kitchenclass, my television-based cookery school in

London. At a reception for Seattle's tourist organisation I served oysters lightly poached in a fruity, buttery chardonnay and then wrapped in basil leaves in a warm brioche. The combination was sensational. The gentle lemony-acidity of the basil elegantly replaced the usual brutal onslaught of lemon juice on the palate, never overpowered the oysters, and added the scented, herbal overtones of its other flavour components. There was some residual acidity from the wine working on the oyster anyway, and the butter-rich brioche provided the final touch of sweetness that everything from the sea needs to taste its best.

How did I know the combination of oyster and basil would work? Because I could follow the trail of the affinities and flavours which made up each ingredient of the combination:

- lemony-citric flavours have a special affinity with seafood
- there's a citric undertone to basil
- so basil will have an unexpected but demonstrable affinity with oysters

The wine and the brioche were taste backgrounds rather than Flavour Bridges, one giving support by its butteriness and light acidity, the other by sweetness and more butteriness. It's as easy as that.

Of course, if you are the sort of brutalised eater who deep-down hates oysters and obliterates their flavour with oceans of lemon juice or raw onion, shallots or vinegar, then oysters and basil won't work for you. If you actually *like* oysters, though, this combination will open new vistas, and yet it's just an *underlying* flavour of basil doing that.

The Pasta Salad Rescued

Pasta salads destroy as many parties and meals as they fill stomachs. The pasta is overcooked or sticky, there is usually nothing much to flavour it apart from chunks of burp-packed, raw red capsicum, perhaps some highly creative apple slices unhappily fighting oxidation with cheap vinegar, some crunchy under-ripe grapes and perhaps the tired stragglers from a school of prawns. Yet properly made, a pasta salad can be the belle and the beau of the ball.

The right pasta treated properly is important. It's the bland background ingredient that makes food bulkier and more satisfying, and allows even quite delicately flavoured ingredients to be tasted. But what if the pasta itself were flavoured more interestingly, and played a part bigger than a mere background? Good thinking. The key to this is knowing how to properly cook and use pasta. The most important time is once it is cooked. It must never immediately be put into a sauce or vice versa but be allowed to steam-dry for a few minutes. The dried surfaces of each piece of pasta thus become absorbent and whatever is then applied is slurped deep inside and flavours the pasta itself. Actually, that's what Italians do without thinking when they bring a big bowl to table with the pasta sitting unmixed in the middle of the sauce; by the time it is mixed and served the pasta will have dried on the surface.

Thus, the simplest thing to do to make a prawn and pasta salad memorably tasty is to dress the warm, drying pasta with something of concentrated zingy flavour. The easiest of these is flavoured olive oil – a mandarin or a lemon oil or a garlic or chilli or anything you can get your hands on. I flavour olive oil with lime oil, but then lime oil and I seem joined at the hip. The flavoured pasta is at once delicious all by itself, and that's a good start – the same as always putting oil and vinegar dressing on to the hot potatoes that are going to be used for cold potato salad, even if it will later be held together by mayonnaise.

Now it's worth adding the prawns, nicely drained and flavoured with salt and pepper plus whatever else you want: I like to add very lightly cooked mangetouts or sugar-snap peas for crunch contrast and then perhaps the concentrated sweetness of sun-dried tomato pieces, the salty surprise of black olives or capers and then a little deconstruction, a suggestion of what flavours the pasta. Extra garlic, finely chopped chilli, orange or lemon or lime zest. And the usual connecting genius of flat-leaf parsley or coriander or rocket or watercress. And perhaps you might have roasted the black peppercorns, too. You'll never burp over bad pasta salad again.

Don't like olive or other oils? No matter. Toss the warm, dried pasta in a really rich concentrated tomato sauce, which will work just as well, or in Italy's *gremolata*, that edgy mixture of chopped garlic, lemon zest and parsley, outstanding as the background for a mixed seafood pasta salad. You could use a curry sauce for a mixed vegetable pasta salad, a sweet garlic–chilli sauce for such as a duck, orange and spinach-leaf pasta salad, or take off to new realms and flavour the pasta with thin liqueur-rich custard, a fruit syrup, or even a velvet-tongued sweet wine, and then make a pasta fruit salad. I'd put jellybeans into mine.

Coriander and Cumin

Here's another example of an affinity based on a secondary flavour rather than the most obvious. Chew some coriander seed and you'll detect an orange-like finish to it, which becomes more noticeable in the mouth when other flavours are dissolving away. That's why coriander goes so well with cumin, which has a residual lemon flavour. It is their underlying citrus flavours that so tightly thread their powerful affinity. Together they are the trusted basis of most cooking east of the Mediterranean, used in any intensity one to the other, because their underlying Affinity Flavour Trail means you really can't go wrong. Few of what we call curries or curry powders start any other way.

Coriander Seeds and Tomato

Once you recognise the orange component in coriander seed, then think of other ingredients with orange flavours, and/or ingredients you know go with oranges. If you've been to Mexico you might have noticed they combine orange and tomato, often in drinks, and it's very good. Thus there's every chance coriander seed will go deliciously with tomato, and it does, brilliantly, and even better when lightly roasted.

Scrunch coriander seeds, roasted or not, on to a simple tomato salad, grind coriander seeds into tomato sauces, or crush them and add to a simple salsa of tomato chunks with a little garlic, orange segments and zest, and parsley. Of course, you could use coriander leaf because its evocative, feral flavour also has an underlying citric bite.

Fruit Salad with Coriander Seeds

The orange-flavour component of coriander seeds is just as useful in sweet combinations. Anything orange has a natural affinity with fruit and so, if you'd like a fruit salad with a difference, roughly crush a teaspoonful or so of coriander seeds and let them simmer in a light sugar syrup for just a few minutes until it is pleasantly flavoured: then strain and cool. Cut your fruit salad pieces into this syrup, including plenty of orange segments, and allow it to sit for a couple of hours at room temperature – the simplest and most reliable way of all to make new flavours – and then chill lightly. You might also roast a few more coriander seeds to crush and sprinkle over the fruit salad; the roasted ones will add an even greater spectrum of flavours but still be within the reliable range of the affinity.

Salt & Pepper Squid with Sumac

Sometimes discovering a new Flavour Trail is as simple as sub-stituting one ingredient for another. Take very basic pepper and salt calamari: these are liked rather more than plain calamari because although there might be salt and pepper right there in the light batter in which they are deep-fried, the real piquancy comes from sprinkling on salt and pepper the moment the pieces come from the fat or oil, the intense heat forcing more flavour from the pepper. All they need is a slight squeeze of lemon juice to brighten up the sweetness of the flesh after cutting back the palate-blinding effect of the residual oil. How might you make your own version of that?

My Australian mate Quentin Dalziell, one of those untrained chefs of casual genius, adds an acid blush of sumac, the red, citric-flavour condiment of Iran, displacing the need for as much lemon or vinegar on the calamari by replacing one acidity with another. In fact the sumac goes well with salt and pepper and, being acidic, also goes well with sweet calamari. Putting the three together makes a new but predictably grateful harmony. All that's needed finally to make this variation perfect is the touch of sweetness all fish like – and that comes from the oil in which they are deep-fried, and in this case from the calamari themselves if they're fresh enough. But if you added another twist, and shallow-fried them in butter rather than deep-frying in oil, even more magic will have been cast, because butter has a fuller sweetness.

Walnuts and Tomatoes

The affinity walnuts and walnut oil have for tomatoes is legendary – except few outside southwest France know about it. Eat a fresh ripe and fleshy red tomato with a little walnut oil and you'll be bewitched by the extraordinary flavours created on your palate. Nothing else is needed.

Using the natural affinity of two ingredients to make personalised dishes means you can rely on them to taste good. All you have to do is ensure the new balance is one where both are tasted. The affinity of tomato and walnut doesn't always have to mean a tomato with walnut oil. You could microwave-roast and then crush walnuts and put these into a tomato sauce, make walnut-studded breads or savoury scones and bury chunks of roasted tomato in them or serve them with tomato butter. Or stuff big tomatoes with breadcrumbs, ground walnuts, a few chopped black olives, a little garlic and plenty of parsley; bake, in a warm to medium oven, 180C/350F maximum, and then pour chilled walnut oil over them just before serving – if you heat walnut oil it loses too much of its veracity.

One of the best first courses ever is to serve a warm, slow-roasted tomato with roughly crumbled roasted walnuts and a drizzle of walnut oil. You don't really need anything else, but crisp, flat-leaf parsley moves the dish on even further by giving aromatic acidity, which both ingredients enjoy. Or you could extend the sweetness of the oil and of the tomato, and so serve the tomatoes and walnut oil on a thick slice of moon-white buffalo mozzarella cheese. But actually you need only a tomato and walnut oil, one of the most resilient of all Affinity Flavour Trails.

Bridging Flavour Trail Routes

Duck with Mango

A hot grilled duck breast will be very good to eat with chilled fragrant mango, perhaps an Alfonso or other sublime aromatic variety from Pakistan – it has to be chilled because that will emphasise its acidity and inhibit its sweetness. Mango's scent at ambient temperature would dominate the plate and its sweetness would be too strong; when heated or cooked mango loses too much fragrance and can taste like lightly sugared damp cardboard. You could argue hot duck and cold mango is an affinity, I suppose, but to me they are merely complementary, that is they might be dating but furtively so, and there's no chance it will get serious and produce something that can be talked about in public. Putting them together is really an arrangement that depends for appeal largely on novelty. That's not enough. But how could you make them into an item, a couple to discuss over dinner?

First, they could be gainfully employed in bite-sized pieces with one of the bland, starchy type of background ingredients, perhaps in a pasta salad. They'd be excellent mixed into a green salad with a whiff of sesame oil in the dressing – then there would be magic to be tasted. Or I'd cut the two ingredients into fingers and strew them in thin pancakes shot through with fresh ginger and lime zest and then quickly browned in duck fat, which would warm the mango but not cook out its flavour. That's definitely more than an arrangement, the cook would have had to think to get things right, each ingredient balanced and complementary, and to have done more than grill the duck and fan out a mango cheek.

Now think about what you have eaten before or read about or imagined might go with duck. What else could make hot duck and chilled mango into something successful? The answers can be very simple. Coriander leaf, that single ingredient with intense flavours, many of them citric, is capable of making a powerful Flavour Bridge between the two. And that signals it's time to move to more creative Bridging Flavour Trails.

Duck and Mango with Ginger

A dead simple bridging ingredient between duck and mango is fresh ginger juice; ginger root peeled, chopped and squeezed through a garlic press. The ginger juice will be a marvellous foil to the fat richness of the duck, and also take the sensual texture, flavour and perfume of the mango and stretch it to unimagined places on your palate. The ginger juice tastes different when warmed by the duck, and different again when chilled by the mango. With the one ingredient on both duck and mango there are dozens of potential flavours on the plate: a forkful of duck with just the juice, a forkful of duck without ginger with an equal size of mango with a little juice, lots of ginger juice on a chunk of duck, lots of mango with a small piece of duck skin, lots of juice on a portion of both. Every mouthful will finesse the three flavours different ways, creating wonderfully exciting eating. But note, no one here is doing any more actual cooking; like the addition of coriander leaf it's just an assembly, an arrangement, yet it stitches the other ingredients together, and it's that stitching that makes a Bridging Flavour Trail and the combination into a real dish – a recipe, in fact.

Actually, some really elegant Sarawak black pepper might do quite as well as the ginger or coriander, for this is the reason we like it so much; black pepper builds bridges between disparate ingredients, and thus makes food seem more intricate than it is.

But you would have to grind the black pepper onto the duck and the mango before serving it, rather than leaving it to others, so they knew it was part of the basic offering. Roasted peppercorns would be more fascinating and even the West's new culinary cliché of sweet chilli sauce would do well as a store-cupboard bridge in a hurry.

To show rather more willing you might have marinated the mango in the ginger juice. If the duck breast had also been marinated before cooking there would then be a quite different spectrum of flavour on the plate, cooked ginger juice on the duck, fresh ginger juice on the mango. And all you did was identify and use a single ingredient to stitch the duck and the mango together. You could have made a sauce with lime and coconut, you could have done a dozen other things, but the simplicity of ginger juice probably gives the diner more opportunities for a flavour surprise with every mouthful.

The objective is to serve a major ingredient with a major complement and something that bridges the two. If there is more than the trio of major ingredient, major complement and bridge in a dish, the other ingredients should pick up and expand an affinity or characteristic of taste or flavour already there in the underlying structures. Yet there is such a thing as a bridge too far, and these should be removed; they'll make the banks on which they rested stronger and more accessible rather than weaker.

Lamb with Raspberries

I recently saw a chef berated by a supposed mentor for wanting to serve lamb with raspberries. While my mind began to race with how to do it, how to build the Flavour Bridge that would make the combination work, the experienced chef tore apart the one with the idea. He said it was an awful idea and anyway was 'so 70s'. But is it a bad idea? And does something tasting good then really not belong quite as well in the 21st century?

All sorts of other fruit and berries are traditional with lamb: jellies of rowan berry or redcurrants are, and so are stuffings of dried fruits, especially dried apricot with mint, so are caramelised quince, apple and mint jelly, and so on, and some of these combinations date to centuries before the 1970s. To me there's no reason why lamb can't be served with raspberries; all you have to do is find an acceptable Flavour Trail that will make the bridge between the two. So let's see how we might serve lamb with raspberries, without making it seem like meat and jam.

My technique is first to let my mind roam freely over other flavours and ingredients that might be served with lamb – the Flavour Trail Lists One to Ten are a ready reference to set you on the same trails.

I know from experience that the mint so often served with lamb also has a great affinity with raspberries, so there's a potential bridge to consider. There's garlic with lamb, of course, and thyme, which can be better with lamb than mint. When lamb is cold, mango and other chutneys work wonderfully well and chutney is, of course, predominantly fruit; somebody is bound to have made a raspberry chutney. Of course, a chutney will also contain vinegar and spices, and perhaps onion, all of which blend superbly with that other great fruit, the tomato, and those are all possibilities. Honey, soy sauce and fresh ginger make a delicious marinade for lamb and with such combinations you can think about adding the aniseed flavours of five-spice powder. Once you add fresh ginger to your thought-pile, you can think about chilli, too, and once you have chilli with other spices you have to think of adding chocolate. And then you have to sieve some of these out.

The first to go is the chocolate, because no matter how savoury the sauce you'd never get rid of the thought of puddings when raspberries are also present. Out of all the possibilities I would lean towards cooked raspberry in the gravy and fresh ones in some sort of uncooked chutney, probably without spices, because they too might remind of desserts. What you need is something that will build a bridge between the lamb and the raspberries, by including both those flavours and a bridging ingredient that goes with both. I think that's a gravy.

For the basis of that gravy, I'd roast the lamb on a really thick bed of fresh mint on the stalk, with crushed garlic cloves and some fresh thyme too, lifting the flavours away from simple mint and garlic. I know all those flavours go with lamb and that the mint content alone would mean they should marry well with raspberries in a savoury sauce. To get that marriage off to the best possible start I would also throw a good handful or so of raspberries under the lamb too, so the resulting pan juices that will eventually include those of the lamb are forming a good blend of complementary flavours. A glass or two of white wine over the bed of mint, garlic, thyme and raspberries will help extract maximum flavour from them as well as stopping them desiccating during cooking.

Once the lamb was cooked, I'd put it to rest for twenty minutes or more (not under foil, which risks overcooking) and thoroughly squeeze and then strain the herbs and fruit cooked under the lamb to get maximum yield for pan juices, and then put the juices back into the pan. Once all the brown bits had dissolved over heat I'd add more wine or stock or some combination and slowly reduce to strengthen and focus the flavour. Here, I suspect a few drops of cider or raspberry vinegar would be all it needed to dramatise the raspberry aroma and set the gravy apart from any accusation of being something more properly spooned over ice cream. I'd then temper the gravy with fresh thyme and mint, and strain them out after just a few minutes so their fresh flavours were complementing the gravy's well-cooked ones; there's more about tempering on page 233–4. That will be delicious, but at the moment it's lamb with a raspberry and mint sauce, it's not really lamb *with* raspberries.

This is where a fresh, uncooked chutney, the sort so commonly served in Sri Lanka, will perform nicely. I'd roughly tear fresh mint leaves, squeeze in a little garlic (perhaps also adding some of the cooked garlic from the pan) and add some grated fresh ginger as a new bridge between the fresh raspberries and the mint/garlic. That would be seasoned highly with black pepper (doing the same job as the ginger but with a different and complementary spectrum) and a bit of salt and then I'd chop in fresh raspberries, not too finely, so they remain recognisable. Depending on my feelings I might sprinkle on some more vinegar, or even lime juice.

And there you are, my first thoughts on a bridge between lamb and raspberries; lamb with a mint, thyme and garlic gravy with an undertone of cooked raspberry served with a fresh chutney of some of the same ingredients including fresh raspberries, tasting totally different. The bridging flavours are themselves a series of Solo Flavour Trails, taking advantage of the natural affinity ingredients have with themselves in different guises. This has been an *ingredient* Flavour Bridge where:

- lamb is the main ingredient
- raspberries are the major complement
- mint in the gravy and chutney was the basis of the Flavour Bridge

Of course, the above is only thinking out loud and I haven't cooked the dish. If you like the sound of it, and try it out, let me know if it works!

Chicken, Lime and Time

If you grill a breast of chicken and then squeeze lime juice over it, that's hardly something that should be called a recipe, no matter how good it tastes. Chicken with grilled wedges of lime is much more interesting and different enough for many people: yet even though it takes a little extra thought and effort to grill the lime, it's still more an arrangement than a recipe. Only the caramelisation of the grilling is working as a bridge, so if I were serving this I would make certain the chicken was also nicely browned and then the twin caramelisation of the chicken skin and the juices of the lime would make a stronger Flavour Bridge with a bigger spectrum of flavours between the chicken and the lime.

This would give you heaps of different experiences to savour as you ate one or the other in different proportions. The arrangement would have become a recipe.

However, if you squeeze lime juice onto uncooked, deeply scored chicken breast and leave it to marinate for an hour at room temperature and then grill it, something quite magically different has happened – new flavours have developed, because the lime juice has penetrated the chicken flesh and truly combined with it. This time the lime juice is unlikely to caramelise as it has soaked into the chicken. The Flavour Bridge used here is the technique of using time to marinate at room temperature, so this is a *technique* Flavour Bridge:

- chicken is the main ingredient
- lime juice is the major complement
- marinating for an hour at room temperature is the technique that makes it a real recipe

Chicken, Lime and Caramel

The alternative to marinating for an hour is to add other ingredients to stitch together the chicken and lime. This might work, but also means more work, more expense for more ingredients and more chance of offering a muddled taste. If you chose to add, say, grilled lime segments you would then further strengthen the technique bridge with an ingredient bridge, stitching together the browning of the skin and the lime marinade by adding fresher, grilled-lime flavour. Of course you are also Solo Flavour Trailing the lime by offering a different version of something already in the combination. Just two ingredients, but what a choice of end products! What simple Flavour Trails to real recipes.

There's one more, which is my favourite can't-be-bothered-to-think dinner. I put a few drops of Boyajian lime oil into a nonstick pan with a generous chunk of butter. When the butter has stopped foaming and spitting I then put a boned, skinless chicken breast topside down, cover lightly, turn down the heat and cook for about five to seven minutes or until the bottom is beautifully browned. This isn't just browning in butter. The oil has caramelised. Turn the breast over and continue frying over low heat until it is cooked through. Let it rest a few minutes while you microwave a mixture of vegetables. Serve with the caramelised lime-butter juices poured over the chicken. A dollop of white wine helps ensure you gather all the crusty bits and if you do this, turn up the heat to reduce and to emulsify the mixture. Salt is a good friend to lime and this is one time I use extra salt as a flavouring, rather than as an enhancement. Good enough to serve to any number of guests if you have a pan big enough.

Fish, Onions and Chocolate

My final Flavour Trail example sounds bizarre, but is based on rock-solid affinities of very few ingredients and has centuries-old heritage behind it: Fish with Chocolate is a traditional recipe from Asturia in northwest Spain, where chocolate probably made its first European landfall with Columbus. It makes sense only when you work out that the main ingredient is fish, the major accompaniment is rather a lot of slowly sweetened onion helped with a little wine or stock, which is then brought back into line by the bridging ingredient chocolate; thus an important bridge acts to perfect the taste and flavour balances of the fish and onion that otherwise might be boring, undimensional and sweetish. The earthiness of wild mushrooms is a secondary, parallel bridge to further tame and dilute the sweetness of the onion, adding a more complicated savouriness. The large amount of butter contributes not just to the sweetness the fish needs but also helps add depth to the caramelisation of the onions.

To work, each ingredient must be perfectly judged and cooked. That's why I am going to include the recipe: it's an absolute paradigm for everything in the book. It demonstrates simplicity, and that simplicity brings with it a great responsibility to know and to treat ingredients the right way. The recipe also shows the importance of choosing the right way to cook an ingredient or a dish. Yes, you could do this in a microwave, and the result would be just as good. But sometimes it's instructive to do things the old way, if only to realise good food did not begin with blokes in white jackets on colour television.

Asturian Fish with Chocolate

500g/1lb firm white fish steaks, boneless and skinless

250g/8oz very finely sliced onion

125g/4oz butter

1 tablespoon mixed dried mushrooms

1 tablespoon flour

150ml/¼ pint stock or water

300ml/½ pint medium dry, fruity white wine

1 or 2 squares 70%, low-sugar chocolate

Salt and pepper to taste

Serves four as a first course, two as a main

Cook the onions in the butter at very low heat for a good twenty minutes or more until very soft and sweet, and then turn up the heat a little and lightly caramelise the sugars now present. If you rush the onions so they are still acidic, or burn them by cooking too fast, the recipe will not work.

While the onions are cooking, rinse a tablespoonful of dried mushrooms very well to eliminate all grit. These can be as simple as dried field mushrooms or as exotic as fairy ring, ceps (porcini) or morels. Then cover them with half the wine and warm slightly in the microwave or over a gentle heat: let them stand, still covered. If these are very dried or in big pieces it's better to do this before you start cooking to ensure they are fully reconstituted.

When the onions are ready, stir in the flour evenly and cook for a few minutes.

Stir in the stock or water and the remaining wine. Now add the chocolate and stir well to blend. Add the mushrooms too, and about half their soaking liquid: beware of using all the soaking liquid as it may not be needed. Season and stir until you have a smooth sauce. The bite of the chocolate wonderfully balances the slow-cooked sweetness of the onions as well as adding delightful colour to what could have been bland and boring to look at.

Cut the fish into two or four pieces, season separately and then sit them on the sauce but do not spoon sauce over the fish, thus protecting the stylish colour contrast. Cover and cook over low heat until the fish is firm – five minutes is probably enough. Serve the fish onto warm plates taking just a little of the sauce as a cushion for each piece to rest on, and then mix the sauce well to ensure any flavour from the fish is evenly distributed.

Serve the remaining sauce around or beside the fish, to get the best contrast of colour and texture. The recipe also works using a fruity young red wine: if you have no dried mushrooms, add a handful of finely sliced button mushrooms a minute or two before serving, so they do not shrink.

This recipe seems so perfect to me I have never once wondered what else I might do with it.

INGREDIENT KNOWLEDGE

The truth about an ingredient is often at variance with common belief.

Ingredient knowledge is vital. It doesn't matter how creative you are, how methodical or how fast you are, without a good understanding of ingredients you'll always be cooking with one hand behind your back. Nothing will ever turn out quite how you imagined. No, not even if your sense of taste and flavour are flawless.

To cook with two hands you have to question everything you believe, even about such basic ingredients as pasta, salt or butter. Often the truth about an ingredient is at variance with common belief. Here are some examples of what you should know, and each of them makes you a better cook, with or without recipes. They are often what you most need to know, but are precisely what other books simply won't or don't tell.

Aioli: once and for all, this is not a nice mayonnaise with some garlic in it. It should start with at least two cloves of garlic per person. Once these were pounded with a little salt only before olive oil was whisked in to make an emulsion, but these days you may also pound in the egg yolk customary when making mayonnaise. When olive oil is whisked in slowly and then more quickly the finished glossy sauce must have a garlic content to assault you, to sting your tongue. It is raw and vulgar and not nice at all, but is wonderfully delicious where it is supposed to be used, as a dip for the raw and cooked vegetables of un grand aioli or when whisked into the cooking juices of a bourride, an all-white fish stew from southwest France. Crushing a few cloves of garlic into mayonnaise just ain't the same raunchy thing.

Allspice: not a mixed spice but a dried berry from the New World, so named because it tastes like a mixture of all the sweet spices from the Old World.

Baking blind: it's usual for blind baked pastry to be anointed with a little butter when still hot, to make an extra layer between the proposed filling and the pastry, thus keeping it crisper. Strawberry and lemon tarts commonly use a layer of chocolate to do this. But I find painting the hot pastry with beaten egg white as soon as it comes from the oven works better – so I often give it two coats.

Beans: it's vital to know all kidney beans (those with kidney shapes) must boil for ten minutes during cooking; boiling red kidney beans is particularly important, because if not they are virulently poisonous. It's best to do this at the start of cooking, so they are not disintegrated by the boiling. Yet another reason to spend the few extra pence and buy them ready-cooked in cans. Also nothing salty, including bacon, should ever be in the same pot as beans until they are soft – salt will toughen them, sometimes permanently. So you cook beans just in water and only when soft do you add the bacon, the spices, herbs, molasses, tomatoes or whatever.

Burghul: this is broken wheat grains that have been precooked to a paste , cooled and then broken up, so it needs only to be rehydrated to be eaten. It is probably man's oldest processed food and still a great thing to have in the store cupboard. It's the basis of tabbouleh, the Middle Eastern salad that's sumptuously heavy on parsley and coriander leaf, but on spring onion too. Leave out the onion, bump up other herbs and salady things, even green peas, and it will be far more acceptable to more people at a decent table. Otherwise, reconstitute burghul with something other than water or stock – try hot, crushed or chopped tomatoes from a can with one of your home-made flavours of oil or vinegar, and then mix in such usual suspects as garlic, parsley, coriander leaf, cucumber, olives, lemon or orange zest and chunks of chicken. Really fast food, that's thousands of years old.

Butter/margarine: these usually have equal energy content – natural oils and fats all have the same calorie/kilojoule content. But one is natural and the other is not and also contains trans-fatty acids, quite as bad for you as animal fats (see Hydrogenated fats below). So why not use butter?

Cornflour: this is generally a much easier thickening agent than flour because it is less likely to go lumpy. When used in clear liquid it gives quite a clear result after a brief cooking – the delicious Danish berry jelly rot grot is a good example. But beware of using cornflour to thicken something that will cook for more than forty minutes, rabbit or fish pie for instance. Eventually, cornflour loses its virtue and the sauce will start to thin.

Cranberries: these last almost for ever when refrigerated (it's their super-high vitamin C/ascorbic acid content) and make a terrific addition to brighten up fruit pies, sauces, and especially stuffings, sausages or patés. But when you make your own cranberry sauce at Christmas time – just so you can add pineapple and toasted pecan nuts, dark brown sugar and cinnamon and orange zest – remember not to add the sugar until the cranberries have popped their skins and these have softened. If you add sugar any earlier the skins will be tough, just as they are when sugar is added too soon to marmalade, plum jam, peach preserves, etc.

Curdling: you will avoid most curdling problems if you always add the thicker ingredient to the thinner. It's usually a good idea to have them at more or less the same temperature, too

De-fatting stock: you don't have to wait until the next day. before lifting off set fat. Let the stock cool and then drop in ice cubes, to which the fat will adhere. Or carefully lay kitchen paper on the liquid fat, and it will take it up neatly. Keep repeating this until no fat remains.

Egg custard: the most important step in making an egg custard is tempering, done when the heated milk is poured on to the prepared yolks or whole eggs, a simple process to make the eggs more biddable and less likely to split into curds and whey.

Eggs: to test if an egg is fresh or not put it or them into a large bowl of cold water. Fresh eggs will stay at the bottom. Those which have been around a while will start to float and should be discarded, returned or checked very carefully before being used; those which hover halfway up are in the some-what mature state most people eat eggs if they continue to resist refrigerating them.

Fish: if you must roll fillets of such flat fish as sole with its skin still on, do this with the flesh side outwards, otherwise a ligament in the skin pulls it into a curve when cooked and it will unravel.

Frozen vegetables: these are far and away more likely to be the freshest and thus the most nutritious you can buy. They were often blanched and frozen within hours of being har-vested and will stay in that condition, but 'fresh' fruit and vegetables are often many days old when they hit the shelves.

Frozen vegetables are not softened or degraded by the freezing process; they are soft when defrosted because they have been blanched or part cooked to make them even safer and faster for you. They are most nutritious when cooked covered but without added water in a microwave. Whispers about microwaves being responsible for fried testicles are as well founded as the moon being made of cheese, blue or otherwise.

Gilding: there are two ways of giving food a golden zhush. The very old way is to let ground saffron colour an egg yolk or two for some time and then to paint that onto, say, a roasted chicken or turkey or goose and then put that back into the oven to set and brighten. If you only have saffron threads, brew some in a little boiling water for ten minutes and mix that into the egg yolks. Or you can use the real thing . . .

Gold leaf: edible gold leaf comes in packs, squares or oblongs beaten almost to single molecule thickness. Totally digestible, it is classically dabbed on to savoury food, hot or cold, just before serving, but is also used on chocolates and patisserie confections. Professional gilders can lift a whole piece and dab it down intact. Most of us are better off dabbing at the leaf with a watercolour brush or with a finger and then dabbing at the food. The casual effect of this is somehow more believable and exciting than presenting food encased like an Egyptian tomb artefact. Silver leaf is cheaper and used just the same way, but invariably makes me worry about the effect it might have on tooth fillings.

Hydrogenated fats: anything made into a solid fat from liquid oil has usually been hydrogenated, which creates trans-fatty acids. These contribute quite as much as cholesterol, but in a different way, to fatal heart disease – in the US it's reckoned over 100,000 Americans a year are sentenced to death because their doctors have made them move from using butter to margarines and such. New York has now banned their use in restaurants and cafés. They have been removed from much manufactured British food but sneakily replaced by palm oil, which contains a high volume of hard fat, a sort of plant-world animal fat that works in the same way as animal fats to infamously affect your heart and arteries.

As long as we expect to buy goods, especially baked goods, which last for months we are sentenced to eat hydrogenated fats and palm oil. Or we could eat fresher, locally made foods that use such natural fats as butter or lard or dripping or any of the vegetable and plant oils except palm oil. That's perfectly possible.

Juices/drinks: anything labelled a 'drink' is largely water, no matter how the lurid packaging and claims seek to disarm you.

Lemons/limes: to get more juice, microwave for five to ten seconds and/or roll them on a hard surface to break down some of the inner membranes.

Long-cooked dishes: there is no advantage in adding a small amount of herbs (in stews) and spices (in Christmas puddings/cakes) to a dish being long cooked, for those flavours will be cooked away. Added five to thirty minutes before serving they are delicious, or you could compensate by using them in greater amounts. But if you are cooking a stew at only 140C/280F or so, the flavour of a very few added herbs stay remarkably vital. Even so, you might want to refresh their flavour at the end of cooking. See Temper, Temper, page 238.

Low fat: this often means higher sugar and so higher calorific value.

Meringue pie topping: sick of meringue topping leaking? The secret is always to start applying meringue to a pie or whatever around its edges, so that is sealed, and then to pile the remainder into the middle.

Onions: their proper, traditional use in cookery is to provide a sweet, unctuous base, and that is only achieved by long, slow cooking, around 40 minutes for 1lb/500g before you turn up the heat to caramelise the sugars thus created. A quick fry-up carbonises rather than caramelises and anyway you still have the sharp, vulgar flavour of uncooked onion in your dish. But that, sadly, is the highlight of so much modern cookery, and often the only flavour, too. Stop using onion, or use it properly, and your food will improve immeasurably; and yes, it is faster to soften and sweeten onion in the microwave, so there is no excuse.

Pasta: traditional pasta extruded through bronze dies (look for bronzato on the label) and then air-dried naturally has a dull caste and feels like fine sandpaper on the teeth, just as natural pearls do. This type of pasta is what pasta should be: it tastes better anyway and then improves further because it absorbs sauce. Thus the most important part of pasta cookery is leaving the cooked pasta to steam-dry for a few minutes on the outside before adding sauce, which is then absorbed – a sauce should be a flavouring for the pasta rather than the pasta being a carrier for the sauce. The classic family way of serving pasta in a big bowl onto which the sauce is then piled in its centre, but only mixed when being served, does this automatically.

Putting oil into the cooking water is a waste of time: cooked pasta will not stick together as long as you use enough cooking water, at least 4 litres per 500g/8 pints per 1lb. And as for the idea of mixing back some of the cooking water into the cooked pasta . . . why? It only dilutes the sauce you have carefully cooked to the right consistency. Someone's not thinking straight.

Although much is made of using high-gluten/hard flour for making pasta, this is only suitable for industrial manufacturing, because it is very tough to roll out. If you are making pasta at home you are quite right to use soft or cake-making flour.

Which shape of pasta for which food is essentially simple; smooth sauces, even when lightly textured, can be served with smooth types, like spaghetti, fettucine, tagliatelle and the like, which will absorb a good deal of the sauce if it has been properly dried before the sauce is added. If the sauce is lumpy then the pasta should have ridges, pockets or folds to catch the pieces, shapes like penne, or conchiglie or orichiette.

Potatoes: if you must cook these in water rather than microwaving, always start them in cold water so the outside does not disintegrate before the centre is cooked. And make sure you choose the right spud for the job: floury ones for mash, for baking and for chips; waxy ones for boiling and, particularly, for potato salads. The key to a good potato salad is to dress the sliced or cubed potatoes with oil and vinegar (with or without finely chopped garlic) while they are still hot, even if you later intend to bind them with a mayonnaise. But why would you boil potatoes? (See Recipes on page 139).

Pepper: Sarawak or Indonesian peppercorns are the most elegant for everyday use and can be found even in some supermarkets. Brazilian are the hottest if that is your goal, Indian are workaday occupiers the middle of the road. All are improved by a greater or lesser roasting, done much faster and more controllably in the microwave. Otherwise the French mixture called quatre epicés, which includes allspice, is a great choice for a second grinder on the table. White pepper is hotter than black but has much less flavour; it tends not to be used these days, unless it's to avoid the dots of black pepper in a white sauce.

Purées: for heaven's sake stop pushing food through a sieve with the edge of a wooden spoon, or worse. Use the back of a soup ladle and it's quantifiably faster and you get a far greater reward.

Ratatouille: if you like to make this in quantity and keep it around for some days, which is a better idea than cooking every day in summer's heat, here's a tip to make it stay safer longer. After 24 hours, boil it again because by then any yeast cells surviving the first cooking will be starting to grow but will not have had time to reproduce.

This second boiling avoids the fizzy fermentation that would otherwise happen and greatly extends the stew's life even without refrigeration.

Rice: please learn the difference between a risotto and a pilaf. A risotto, made with short-grain arborio, carnaroli or vialone rices, is always a first course or a stand-alone course followed by fruit or pudding. It is rice cooked al dente and bound together with a rich sauce of emulsified butter, stock and starch from the rice. And it's always finished with more butter and Parmesan cheese to perfect that sauce. It can be all'onde or wet enough to make waves when you put a fork through it, or it can hold its shape – but the grains will still be bound by the sauce. It should be made on the hob, can be made very successfully in a microwave, but cannot be baked in the oven, for the correct emulsified sauce can only be made by whisking.

A pilaf, pilau, pulao, etc. is made from long-grain rice of different sorts; it is not whisked while cooking and thus the grains should be fully cooked and perfectly separate. A pilaf can be made in an oven and it is into a pilaf you can safely add whatever the refrigerator and the dog refuse any longer to contemplate. Basmati rice makes the most elegant pilafs of all, quite aristocratic enough to be dabbed with edible gold and silver if this takes your fancy.

Rice pudding: if you don't care much about the skin on baked rice puddings you can make a really creamy one in a saucepan. Use low heat, stir from time to time, and when the milk has been absorbed, add the same amount again. The rice will always have an unctuous sauce coating the grains, so it is a kind of risotto. Do the milk thing again and again and again and you make an Eastern Mediterranean rice pudding, which is then sensually flavoured with orange-flower water, perhaps with mastic, or coloured and flavoured with saffron and then scented with rose-water and scattered with pomegranate seeds or shards of green pistachio. It is one of the most beguiling things I know and even better when served chilled, which means the fragrances and aromas are largely hidden until they meet the warmth of your mouth. Add touches of gold leaf and it's as close to sensory nirvana you can get with your pants on.

Salads: these should not leave a puddle of dressing in the bottom of the bowl. In fact, the professional way to dress a salad is to have the dressing in a large bowl, to dip in the salad a handful at a time, shake it well and then put that into the serving bowl; when this is empty there should be no puddle on the bottom. I hate the idea of shaking salad dressings in screw-top jars with a passion. Why do the ingredients need to be emulsified, which, anyway, tends to make the salad leaves look dull.

For salads that can't be dressed the above way, like a tomato and walnut salad, just take a few steps back from all the smarty-farty nonsense peddled about, pour the ingredients directly into the bowl and stir, mix, blend and toss with care. Remember, even done like this there should be very little dressing left over. If there is, transfer everything to another bowl.

Salt: in case you are skipping through, go back, and you'll learn why salt does not bring out the flavour in food, but merely makes your tongue more sensitive to what is to be detected.

Tomato purée: an Italian chef taught me always to fry tomato purée in a little oil until it thickens and brightens in colour before adding it to anything, especially to pasta sauces. Somehow this prevents the purée from going brown and adding dullness rather than brightness.

Truffles: summer truffles, tuber aestivum, have virtually no flavour and so they masquerade as the real winter black truffle, tuber melasporum, but deliver nothing. Any paste of summer truffle you are offered that contains onions and vinegar is a double bluff to screw you out of your money but give nothing in return. Go for the real thing. Or use truffle oil,

Wholemeal flour: bread made with wholemeal flour should not be kneaded, as this destroys most of its special nutrition. A loaf made with mixed flours is a careful balancing act, best solved by kneading a soft dough of the other grains and then mixing in the wholemeal flour at the last minute.

Discovering the truth of ingredients is one of the most exciting aspects of cooking and often saves you heaps of time while actually delivering much better flavour.

Question everything until you are sure you know the truth. A copy of my *Real Flavours – the handbook of gourmet and deli ingredients* would be a great help. Well, I would say that, wouldn't I, but Tom Parker Bowles in the *Daily Mail* said it's as 'important to the kitchen as a sharp knife'.

BREAK AN EGG

Eggs are not an enemy. As well as being the single most divinely comforting of foods, eggs are downright good for you in a varied diet. Do you honestly know anything more soothing than eggs with toast and butter? They are also the most perfect example of how really knowing the possibilities each ingredient offers is always the fastest way to cook without recipes.

For many years scaremongers have warned we should eat but a couple of eggs a week — if that — because of cholesterol. Yet as long ago as 1999 the Journal of the American Medical Association reported the Harvard School of Health found no relation between egg consumption and cardiovascular disease in 117,000 people who were followed from eight to fourteen years. Even those who ate two or more eggs a day seemed at little risk. The conclusion was that 'consumption of up to one egg per day is unlikely to have substantial overall impact on the risk of CHD [coronary heart disease] or stroke among healthy men or women'. There are similar results from equally substantial sources, but because this is good news scarcely a newspaper in the world picked it up.

Eggs are basic to our dietary choice, and for vegetarians, particularly teenaged vegetarians, they are vital, absolutely vital sources of essential protein. And they give you the essential Vitamin D when there's not enough sun for your body to make it. There is no inherent downside to eggs other than how some of them are produced, and that is being addressed. Regard eggs as if they were red meat, butter, cheese, milk or cream, and averaging out one a day is more than OK: if you have four one day and three the next, both on days you don't eat red meat, cheese, etc., then a total of seven a week remains a very good thing.

Best of all, an egg is an icon of what our food should be — once laid it comes to us entirely unprocessed. We are the first person ever to see what is inside the shell.

The Eastern Mediterranean and related countries do great things with eggs: I specially like Hamine Eggs, eggs in their shell which are simmered in water with a few onion skins for a very long time, overnight even. The onion skins first colour the shell and then the whites and the eggs develop a quite different texture — smoother and silkier, and with more complex flavours. They are used as any other hard-boiled egg — shelled and served with dips, sliced into salads, or chopped to spoon into pitta pockets or other sandwiches.

Whole eggs also go into long-cooked stews, like the hearty bean and meat cholents that cook through a Friday night, so observant Jews do not have to cook on the Saturday Sabbath. The eggs absorb the complex flavours of the stew through their shells and can be served with the stew or separately. They, too, are excellent picnic fare, but no hard-boiled egg is more excellent than a Golden Net Egg.

For Golden Net Eggs, you hard-boil eggs, shell them under running cold water and then pat them dry. Slide each from a spoon into at least 1cm of hot olive oil in a large pan, and when they begin to colour, roll them from time to time to ensure all the eggs colour up, not evenly as you'd expect, but with an intricate net of gold. Serve them when cold with tasty dips, one or many, including a mixture of herbs and spices – parsley plus salt, pepper, cinnamon and cumin is a great start.

In our part of the world, people often say scrambled eggs but mean buttered eggs. Buttered eggs are lightly beaten and poured into melted butter that has fallen silent: only when heated butter stops spluttering is it at the perfect cooking temperature. Stir and fold the eggs into the butter as the eggs coagulate, until the butter is incorporated and the eggs are almost set. Get them out of the pan and onto toast quickly. They set more firmly than scrambled eggs.

Scrambled eggs require infinitely more care. First, you whisk the eggs making as little froth as possible, and then stir in a tablespoon or so of milk or cream per egg. You can add much more, up to 150ml per egg, but don't.

I make scrambled eggs in a wide-mouthed saucepan or a nonstick frying pan. There must be generous butter, in even, small, solid chunks this time, two or more teaspoons per egg. Hot plates with properly crisped toast standing to attention in a rack (never lying down to sweat and go soggy) must be on full alert. Pour the mixture into a heated pan over medium heat, and then use a spatula with a straight edge slowly to move the liquid, first one way and then another, so that the eggs exotically meet themselves both coming and going. When the mixture starts to coagulate, use the flat edge of the spatula to scrape up long, languid curds from the centre and then to tip them into the outer cooler edge. The eggs are now doing one of my favourite things – flocculating. An excellent word that, and it means making clouds. Keep the clouds of curd as big and undisturbed as possible as you tip and fold. The eggs should be cooked at about the same time the last of the butter has melted; that's the secret of scrambled eggs.

Remembering that eggs continue to cook off the heat, you should serve when there is still a little liquid and a little butter to be seen between the curds. Tongue-crushing the unresisting warmth of silken and suppliant scrambled egg curds is sexier than most things I can call to mind.

To my mind, additives like bacon, smoked salmon or grilled tomatoes should go under or beside the scrambled eggs. For some reason the women of the previous generation of my family all thought it a good thing to add sliced tomatoes to scrambling eggs. The red-weeping eggs looked as though a truck had hit some small sad animal as they scrambled to escape the pan. Manfully we ate on, and some even liked the combo of rubber eggs, battered tomatoes and torrents of whey: one turncoat cousin cooks them still.

Not a million miles from the theories of scrambling eggs are the richest kids on the egg block, those aristocratic twins of eggy superiority, the crème brûlée and the crème caramel. But these are baked, so the flocculation is solitary. From there a sugar-free step takes you to baked egg custards, most often enjoyed in pastry. Neither crèmes nor tarts should ever be cooked at 180C or above, because the egg will rise and cook into a rubbery foam or can even split into curds and whey. The low baking temperature is why it's essential to blind-bake any pastry first, or it's got no chance of forgetting it was once pale and pasty. Thus 170C is best for your quiche or flan, or your sweet or savoury tart, even if it takes for ever to bake. Still, you can predict this – the greater the salt level the faster baked egg mixtures cook, the greater the sugar level the slower they cook.

Of them all, the crème brûlée is the richest sweet custard and properly has a mirror of caramelised sugar on top, but making that crunchy coating is too difficult for most domestic cooks, so I make crème caramel with a crème brûlée mixture, that is a baked custard with runny caramel on its bottom. You turn these out to serve, although Fletcher Christian's grandmother had a recipe with a runny caramel bottom plus a crisp caramel topping, and flavoured the custard with orange-flower water. It's exceptionally good.

Crème caramel is usually much less rich than the brûlée, for while the brûlée is made with cream, the crème caramel is usually made with milk – but you can do what you like. I know some want their crème caramels made only with condensed milk, and the kitchens of the late Jai Jaipur, the handsome polo-playing Maharajah of Jaipur, would boil down two pints of cream to make just four small crèmes brûlées for His Highness' table. There are French and Japanese equivalents using neither milk nor cream; the egg-yolk-bound French one is made only with sweet muscat or Sauternes wine, while the Japanese is made with concentrated stock and egg yolks. Using only egg yolks give a better mouth-feel than whites, but there will be success using all egg yolks, whole eggs or whole eggs with some added yolks.

If you use all yolks, you are rewarded with a silken texture that's matchless, but then you must flavour highly to counterbalance the palate-blinding effect of the richness or the results taste like, well, like egg yolks. The French baked custard reduces the sweet wine by at least half before mixing it with egg yolks. You must never use only egg whites or too many egg whites when making any sort of a baked custard: crème brûlée in particular fails, becoming a legless, deathly pale scramble of egg and sugar. (If you'd like to try this, there is a clutch of restaurants I can recommend, all around the world.)

Rich Crème Caramels

You can make these even richer by using only four egg yolks, which will give a light set, or five for something firmer.

HOW TO DO IT:

6 tablespoons caster sugar

2 tablespoons orange juice or water

½ cup caster sugar

½ teaspoon real vanilla extract

2 eggs

2 egg yolks

600ml/1 pint milk or cream, hot

1 or 2 bright navel oranges

Makes four to six servings

Use milk or a combination of milk and cream to make the richness you prefer: orange and vanilla might seem old hat but there's really nothing quite as good.

Finely grate enough bright orange zest to lightly sprinkle into the base of individual ramekins; this time a ½ teaspoon per ramekin is about right. Melt the six tablespoons of sugar in a small saucepan until it is a definite dark rather than light golden colour. Remove from the heat and add the orange juice or water: it will sputter dramatically. Stir until nicely mixed and then pour evenly into the ramekins. Mix together the second lot of caster sugar and vanilla extract and then mix in the eggs and egg yolks. If you whisk sideways rather than in a circle you make fewer bubbles, and that gives a smooth, unpocked result. Once the caramel has set, stir the hot milk or cream into the egg mixture, strain into a jug and then pour carefully into the ramekins.

Put these into a roasting tray, put that in the oven and then pour in boiling water to about halfway up the ramekins. Cook at 75C/170F maximum until set, which will take up to an hour: the more sugar you use, the longer they will take.

Turn out to serve at room temperature, standing each ramekin in hot water for a few minutes if the caramel is recalcitrant. Serve with shredded and blanched orange zest, cold, thin cream or some mixed berries – the frozen ones are just great, but defrosted, of course. For an olden-day touch, flavour the crème caramels with orange-flower water, in which case they are best lightly chilled.

Serve with ice-cold, peeled, sweet dates onto which a little outstanding vodka has been dripped.

Excellent Microwave Mash

When potatoes or other root vegetables are microwaved, they come out of the cooker ready to mash – and serve – in the same container.

HOW TO DO IT:
1kg/2lb starchy/floury potatoes
Serves four to six

Peel the potatoes and cut into pieces about the same size. Ideally they should cook in a large microwave-safe dish or bowl in which they can lie in a single layer: if that's not possible, turn the potatoes around once or twice during cooking. Because of the long cooking time compared to other vegetables, it's worth adding a few tablespoons of water, which stops the outers of the potatoes becoming too dry. This is mashed up with the potatoes. Cover and microwave on High for twelve minutes. The potatoes should be cooked through and beginning to break up and dry a little. Perfect.

Mash or crush lightly, let them steam-dry a little more and then continue. You can use a potato ricer, a vegetable mouli, a hand-beater or plain elbow grease (but not a food processor) to finish the task of making a complete mash, adding butter, hot milk (which helps keep the mixture light), extra-virgin olive oil or all of them.

Reheat in the microwave before serving. A grating of nutmeg is always a good thing.

Recommended Detours

- Olive oil and garlic: Microwave starchy potatoes with eight or more sliced cloves of garlic as above. Mash them together until as fine and dry as possible and then beat in olive oil – at least 150ml/¼ pint and perhaps more. Season. You can make this without the garlic and very good it is too, and you can also use half olive oil and half hot milk.

Crushed Potatoes

To triumphantly present crushed potatoes, you need only cause some slight damage to microwaved (or boiled) potatoes with the back of a wooden spoon and then serve. They should be very lumpy and uneven, and this can sometimes take rather more care to look good than making a smooth mash.

Crushed potatoes look particularly good if you have left the skins on the pieces, but that means you might have to cut through them with a knife as well as crushing. Dab on a bit of butter if you must. The place to serve these is on any plate where there is lots of juice, so this can be absorbed by the potatoes. Less fat, but more flavour. A winner.

Recommended Detours

- Garlic and olive oil: Microwave starchy potatoes and up to eight cloves of garlic as above, and when done injure the potatoes but do not bash or mash the garlic too much – they are like treasure chests to be discovered. Drizzle a little olive oil over each serving for flavour or effect, and add flat-leaf parsley.
- Horseradish and nutmeg: It's taken over thirty years for me to be fashionable – that's about how long I have been serving crushed potatoes with horseradish and nutmeg. Microwave starchy potatoes with garlic as above, crush roughly, and

then mix through lots of creamed horseradish, one of the less hot types. A little milk or cream is an advantage as is parsley, and freshly grated nutmeg is a must.

- Mediterranean: top the crushed garlic-potato mix with chopped black olives, capers, capsicum, flat-leaf parsley and torn basil. Drizzle on plenty of olive oil, which is all the better for being heated.

CHAPTER FOUR

HOW TO TASTE
PART TWO

GIVING IT TONGUE

Knowing what sort of tongue you have is vital to exploring Flavour Trails.

Now you know more about the tastes and flavours you will use to create Flavour Trails, you should learn as much about the tools with which you will be driving them, your mouth's tongue and palate. In the end you cook with your tongue, but who knows much about their own?

Just as everyone sees, hears, thinks, runs, laughs or writes differently, everyone's tongue works at its own speed. In those last seven words lie all the woes and troubles of cooks and chefs, domestic or professional. It's a bit of a bugger really, because it means five or twenty or two people eating the same dish will each taste something different, according to how sensitive, or fast, their tongue is. Even those attributes can change from day to day, hour to hour, and environment by environment.

If your tongue works at an average speed, the food you cook is likely to please most people. If your tongue is very fast or very slow to taste what is in your mouth, your food is likely to please a few but confuse or disappoint most others. The greatest cooks – and chefs – have tongues behaving somewhere in the middle of the spectrum.

Culinary skill is not based on how fast you can recognise flavours or how many you can: blindfold many a famed chef or wine expert and they would have huge problems knowing what is put in their mouth. Their skills lie in the creative but always ultimately lucid way they combine and build flavours and in the way they ensure – as a professional chef must – the same dish tastes the same, time after time. This latter point might be precisely what the home cook doesn't want.

So first, a guide to knowing what sort of tongue you have and why other people's food can be so disappointing, or always better than yours.

THE SPEED OF YOUR TONGUE

Someone using very little salt and someone using rather a lot might have the same flavour in their mouths.

There are three types of tongue: fast, slow, and every other sort of tongue.

Fast Tongues

Active, awake, supersensitive fast tongues are ready to taste any and everything fully with little or no salt. Essentially they are faster not just because of supersensitive taste buds but because they actually have more of them than other people. Yet all of us lose the potency of our taste buds as we grow older and as fast tongues age they often develop a need for a little salt to help them taste flavours the way they used to. This can happen to the most refined palate.

When the late great Robert Carrier put together *New Great Dishes of the World* towards the end of his life, he crumbled alarming amounts of red chillies over dish after dish. He was getting heat rather than flavour, but at least something was happening in his mouth at a time his taste buds were giving up on him. A younger Bob would never have used any chilli, let alone the amounts he specified.

Slow Tongues

With fewer taste buds at your service, slow tongues can need big helpings of salt to get into action, sometimes so much an eater is more aware of the taste of the salt than the flavour of the food. Because they would taste nothing if salt were not in their mouth, they put up with saltiness, and anyway, to them this is normal. A greater problem than the false flavour spectrum they experience is the harm excessive salt does to arteries.

As these tongues get older they, too, will need even more salt to switch on their taste buds, putting their health at even more risk, particularly because they have almost no way to recognise when their mouth has been satisfied. A great many overweight people eat too much simply because they taste so little and thus are never gratifying their mouths. There are some solutions, including MSG – see page 41.

Every Other Tongue

Most people have tongues neither too fast nor too slow – but don't think this simplifies anything. Someone with a very salt-sensitive tongue might have a sweetness-blind tongue, and vice versa.

And as well as tongues changing in sensitivity as they grow older, their potency changes when you are sick or tired or inside or outside. Nothing is harder to please than a table on the terrace for the whole family, from grandparents to grandchildren. The best thing to do for any group is to season lightly and to then invite everyone else to season to their own taste.

The confusion is an absolute. Someone using very little salt and someone using rather a lot might have the same flavour in their mouths, something entirely dependent on the speed of their tongues and not on what someone else deems to be the right amount of salt.

Throughout the food writing and professional culinary worlds there are men and women who do not understand their own palate is not a standard for the rest of us. When the judges of such a popular BBC series as *Masterchef* berate a competitor for not using enough salt they are not judging the dish but exposing their own palate's private shortcomings: they should be judging the merits of the combination of tastes and flavours and then be seen to add salt if they need more than the cook has used. Judging food solely by its salt content is as accurate as weeding an herbaceous border with a bulldozer.

As for you, once you can clearly identify each of the tastes in food and drink you will have an outstanding tool to help you create or judge recipes. Not only will you know where your tongue is being stimulated, you will also recognise where there are shortcomings and thus know (a) the *tastes* needed to balance the base of the recipe and then (b) be able to identify the sort of *flavours* needed to round out the recipe into something with a long, satisfying finish.

TESTING YOUR TONGUE

. . . to get a broad perspective on your palate.

It's not the sort of thing to be obsessive about. But knowing how sensitive your palate is to what and where, is the key to being a better cook. It will empower you to make better choices about how you cook, and thus make eating more enjoyable for you and others. To be serious you need a trusty companion to help with the tests.

Note, there are professional taste tests, using especially saturated paper strips, but these involve time and money to locate and aren't half as much fun to use. These are informal tests to do at home, to get a broad perspective on your palate.

For some the following test will mean hitting a culinary wall, beyond which no progress will ever be possible, but it will at least explain why they fail to see the point of certain ingredients or dishes which drive their friends into paroxysms. They simply have to accept they have fewer or older taste buds.

The number of taste buds we have is genetically determined. The more taste buds anyone has, the greater intensity of flavour they can taste: those with fewer simply don't get as much taste in their mouth. Counting your taste buds is a good way to begin understanding your palate and the palates of others. The result is something you just have to accept, like being short or tall, fat or thin, red, blonde, brown, or black-haired. It's you.

Test 1

The tools you need for counting your taste buds are:

- Food colouring
- Clean handkerchief or kitchen tissue
- Paper file-hole reinforcers
- A mirror or a trusty friend
- A big magnifying glass

Dab a little food colouring – blue or green are the better choices – on the tip of your tongue and then rinse out your mouth with water. Blot your tongue dry and then put a paper file-hole reinforcer onto your tongue, no further than 5mm from the tip. Ask a friend to use the magnifying glass to count the colour-defined taste buds within the circle; they look like tiny mushrooms. Or look in the mirror and use the magnifying glass to do the same for yourself.

The tongues of so-called Super-Tasters generally have more than 25 small evenly clustered taste buds within the circle. Slower tongues will have bigger but fewer buds. The fewer your taste-bud count, the slower your tongue will be and, generally, women have more taste buds than men.

But this has tested only the buds in the sweetness-detecting area of your tongue. It is worth looking to see what the count is in other areas, too. Matching this result with the next tests will be very informative. But keep these results from each person secret if you are then going on to the next tests, so they do not go into those with heightened or lowered expectations.

Test 2

If you simply want to be certain you can identify each primary taste, make up the following solutions and taste them one by one, thinking about the definite changes of mouth-feel that each primary taste also has, and where you most taste them. Or keep the identification of each solution hidden and make the discoveries a friendly game. Let's not bring 'reality' television's manipulated confrontations into the kitchen.

The tests will not only help you recognise and differentiate tastes but show which ones you taste more intensely: comparative speed and intensity of taste are what change from person to person according to the number of taste buds they have. Those with the greatest intensity of taste experience can taste at a much higher dilution and thus have more fun than others because they literally get more taste in their mouth whatever they are eating. Conversely, they will be more easily nauseated by over-sweet food or distressed by high bitterness in beers or in badly cooked cruciferous vegetables.

First, one person should make up the following solutions, unseen by the other or others – if more than a couple is playing, the amounts below might be doubled, tripled or more. The controller should be exceptionally careful he or she can always identify which is which – put a stick-it label on each (not under) with a different number or symbol and keep the key to these hidden until needed.

Everyone taking the test should be given paper and pencil. Strong smells, including aftershave, scent, soap or deodorants, should be washed away. Neither should there be competitive aromas of cooking, candles, flowers, fabric softener (ugh) or smoking.

The solutions should all be in the same sort of container – opaque paper cups are the ideal. Tasting should be done with a small plastic or silver teaspoon. For hygiene's sake, each dip should be with a new spoon; double-dipping with the same spoon is forbidden.

These are the solutions you need: if you want to take the tests to a more challenging level, make up three separate but equal amounts of each before you start.

- **Sweet**: ½ teaspoon white sugar dissolved in two tablespoons water
- **Salt**: $^1/_8$ teaspoon table salt dissolved in two tablespoons water
- **Sour**: ½ teaspoon vinegar (or lemon juice) dissolved in two tablespoons water
- **Bitter**: a big pinch of instant coffee powder whisked into two tablespoons water
- **Umami**: a big pinch of monosodium glutamate dissolved in two tablespoons water*

Each person takes a teaspoon or so of each solution and must then identify the taste, by writing it down in the order tasted. They should not say anything that others might use as a clue. It is as well to put a time limit, say ten seconds for each taste, on each contestant; remember, if they want a second taste they must use a clean teaspoon. When each person writes down their identification, it's not a bad idea for the invigilator also to note if the recognition was fast, medium or slow – i.e. was it less than three seconds, less then seven seconds or more than seven seconds.

The next person then does the same.

You can stop here, but tasting again with the liquids diluted, gives a clearer picture of the individual sensitivities of each palate.

Note: Resist all resistance to this test. It is very difficult to isolate umami taste, it is a small amount of MSG, and anyway you will have read how exceptionally safe it is. The first taste is somewhat salty but the aftertaste is indeed brothy, probably the detection of remnants of some meatiness you have eaten earlier. Otherwise make up some superior dashi and tell everyone to ignore the fishiness.

Test 3

The next stage is to take the second lot of solutions and then to each container add a further tablespoon of water. Mix up the order of the containers, noting the identification of each, and then let everyone taste again. This is where individual palate sensitivities or blind spots start to become obvious.

Test 4

For a real challenge, start again with a third lot of solutions and then add two extra tablespoons of water to each. Mix up the order, noting that down, and then let everyone taste again.

Those who can identify a taste at its greatest dilution clearly have the most sensitive tongues – but most people will now have demonstrated quite different spectra. Comparing overall correct identifications and examining each person's strongest and weakest taste sensitivity will be very informative, particularly when the comparative number of taste buds in each taste area is related to actual tasting experiences.

Test 5

This next test is to find if palates are good at recognising two tastes at the same time. Make up these solutions three times and then proceed as above.

- Sweet and sour: ½ teaspoon sugar and ½ teaspoon vinegar in two tablespoons water
- Bitter-sweet: ½ teaspoon sugar and a pinch of instant or ½ teaspoon brewed coffee in two tablespoons water
- Sweet and salt: ½ teaspoon sugar and ½ teaspoon salt in two tablespoons water

Test 6

The Eyes Also Have It

Our eyes help our brains predetermine the taste of what is going to be put into our mouths – that's why we can get so much pleasure from merely looking at pictures of food or from seeing it through a shop window. By promising pleasure based on its recall of past experiences the brain is ensuring we will eat and thus keep it healthy and alive. But it's very easily fooled.

The following is a bit of a party game, and very startling. Choose four or five clear liquids with contrasting tastes, for instance, apple juice, white wine, tonic water, lemonade and water. Pour equal amounts of these into as many clear glasses or tumblers as you need – ideally each person taking part should have a set of all five. Then add the same amount of tasteless blue colouring to each. Most people will be able to recognise the five flavours at once when in their original state, but guess what happens when they are blue . . .

Test 7

Knowing the Nose

The most astonishing way to test the importance of the nose to the perception of flavour is to taste something with the nostrils pinched. The ideal is a good swig of white wine from a coloured container, so there are no visual clues to what is being tasted. It should be nowhere near each participant before they taste it and no clue should be given.

Make the participant hold their nose and then give them the container and ask them to take a sip. Then, keeping the wine in their mouth and keeping their nose held tightly, they must immediately write down what they think is in their mouth. As soon as they have, let them release their nostrils and swallow. The full flavour is magically revealed.

There is no other experiment that will so dramatically demonstrate the importance of the nose to the overall perception of flavour. The effect is heightened if the white wine is one of the aromatics, like a Riesling or Gewürztraminer.

Because the nose is so important to our perception of taste and flavour, food eaten outdoors needs to be tastier than food eaten indoors. Wind makes it harder for the nose to get to grips with what is going down – the virtues are whisked away before it has time to get into gear. If it's a woodland or seaside picnic, or a filled roll on a park bench, air that is scented with pine or with salt-foam or exhaust fumes will make everything taste subtly different when you first arrive. After that, other curious physiological effects come into play, which are the unsuspected bane of those who cook in small kitchens or in large unventilated ones.

WHAT ELSE INFLUENCES THE TONGUE?

One of my prized possessions is an official receipt for cocaine. It hangs discreetly in the hallway and always creates a frisson when it is noticed. I keep it there as a memento of the time I was most forcibly reminded that without a nose on your face nothing delicious would ever happen in your mouth.

I had had a bit of a nose job and the thing they do after your septum has been straightened out is to stuff the affronted tubes with yards and yards of gauze, an intrusion made more bearable by first sprinkling the membranes with cocaine. I'd like to tell you it was a bit of a buzz but I knew nothing about it until I got the bill. The point of telling you this is what happened when the very expensive clinic in Brighton, Melbourne, then served very good food while my nasal tubes were so stuffed. Nothing.

Olfactory sensors in the nose and throat are dedicated to different experiences of taste and flavour from those of the tongue but without their contributions food tasted just by the tongue would be very ordinary or nonexistent. Think of how little you tasted the last time you had a cold and your nose was blocked.

The generally accepted families of smell recognised by the nose are: Camphor, Musk, Floral, Mint, Ether, Acrid, Putrid.

It is nuancing the amount of each, combined with what we taste with our tongue, that gives us the full potential from eating and drinking.

TONGUE AND NOSE BLINDNESS

A curious trick played by our tongue/nose tasting system is to get bored with a flavour or an aroma and then to put up CLOSED signs.

Nose and tongue fatigue are why people never smell the horrors of raw onion on their own breath or of garlic on their body being exuded from their skin and hair.

Such self-deception is why blokes think their own farts smell delicious or are unaware their armpits stink, why women think no one will know they've worn that top a few times before or haven't washed their hair, and why neither men nor women can smell stale aftershave or scent on their clothes or body. Their noses know, but have had enough and have gone out to play with someone else.

Infuriatingly, the nose behaves quite as selfishly when the smells are good. That's why a room seemingly overladen with the gorgeous scent of flowers to a newcomer is very ordinary to those who have sat there for a while. Their noses have put petulant hands to their hips and refused to smell any more. It is why some people famously cannot eat food they have cooked – it seems bland to them because receptors to it have been switched off and are taking ages to be persuaded back into business. It's why some people serve food so very much overseasoned and why so many cooks fall upon chilli so gratefully. Their smell and taste sensors have rebelled and put up that CLOSED sign: they don't want any more of what's on offer. When the food is ready and at the height of deliciousness, the cook then mistakenly feels the food has no flavour and panics . . . and you get your tongue conflagrated, or over-salted or insulted with hoary mixed herbs from the back of the cupboard.

Some cooks have to wait for hours before properly tasting what they served to others: a few even have to wait until the next day before their tasting organs have got back to normal.

If you have been cooking in a kitchen for hours it is often a good idea to get a new arrival to do any final tasting. And the more ventilation you have, the better are your chances of tasting what is really in the pot. Thus, the old kitchen maxim of taste, taste, taste can actually work *against* you. Taste too often in an unventilated kitchen and you will actually taste less and less of what is there, getting more and more immune because all your tasting systems have become more and more profoundly insensitive to the very thing most important to you at that moment.

All the above is a natural trait over which we have little physiological control. Going for a walk in the fresh air is about all you can do, hoping things are back to normal when you return to the kitchen.

Avoiding nose and tongue fatigue are why meals and menus must be planned with no repetition of ingredients or garnishes, and why contrast of texture and colour is vital. It was shocking even to quite ordinary family cooks to see a much-vaunted British menu served at the spectacular British Embassy in Paris feature peas and mint in both the first and the main course. Did that mean even luminaries make mistakes? – or were they relying on celebrity status to blind us to the thumbing of their noses at convention?

An extreme example of nose fatigue is found with violets. Pick or buy a bunch and after keeping them well away from you for twenty minutes, bury your nose deeply and inhale; it's one of the world's greatest pleasures. But smell a second time and . . . nothing. There is something in the scent of violets that stops the nose registering it continuously, and for some noses the barrier goes up for as long as twenty minutes before they can smell the violets again. This is why violets are so associated with things past – you remember the scent far more than you experience it.

Violets demonstrate just how capable the body is of filtering out what it does or does not want, but food and drink flavours and aromas don't generate such extreme cases. Remember onion breath? You can't smell it or taste it, but your neighbours can and until they too develop fatigue towards it, *your* raw onion will affect everything *they* eat and drink for some time. Not very nice of you, is it? It's another reason raw onion, including spring onions and chives, should never appear on or amidst decent food and wine.

I know hundreds of thousands of people protest this, saying onions give a nice edge to a dish . . . No it doesn't, it becomes the principal taste and flavour, overpowering everything else, including that expensive wild rice or saffron, including the home-grown tomatoes, and it particularly ruins wine – and not just your own, but of other persons who are within the borders of your onion cumuli. Believe me, many recipes that include raw onion are far better without it: just as many are revealed as tasteless without it and thus not worth eating anyway.

MOUTH-FEEL

*Personally I like to have a variety of textures
– and so of tastes and flavours –
in anything I eat.*

It can be a great mystery to watch diners in China and other Eastern countries thoroughly enjoying an apparently tasteless and flavourless dish of something like sea slug or jellyfish. What the diners are enjoying is texture rather than flavour, just as some of us might enjoy the biting cold of an ice cream or the biting heat of chilli rather than any actual flavour.

Most Westerners would not thank you for serving up jellyfish, with or without chopsticks, even though texture is one of the important building blocks of our recipes and menus, too. Some of our recipes are meant to be uniformly smooth, such as a mousse or scrambled eggs; those bland textures are, at least, the carriers of delicious flavours. Accompaniments add the necessary textural interest: fruit and wafers or biscuits with the mousse, buttered toast or bacon for the eggs. If you were planning to serve either without such textured partners you would probably have added something to the mousse (toasted hazelnuts) or the eggs (smoked salmon). Unless you needed comforting, and then there is little greater than a solo plateful of scrambled eggs, but only if you can scramble eggs to the correct voluptous texture.

The advantage of texture is that it keeps the eater's interest. As strongly textured ingredients are chewed they usually release other flavours, other textures. There is ever-changing flavour *and* mouth-feel, which continue to change as you chew more and more. Such experience should be a major consideration in putting together your own recipes. Personally I like to have a variety of textures – and thus of tastes and flavours – in a main dish, so every mouthful is different, changing in texture and flavour as it is eaten, giving the mouth, palate and tongue a constantly stimulating spectrum. But the simple addition of a textured ingredient won't save a dish if there is no underlying affinity of flavours, no traceable Flavour Trail; it will instead taste like the thousand-and-one heavily textured dishes offered by earnest vegetarians, who believe more ingredients is a higher nirvana than good ingredients. Each might be very good for you, but take an age to chew without any degree of rewarding flavour. So you eat on, chomp, chomp, chomp, until any feeling you have is only one of exhaustion.

That's not what I want food to do.

ORDER, ORDER

*. . . layering of taste and flavour in a single
dish is one of the ultimate objectives . . .*

A useful talent to develop is an awareness of the order in which
tastes first appear on your palate. When the food is sweet the
order of recognition by the palate is:

- Sweet
- Acid
- Bitter

When the food is savoury the pattern is:

- Salt
- Umami
- Sweet
- Acid
- Bitter

As you would now expect, the speed of detection is inextricably
linked to the number of taste buds you have, and how old you
are. Concentrated flavours are detected much faster than the

same one in dilution – again, no surprise. Taste recognition can be as fast as 300–400 milliseconds for salt and umami tastes, but the bitter taste can take as long as a second or more. Yet even these seemingly negligible differences can play a part in how dishes are constructed. In one of the very few tests made on taste detection, women were notably faster than men at identifying both good and bad tastes, and they got even better and faster as tastes were diluted.

Clever, confident cooks thus use these effects to entertain the mouth, combining ingredients with especially strong *taste* characteristics to make their presence felt in dramatic order and seemingly quite individually. At its most extreme you will then detect different and separate *flavours* as well, something quite magical.

The most memorable example I've encountered was a chocolate made by *chocolatier* Damian Allsop of Marlow, on the banks of the Thames. His chocolates are unique because he uses no butter, milk or cream in fillings, believing these get in the way of the pure flavour of chocolate and of its accompaniments. To get the creaminess of a ganache he uses only water. With no dairy fat to coat the palate or to cloud direct appreciation, the resulting clarity of flavour is astonishing. Damian's showstopper looks like a small rugged truffle, which you are instructed to put into your mouth whole and then to bite firmly. First there is an explosion of sweet tropical passion fruit, which quickly dissolves to its gratifying acid finish, but as that fades you start to taste the bitterness of the coffee in the outside layer. There's a knife-edge clear progression of flavour and taste, and by the time you are enjoying the final combination of chocolate and coffee, the flavour of the passion fruit is the subtlest of memories.

Such layering of taste and flavour in a single dish is one of the ultimate objectives of good cooking. When you create something somewhat one-dimensional, go back and identify the basic *taste* profile, detect which tastes are missing, and then find *flavours* that come with those missing tastes.

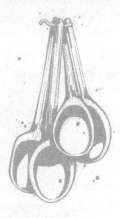

FINISH LENGTHS

For real oral gratification, at or away from the table, aftertaste is paramount.

You might not have realised your favourite biscuits, best salad, yummiest puddings or most delicious wines all offer the bonus of long aftertaste, but they do. It's why you like them so much. All the world's best food and drink leave culinary echoes, sometimes lasting on the palate and tongue for an hour or more. It's common to call this effect a long finish, a phrase usually associated with wine tasting.

Creating a recipe first delivering a mouth full of flavour, and then leaving a good lingering aftertaste is perhaps the ultimate goal of making something nice to eat, whether it be a cheese sandwich or a ten-course royal banquet.

Disappointing or unsatisfying food and drink usually have a short finish: in this frustrating effect the aftertaste comes to an abrupt stop very soon after the tongue tip. Beyond this nothing happens.

More common is the frustration of mid-finish and, as it suggests, the sensation of taste seems to meet a wall halfway back along the tongue: there is little or no taste registered behind that wall, neither on the back of the tongue nor down the throat.

This mid-finish is called a short finish when judging wine – taste and flavour sensation abruptly stops halfway back along the tongue. You have probably experienced this without being aware of it: so-called quaffing wines usually have this short finish and this is why there is an urge to drink so much of it. A short finish in wine or a medium finish in food is ungratifying to the palate, which knows there should be more. This is why it is easier to overeat when food is bland and/or has a mid-finish.

A pleasurable long finish of food and wine is long because of two attributes. The tongue is being used from one end to another, with a continuous exchange and interplay of flavours as you drink or eat: once you have swallowed, there will still be wonderful things to enjoy and this lingers deliciously past the back of the tongue and down into the throat, more often than not because of some oil content. The effect is the best way to judge the quality of food and drink. Whether bread and butter, caviare and vodka, or roast beef, any of these with real quality and depth of flavour will leave a glorious mouth-long taste behind. A cheese sandwich might not last quite as long on the palate as you'd hoped and neither might a £5,000 bottle of wine, because price is no guarantee of gratification. But another sandwich and another bottle might. Whatever the price, the best food and drink always offer a long mouth finish, longer than ordinarily imaginable, every time.

When fat as cream is frozen in ice creams, there is a double flavour sensation; first the slow build-up of flavour as the ice cream is warmed in the mouth, which increases the sensitivity of the taste buds, and then the slow clearing of the fatty cream away from them, leaving the intricacies of its underlying acidity and other complications to be savoured. The acidity that has been sharp when frozen now softens, too, the sweetness is intensified and the creaminess wallows about on the palate for ages with aromas and fragrances of the special added ingredients, reminding you again and again why you chose that particular flavour. It lingers. No wonder you like ice cream so much – it's an almost perfect entertainment for your tongue.

The following simple recipe is a brilliant way of introducing the young and the doubter to the concepts of the effect of cold on taste and flavour detection, and of the masking effects of fat, and thus is also a perfect example of the heightened wonders of food with a long finish.

A Simple Ice Cream

Don't be alarmed to see condensed milk in this recipe. The point of most ice cream recipes is first to make a thickened, sweetened custard – and here it is with no cooking. The basic mixture will hold up to 300ml/½ pint of fruit purée, fruit chunks or whatever, so let your mind wander freely. If you add only dry ingredients, like nuts or chocolate or dried fruit, increase the cream content by another 75ml or so, or the ice cream will be a bit too solid. A version using canned plums was one of the most popular of the hundreds I created for *Breakfast Time*.

HOW TO DO IT:

Makes about 600ml/1 pint

200g/7oz can sweetened condensed milk

150ml/¼ pint double/heavy cream

2 tablespoons lemon or lime juice

Flavouring

Refrigerate the condensed milk and the cream, overnight if you can, to ensure they are as cold as possible. Chill the bowl in which you will make the ice cream, too. Otherwise a short supervised stint in the deep freeze will do what is needed for both the can and the cream. Turn the condensed milk into the bowl and beat it with the lemon or lime juice until it's very light and frothy. Add the cream and beat until the mixture is the consistency of lightly whipped cream. Stir in your flavouring – or fold and swirl it to make streaks, which I prefer. This ice cream mixture does not need to be whisked when part frozen, but you will get an even smoother texture if you can be bothered and have the sense not to add anything chunky until the final beating up.

Recommended Detours

- Banana: mash two or more very ripe bananas with a generous teaspoon of vanilla extract – add passion fruit pulp, too.
- Plum: drain and then sieve the contents of a 600ml/20fl.oz (approx.) can of Victoria plums and stir in a teaspoon of very fresh ground ginger, allspice or cinnamon.
- Mango: flavour 300ml/½ pint thick chilled mango purée with freshly grated lime zest, or mix purée and random chunks of fresh mango; and that's with or without passion fruit pulp.
- Coffee strudel: mix 300ml pint apple purée with 1 teaspoon very fresh mixed spice, 1½ tablespoons coffee essence and 2 tablespoons of seedless raisins, which might have been plumped in rum. Some breadcrumbs, gently fried to a golden crispness in butter, make this even better. If you've no coffee essence, use 1 tablespoon of strong instant coffee granules and dissolve in a half-tablespoon of hot water.
- Exotic avocado: flavour with orange-flower water, stir in one or two ripe and well-mashed avocados (making sure you harvest and use all the scintillating green of the inner skin) and a handful of toasted almond or pistachio shreds; use honey rather than sugar if this mixture needs extra sweetness, or serve with a dribble of honey.
- Lychee and roses: flavour with rose-water and stir in plenty of roughly chopped fresh or canned lychees. Very sexy.
- Christmas pudding: fry crumbled leftovers in butter until crisp here and there. Allow to cool and stir in, together with a little something sweet, ideally cream sherry or port – but not too much or these will prevent a good freeze.
- Rice pudding: stir in 300ml very creamy rice pudding (yes, out of a can if you like) and stud with seedless raisins, chunks of glacé or sliced dried apricot. It's rather more wondrous if you have some leftover Eastern Mediterranean rice pudding,

flavoured with saffron and rose-water.

- Hot Rocky Road: stir in a selection of marshmallows and chocolate chunks, with or without coffee essence, and then add Tabasco drop by drop until only just detectable.
- And – chocolate and other syrups can be swirled (crunchy peanut butter and maple syrup?), so can crushed fudge of any flavour, high-quality jams, especially thick-cut marmalades, black cherry jams and Tiptree's Little Scarlet strawberries. Thick yoghurts and orange, lemon or lime curds also give worthwhile results.

THE BITE-BACK PRINCIPLE

I try never to put anything into my mouth that doesn't bite back with flavour. When we eat there are two hungers to feed. The most commonly recognised is stomach hunger, and we know – or should know – when this has been appeased. The other is mouth hunger. It is quite separate and requires quite separate gratification, and ignorance of this is another deadly contributor to the evils of overeating and obesity.

What the tongue and the palate need most is food and drink with so much flavour they bite back in the mouth. Bite-back food and drink fill the mouth with flavour and excitement, gratify and satisfy and leave a good long aftertaste. Doing this quickly convinces the stomach it has had enough. Not gratifying the mouth means the stomach stays expectant and you must then eat more and more until it reluctantly signals it is not satisfied but stuffed. Bite-back food or drink mean you eat well and feel satisfied – but with less food or drink.

The bite-back principle is equally important to anything you might drink. A really good half-bottle of wine with captivating complicated flavours keeps the palate entertained for ages because you have to drink it slowly. You are always better off ordering a decent half-bottle than a full bottle with a boring short finish. I remember a single bottle of red Bordeaux at a dinner party that took eight people an hour to finish. Yep, it really was that good. See? The bite-back principle helps control alcohol consumption too.

So, this might be a good time to think about what is a recipe, and what is not a recipe.

CHAPTER FIVE

HOW TO COOK IT

HOW TO COOK IT

It's difficult to get an edible result from poaching red meat, fish are notoriously easy to overcook – or undercook in a grill, frying asparagus is not a good idea, and then there's the microwave . . . and that's often the best bet of all.

There's a lot to think about in this section, because you are certain to find great surprises – like learning that a second helping of muffin mixture might badly affect how high they rise, that sort of thing.

I've included some more recipes for your basic repertoire, each of which is capable of being led deliciously astray by my or your Flavour Trail Detours.

Before we get down to the techniques of cookery, there are just two more of the scientific principles of cookery to look at. The effects of temperature and the effects of fats and oils are vital to understand if you really want to be in charge of what you are producing to eat.

THE EFFECTS OF TEMPERATURE

At extremes of temperature the flavour of most foods will seem very different in the mouth.

You must season food for the temperature at which it will be served, and not the temperature at which you prepare it.

The warmer food is to be served, the less help it needs from salt to be tasty or from sugar to be sweet, and the less extreme the flavour of other ingredients can be; the converse is true, too. In other words, sweet and salt flavours are intensified at higher temperatures, but diminish when food is chilled or refrigerated. The temperature effect is why you have to use so much more sugar in an ice cream than you would use with the same ingredients at ambient or hotter temperatures.

But note the optimum hot temperature is less than half the most usual oven setting of 180C/350F.There is absolutely no advantage in serving food directly from the oven and 'piping hot' because there's no way we can get maximum taste and flavour pleasures until it has considerably cooled. It's a curious self-protective mechanism the tongue has to prevent injury from heat:

like a strict Mummy, it warns you not to eat it directly from the oven, and then rewards you for waiting, but also punishes you if you don't wait.

At the lower end of the temperature scale acid and bitter tastes are especially exaggerated. You only need sip a cold black coffee to prove this and it's why iced coffee is usually served sweetened and with milk, ice cream or whipped cream.

Thus, once chilled, a lemon sorbet or tart can be much sharper than you expected, for two reasons – the acidity has been lifted and the sweetness diminished. Pairing something sharp-tasting with really ripe fruit at room temperature or with lightly sweetened cream will sort that out. Or you could just sprinkle on a little more sugar.

In summary, you should use less sugar or salt for hot foods, more for cold foods. Use less acidity or bitterness when a dish is to be served cold or chilled.

THE JOKERS

A few ingredients do very curious things to our palates. MSG increases our enjoyment of savoury, salty and bitter tastes but won't be of much use to heighten sensations in sweet and acid-sweet dishes. The artichoke component *cynarin* blocks everything but sweet flavours, making other foods taste comparatively sweeter: at the same time it wrecks wine. The herb sweet cicely does the same thing, rather magically making rhubarb taste sweet even though you have added little or no sugar.

THE EFFECTS OF FATS AND OILS

Fats and oils coat and inhibit the taste buds,
slowing down their reaction.

Fats and oils can have such arresting flavours we often don't care what else they are doing in our mouths – think of butter and cream or of walnut oil and hazelnut oil. No wonder we like to eat so much of them. Other oils and fats bring rather less pleasure. Indeed they are often chosen because they have so little flavour, like the oils used for deep-frying. Yet all oils and fats coat the palate and thus inhibit us from detecting other flavours. That's why we often use such inordinate amounts of salt on greasy or oily food – fighting a losing battle against both the blandness and the coating qualities of the fat and oil, we opt for salt as an easy option and then salt is often the only primary taste and only flavour we experience.

High fat or oil content and low flavour combine to define stodge. We do get a full comforted feel from eating them – that's why they are called comfort foods, and there's definitely a place for them. But the comfort in our guts is what later becomes uncomfortable pot bellies, because comfort eating is the basis of most obesity – that and the undeveloped palate fixated on sweetness above other tastes. Better food education early in life at school, which included tutored tasting of a wide variety of fresh foods, would go a long way to eliminate the undeveloped palate common to many overweight people.

Adding vinegar to fish and chips, at first the most baffling of Britain's curious food peccadilloes, also has its genesis in the palate-blinding attributes of fats and oils. The vinegar cuts the fat, certainly, and thus exposes our taste buds rather more, but the vinegar or 'brewed condiment' is often so one-dimensional in flavour it again sets up the tongue for nothing but disappointment. The tongue is ungratified, whatever the calorie content slipping by, and the stomach is still not satisfied: 'Gimme another deep-fried Mars bar, mate, and double chips' . . .

This is a simplified but true explanation of why we eat so much fish and chips or other fatty fast foods: if the fat wasn't there we would eat less and be just as satisfied. On the other hand, fats and oils are often beguilingly flavoured and the pleasure of their lingering in the mouth is the highlight of many good things we eat – like a good olive oil, or of butter baked with flour and spices in a biscuit or cake.

COOKING BY DIRECT HEAT

Grill/Broiler/Griller/Griddle/Barbecue

For most of history mankind cooked almost exclusively by direct heat, either in a cauldron of sorts hanging over a fire, on a spit in front of the fire, or on a box of some nonflammable material with a fire inside and a pot sitting in a hole directly above the flames – you can see rows of such constructions in the kitchens of Hampton Court Palace. The only exceptions were wood-fired ovens, where the fire was lit in the oven to heat the brick walls and then withdrawn and replaced by the bread or other goods to be baked.

The griddle and the grill mean different things in different societies. To some, to grill means to cook with top heat and a griddle is something metal without sides on which you cook food. A griddle can also be a girdle and may be either corrugated or flat. For others grilling can mean cooking in a ridged pan or over the grilles of a built-in kitchen barbecue

Grill/Broiler/Griller

Essentially you cook with a direct heat source only from above and the food is close to the heat source.

Many grills on a modern cooker are constructed like a small oven, and the makers recommend grilling with the door open. This is not only to allow fumes to escape, but also so steam can escape. Anyway, a closed grill with food cooking close to the heat source builds up fatty smoke and, together with over-heated fat in the food, can burst into flames. It's become an oven, but not as we should know it.

Grilling is an excellent way of reducing fat intake, for melted fat escapes into the pan below. But just like frying or griddling, this fat is likely to become overheated and smoke. If it does you are cooking at too high a temperature or too close to the heat.

The grill/broiler/griller doubles as a modern equivalent of the salamander and the village baker's shop. The salamander is a heavy metal disc on a long handle a cook would heat until red-hot and then run lightly over the surface of dishes, to create an appetising golden-brown finish. These days it is fashionable to do such browning with a culinary blowtorch. This is not as pretentious as many a TV chef makes it appear, because such blowtorches are remarkably cheap. Although the quick blowtorch blast of direct heat by a flame to only small areas at a time is like the effect of a salamander, it won't give the deep crackling crust achieved by the more even heat of a grill, or by long baking. This time, the relatively new grill and closed baking oven are definitely the best.

Generally it's taken that when Americans say broiler they mean a grill. Except, a flat metal sheet over heat was once a broiler, and in some parts of the States may still be. That's quite the opposite of what we think broiler means, and another example of the broad general knowledge of food and cooking you must develop if you want to read cookery books from other civilisations.

Griddle

Much traditional griddle cooking was done on a flat slab of cast iron sitting over a fire or, latterly, over the heat of a coal range or gas cooker. It can be thought of as a frying pan without sides. You do need a good extractor hood in attendance because to cook meat or vegetables through you need a good whack of heat, and a griddle at the right heat will vaporise excess fat and make smoke of it.

YOUR STEAK AT STAKE

How do you know when your steak or chop is just right? There are two main ways and both take practice, so don't expect to do it right the first few times. But note that neither really works with a thin steak or chop, for which you must rely on sense.

The worst thing you can do to steaks, chops or any other grilling cut is constantly to move, prick or turn them, perhaps the most common of all cookery mistakes. Neither should you press down the meat with the back of a tool – what is more likely to express the meat's moisture and its flavour?

The Touchy-feely Test
This is the usual way chef's test:

- Press a raw steak with your forefinger and it feels soft, and the impression tends to stay there. Remember how it felt and looked.
- When it is half-cooked – medium-rare – it resists your finger a little and goes back into shape; the feel and look is said to be the same as when you press the fleshy muscle in your hand directly under your thumb.
- If the cooked steak barely yields to your finger and springs back into shape it is well cooked and well on its way to being ruined.

The Bead Test
Provided the steaks or chops are at least 2.5cm (1-inch) thick, there is a better way. It works only if you are cooking in a pan or on a griddle, that is with the heat source beneath, and you must accept that meat needs only to be turned once, yes ONCE.

Keep the temperature high enough to ensure the meat really is not merely stewing in its own juices – the fat should be smoking a little but if there are dampish bubbles around the edge turn up the heat or you'll be eating steamed meat. Leave the meat until you see tiny beads or pools of juice breaking the surface; some will be red or pink. That's the time to turn over the meat. Immediately the same effect is seen on the other side, take it out and rest it. It will be perfectly cooked through, but still very pink, sweet and savoury. Experience will tell you how much beading you allow before you turn or remove the meat – the more there are, the more the meat is cooked. Remember, in the five or six minutes you rest the steak before serving it, residual heat will cook it a little more and the pinkness will even out.

As with boiling, steaming and poaching, it is a common fault to cook at too high a temperature. The food should be sizzling a little but if there are billows of acrid smoke, the heat is too high. However, if you are cooking very thick steaks or chops you *must* keep the temperature high or the flesh will steam and simmer rather than cook quickly and this makes the outside taste like wet cardboard. Open the windows and put the extractor on to high.

Today griddles are likely to be ridged and are becoming very popular as a way to cook meat, fish, poultry and vegetables because oil or melted fat drips into the channels and is not absorbed by the food. The cooked food has a nice ridged pattern on the surface, usually associated with restaurants and thus greater expense. Increasingly a griddle option is being offered on new cookers, but you can't make pancakes or griddle cakes or drop scones on these.

If you don't have a barbecue griddle as part of your cooker's hob, add a nonstick griddle pan. They have thick ridges on which food cooks. The food gets golden-brown scorch marks and fat drops away into the hollows between the ridges. The fat will still smoke and so to use such pans an extractor fan is a must. A caution though. Charred meat is a proven cause of stomach cancer. Use grills for cooking meat, poultry or fish only once or twice a week – even better is to cook your protein another way and to use the grill only to cook or to finish vegetables.

Barbecue

The world thinks differently about what is and what is not a barbecue. Some even include true roasting – cooking in front of a fire – in this category.

To many in Australasia barbecuing means any method of cooking outdoors, repeatedly translated as a slab of sheet metal under which you encourage an inferno of household rubbish, trees and any part of an old boat or truck that can't be used again. Needless to say, only blokes are deemed capable of ruining food to such a profound degree, and most march up to qualify from a frighteningly early age. The idea of barbecuing on bars, over a fire that has been allowed to die down to whitened ashes, is thought sissy, like wearing a shirt over a singlet. In the United States, massive men run massive barbecue events and competitions, but here the animals – they must be complete animals – are cooked in front of flames, rotating as they do. That's actually roasting, but I've never dared point this out.

The most disquieting fact to learn is that regular eating of any charred flesh (animal, poultry or fish) is a major encouragement to stomach cancer; it's a fact published in *Food, Nutrition and the Prevention of Cancer*, jointly published by the World Cancer Research Fund and the American Institute for Cancer Research, and the warning includes juices and gravies made from the charred encrustations of roasting pans. Curiously, the substances in charred flesh that cause the problem can be counteracted before cooking if you lightly microwave your steak or whatever, just to cook through the outer surface. This changes its chemical composition and what is created does not form carcinogenics so readily.

Otherwise it's smoke that most gets up people's noses, and that's caused by fat dripping down onto the heat source. The proper way to cook over the direct heat of coals is by *indirect* heat. That means when the coals have reached the state where they are covered in white ash, they should be moved to one side, or to both sides, and the food cooked over the vacated space only. It's good to put a tray under the food, so the juices are caught, to use when serving and so they don't stray onto the coals. If you use a device with fixed coals then you put a foil tray on the coals, to catch the drippings. For a touch of extra smokiness in the eventual flavour, tip some of the juices out onto the coals a few minutes before serving, perhaps adding something containing aromatic oil, like rosemary sprigs, or hickory-wood chips.

The knee-jerk belief in marinating meat to be barbecued is in no small way associated with the awful, unsuitable cuts usually sold as 'ideal for barbecues'. Marinades certainly punch up what little flavour is in such cuts but the sugary content chars well before the meat is cooked, which seems senseless to me. Buy better meat and enjoy its flavour with only salt and pepper and the prehistoric pleasures that come free of charge with cooking and eating outdoors. If you want the added zesty flavours eating outdoors invariably demands, then add a marinade as a baste for only the last few minutes of cooking; or keep it warm on the back of the barbecue and use it as a sauce for the beautifully cooked, non-charred result of such thoughtfulness.

The best compliments for barbecuing have always come when I used the barbecue only as an outdoor heat source, using it to keep soup hot on Guy Fawkes Night, to keep spiced wine mulling over itself, or water simmering into which meaty, juicy Polish sausages might be heated through. No, it might not be very blokey, but you make many more friends, not least because you can actually see one another.

COOKING IN HOT AIR

Baking and Roasting

Different countries and different decades use both roasting and baking of meats as interchangeable cookery terms, sometimes on a whim it seems. There is, or was, a difference.

Meat described as being roasted would always have been cooked on a spit *before* an open fire. For virtually everybody in the Western world, roasted meat was all they knew until the middle to late nineteenth century when enclosed ovens as part of coal ranges began to be seen in kitchens: well into the twentieth century coal ranges were still designed with a spit attachment used for roasting in front of the central fire.

Baked meat became the term when everyone started to cook in an enclosed gas or electric oven: the meat was being cooked like bread. Gradually personal preferences for something new or something old, and old-fashioned confusion, mean some places call meat baked or oven-roasted, and others call it roasted. If meat is cooked in an oven it should really be called baked or oven-roasted rather than roasted, whether chicken, hogget, venison or anything else. But you wouldn't want to seem pedantic or a know-all, would you?

A big roast of lamb, pork, beef or venison should be started bottom up; the side you want eventually to the top should start on the bottom and then you turn the piece halfway through, using anything helpful to hand, NOT something that pierces the flesh and allows juices to escape. For really big joints the answer is to don thick oven gloves and turn the meat by hand. By turning a large joint during cooking, the juices remain more evenly distributed through the meat. Small roasting cuts give best results if they are browned in a pan before going into the oven.

Opinions vary on how to oven-roast: low temperature, high temperature, or a mixture. As long as the oven is hot enough to cook the meat safely and you are watching carefully, personal preference may prevail: the single most important thing you can do to roasted, oven-roasted or baked meat is to rest it after it is cooked and before a single slice is removed.

Resting means to let the cooked meat sit undisturbed before it is cut. All the juices attracted to the outside of the joint or bird by the heat source return to their rightful place and flesh toughened by the uneven heat relaxes to its normal tender self and reabsorbs those juices. Result, no more pools of liquid when you carve, and very tender and juicy meat. Provided it is not cut, a joint can relax without losing heat for 20 minutes or more, and a turkey is still piping hot 45 minutes later. Most people disappointed by the dryness of a Christmas turkey would have been ecstatic with delight if someone had waited 30 to 45 minutes or more before carving, ideally with the cooked turkey on its breast so juices slither into the muscles rather than drip into the cavity.

One excellent cook I know says he will not carve meat if steam rises from the cut – that's moisture he believes should be in what you eat rather than what you breathe. He rests a leg of lamb for at least an hour before carving, and relies on gravy and hot plates to sort out any potential complaints. I find this very hard to argue against.

Resting works for smaller cuts equally, for grilled lamb chops or chicken pieces, and the time you take to serve and sit is generally enough time for the resting to have worked. Small birds, game birds, should never be cooked on their backs and should also be rested upside down.

Chickens and other birds need a bit more attention. They are the ideal way for anyone to learn to bake or roast.

The Roasted Bird

Never think of roasted chicken as a default choice. It is one of the most assured ways of giving a treat to others. Serve them something grain-fed and free-range and the rewards are much bigger than any effort made by you really deserves. Great. Go for it.

To get the best chicken meat you really have to forgo any idea of serving crisp skin and you won't get it if you cook it this way. Anyway, the skin is where more than 60 per cent of the fat lies and many people simply put it to one side anyway. Or should.

But first a summary of best practice for roasting birds, including the turkey and goose:

- Never put a bread-based stuffing into a bird – if you like such accompaniments, they should be made into balls and cooked around chickens, turkeys, etc.; Americans always do this correctly, echoing the way the drippings from a spit-roasted bird were once thickened and served.
- Only put into a roasting bird something that creates moisture and will give flavour to any gravy you make – a cut lemon, orange or lime, chunks of an acidic apple, quince or pear, onion, garlic, sweet chutney, chopped sun-dried tomato and/or black olives in oil . . . that sort of thing
- Get rid of any trussing. This is a leftover from the days of spit-roasting, for it made the shape even and compact. When roasting it prevents the heat getting into the thick inner parts of the leg and thus overcooks the breast while you wait for this to happen.
- Think carefully before wrapping a chicken or any other bird with bacon – the flavour of the bacon will mask the finer

points of a high-quality bird and it certainly isn't needed to keep the flesh moist.

- Ban foil. Cooking under foil means you are steam-roasting and this does not give the good, firm flesh of a roasted bird, moist though it may well be. It gives a curious watery flavour, too.
- For real extra moistness and flavour the proper place to stuff a bird is between the skin and the breast meat – see Stuffing Your Bird, below.
- Don't bother with basting as this only browns the skin and does nothing at all to keep the flesh moist – how can it when the skin is impervious?
- Most of all, plan for plenty of time to let the bird rest before you carve it.
- For maximum ease of carving, take the time to remove the wishbone before you cook. You can always fudge this by putting it back under the neck skin later, to be 'discovered' by you when serving your favourite or soon-to-be-favourite guest.
- And DON'T rest the bird wrapped in foil or anything else; by retaining heat you can overcook and the muscles can't relax enough to reabsorb the juices forced out by the cooking heat.

Stuffing Your Bird

Quickly rinse the bird under running cold water. Pat dry. Frankly, I never do this as I reckon you risk dissolving away some of the bits inside that would add flavour – but hygieniks and Americans insist. (Neither do I salt a bird, as this only flavours the skin and does nothing for the flesh.)

The only place to stuff a chicken – or other bird, including the Christmas turkey – is under the flap of skin where the neck once was, and/or between the skin and the breast, which will result in notably more tasty flesh and a great look. Anything you put over the breast and under the skin must be moist and capable of expressing either more moisture or a degree of fat, oil or butter.

To prepare the bird lift the skin at the neck end and then, using your fingers, gently stretch the skin away from the flesh – it's remarkably elastic so you have to be very careless or anxious to tear the skin, not that it matters a lot if you do. It's possible to continue on and to lift some of the flesh over the top of each leg, too. When all is lifted but the last extremity of skin over the back vent, put in your stuffing as evenly as you can.

To stuff the neck end, remove the wishbone altogether and bundle on enough stuffing so it can be held in place by the spare neck skin, and then hold this in place with sharp toothpicks or by stitching.

Stuffings under the breast can be as simple as Boursin cheese with or without extra fresh herbs and perhaps some lemon zest, or it can be butter into which you have worked herbs, garlic and the like; the most sublime combination for chicken is simply butter and tarragon, a marriage made in culinary heaven. Both the Boursin and butter will melt into the flesh without you having even to remember how to spell baste.

Otherwise, anything looking like a sausage or a paté does very nicely for breast or neck and these add a contrasting layer when you carve the chicken. Tops for looks and flavour is a squidgy black pudding to which you have added chopped apple and more Calvados than is good for you (but without making it into a swill). I've used the excellent Toulouse sausages with fresh herbs from a supermarket and almost any of today's meatier sausages, taken from the skins, do a fabulous job as a stuffing under a skin. This means any good paté can also be used – a chicken liver, perhaps.

Otherwise, grated courgettes, well drained, squeezed in a tea towel and then mixed with cream cheese or Boursin, is great and . . . well, you can make up your own from here. As long as the stuffing includes nothing that will absorb moisture from the bird, like breadcrumbs, you can hardly go wrong.

If you do put something like this under the skin of a bird,

you really are better also to have removed the wishbone before cooking, so you can easily make long impressive slices with the contrasting stuffing layer intact.

If you add a tasty stuffing it stands to reason it will better season the bird's flesh if it is allowed time to do so – overnight in a refrigerator is best – otherwise at ambient temperature for however long it takes the bird (and stuffing) to reach room temperature. Putting a refrigerator-cold bird directly into an oven is the major reason for undercooked or overcooked birds – and if you have also left on the trussing you will reap the full disaster.

It's simple things like that, not complicated stuffings and sauces, which put delicious food on the table.

The Cooking

Calculate the cooking time at 15 to 20 minutes per 500g/1lb and divide this into three equal portions of time. The oven should be set at 190C/375F and the bird must be at room temperature before it goes into the oven.

Cook the bird on one side for a third of the time – you have to jiggle the leg and wing a bit to get it to sit firmly but, again, this is a technique you develop with experience. Then turn the bird over onto its other side and cook for another third of the time. Instead of fiddling with forks and risking piercing the flesh, I turn the bird using two oven gloves and holding the whole bird firmly: this is a faster and safer way of handling a turkey. I'd rather wash a pair of gloves than serve dry poultry by piercing it with a fork so juices escape.

Next time you open the oven take the roasting pan out and then turn the bird on to its back, slice into the skin between the thighs and the chest, and pull the legs away from the main carcass. You'll see the inner thigh is not cooked – but now it is exposed directly to the heat it will do so quickly and without drying out the breast flesh.

Once the thighs are cooked through in more or less a third of the original cooking time you calculated, take the bird from the oven and turn it onto its breast. Let a chicken sit for at least twenty minutes before you even think about carving it.

The ideal is to rest it on its breast but this rather depresses the flesh if it is a heavy turkey or a capon. The best thing to do is remember the old advice to gentlemen always to take their weight on their elbows; so put a raw potato or similar under the wings to take the weight of the bird and keep the breast meat the way nature intended.

Turkey or goose can sit uncovered in a warm place for at least 45 minutes and still be piping hot. This gives you unflurried time to make the gravy, sit to a first course (or have a drink and a sit) and then to serve a perfectly succulent bird. Whatever you do, don't simply open the oven door and leave the roasted bird there: there is more than enough heat to continue the cooking and dry out the flesh.

For a good old-fashioned look and flavour you must now make a pan gravy.

Pan Gravies

Empty everything you put inside the bird into the roasting pan, and put the bird to rest on its breast. Let the pan rest a while so the fat floats to the surface and then tip the pan and spoon off the excess fat – quite how much is excess is entirely up to you and I know people who totally ignore such instructions, arguing that fat has the most flavour of all. Put the roasting pan on a lowish heat, still with the flavourings from the pan or from inside the bird, and then stir and stir until you have dissolved most of the crusty brown bits: they might not disappear completely until you add liquid.

Sprinkle onto the fatty mixture about a tablespoonful of flour – a heaped one if it is a big pan and there are plenty of guests, a level or a scant one if it is a small bird you have roasted. Stir like mad until the flour is all incorporated and no lumps remain and then gently cook for a few minutes, which relieves the rawness of the flour. Turn up the heat and then add your gravy liquid, stirring or whisking all the while.

The liquid can be the cooking water from your vegetables, but I never have any of this because I always cook vegetables by microwave or by roasting. Instead, use wine, wine and water, or stock. Apple juice or cider are both excellent additions to chicken gravies, as they are to pork or lamb. Add much more liquid than you want and let it reduce to concentrate, remembering the gravy's flavour will be diluted by the meat or vegetables with which it is eaten. Only experience can teach you quite how concentrated a gravy should be, but it is definitely better to serve something too strong than it is to serve a watery and pallid gravy.

When all is satisfactory, strain the gravy and then return to the heat. Now is the time to tweak it, adding quince or redcurrant jelly and fresh mint leaves if it is for lamb, adding extra garlic, parsley and perhaps horseradish for beef, adding lemon or orange zest and fresh herbs if it is for chicken – this is, of course, tempering – see page 233–4.

Remember, the time you take to do this is giving your roast time to relax and tenderise.

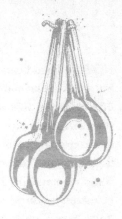

BAKING CAKES

Baking muffins and large or small cakes is quite another way to build up a repertoire of basics that you have tweaked into something of your own. In fact, this kind of baking is where most people begin, for little is so gratifying as the smell of a house when something is cooking in the oven – and if you choose carefully, you don't have to wait long before you can taste the results.

Spelt and Oat Bran Muffins

When muffin-cakes first hit the scene in the 60s and 70s they were touted as being healthy, and they were in a way – earnestly healthy and heavy with bran or other roughage. But now most are universally sweet, often sickeningly so. It's unlikely this trend will be reversed, but at home there are ways to make them *seem* better for us. Even if you are radiant with good health you will find these the most comforting muffins you have eaten for years, especially if you have added banana, or a mix of banana and blueberries.

You don't have to use spelt flour, which is pretty much the original flour we all used until modern machinery required different varieties, but it does seem to have a more comforting flavour and is much easier to digest by those with gluten-absorption issues. This recipe is quite as suitable for savoury as for sweet mixtures, so gives every opportunity for your originality to shine forth.

HOW TO DO IT:

Makes six jumbo muffins

225g/8oz spelt/plain flour

120g/4oz oat bran

2 generous teaspoons baking powder

2–3 tablespoons fruit sugar (or caster sugar)*

2 eggs, room temperature

600ml/20fl.oz milk, room temperature

1 tablespoon melted butter**

1 tablespoon canola oil**

300ml/½ -pint cup mixed dry ingredients – see Recommended Detours

* For savoury mixtures reduce or leave out the sugar.
**Two tablespoons melted butter only or two tablespoons of oil only can be used.

Mix together very well the flour, bran, baking powder and sugar. Whisk the eggs lightly and then whisk in the milk. Add the butter and/or oil to that liquid and blend thoroughly, then put to one side.

Stir the flavouring ingredients lightly into the dry mixture until they are evenly distributed and lightly floured.

Pour in all the liquid mixture and stir very quickly – if you over-mix the muffins will be heavy or channelled inside – a few lumps of the flour mixture here and there doesn't matter.

Use a cup or large soup ladle to measure an equal amount into each of six muffin tins or paper cups, trying not to add a second amount to any of the containers as this can prevent rising (no, I don't know why).

Bake for 30 to 35 minutes at about 190C/375F – slightly less in a fan oven.

Recommended Detours

Whatever you see offered in greasy commercial muffins will taste much better in this mixture: bigger chunks are tastier and look more interesting than little nuggets.

- Chunked bananas with toasted nuts
- Banana chunks, blueberries and cinnamon
- Goats' cheese cubes, sun-dried tomatoes and chopped black olives
- Blueberries, banana, ricotta clumps
- Raspberry and white or dark chocolate chunks
- Mixed summer berries, cinnamon, clumps of ricotta
- Pineapple chunks with roasted pecan nuts
- Morello cherry jam swirled through the mix
- Blue cheese chunks with fresh pineapple chunks
- Cheddar cheese cubes with swirls of Branston pickle
- Goats' cheese with toasted walnuts and halved grapes

The Ultimate Chocolate Cake/Dessert

As rich and as dark as any chocophile could possibly want, this is a cake guaranteed not to go wrong – it is supposed to be squidgy and can even be uncooked and runny in the middle. This moistness means it can safely be warmed to serve, and the possibilities to deviate onto personal Flavour Trails to make this your own recipe are many.

If you bake the mixture in two pans you get a lighter result; if you bake in just one it is heavier and more likely to be mousse-like in the middle. Of course, to serve it very soft in the middle you and your guests must be cool about eating egg that is not thoroughly cooked, but isn't perfect pleasure even greater when the *frisson* of danger is present?

HOW TO DO IT:

Makes eight or more portions

200g/7oz 70% cocoa solids chocolate

175g/6oz unsalted butter

175g/6oz caster sugar

5 large eggs, separated

75g/3oz ground almonds, hazelnuts or walnuts

50g/2oz plain flour

Your chosen flavouring – see below

First prepare a 20cm (8-inch) round cake tin or two 20cm (8-inch) sandwich tins by lightly buttering them and then dusting with cocoa, so you don't get the nasty white marks left by using the usual flour; do this even if you have nonstick baking pans.

Melt the butter, remove from the heat source and then stir in the chocolate, which will melt in the residual heat. Let it cool to ambient temperature. Then beat in the egg yolks only one by one, stir in the ground nuts and then the flour.

Now, choose and add your flavouring. A half-teaspoon or so of genuine vanilla extract is always right, but think also of Boyajian lime or orange oil, of orange-flower water or rose-water. A few tablespoons of Cognac, dark rum, Calvados, crème de menthe or any of the orange spirits or liqueurs all work well. Be courageous, for whatever you add will lose a little of itself in the oven heat and a bit more when the cake is served cold.

Whisk up the egg whites until firm but not dry, that is until they hold their shape in a slovenly, uncommitted sort of way but aren't so stiff they expect a salute. Take a large spoonful of the beaten whites and stir them evenly into the mixture, which lightens it somewhat. Fold in the remaining egg whites, using a light action like a figure of eight lying on its side. When it's pretty even ladle rather than pour the mixture into the cake pan or pans and bake in a 170C/340F oven until the sides begin to shrink from the tin. This will take about 25 minutes if you are using two cake pans and about 40 minutes in a single pan. The top will be crusty and the centre still very moist – cook on for a while if you'd rather it were less squishy. Only making this a couple of times in your oven will tell you what's right for you.

Let the cake rest for ten minutes before turning it out to cool, ideally on a wire rack. Serve in thinnish slices with raspberry purée, with a hot chocolate sauce or with whipped cream.

Recommended Detours

Each of the recommended nuts will give a different result so don't overlook the possibilities of pine nuts or pistachios, even of peanuts, to make a flavour entirely your own; but do microwave-roast the nuts before you grind or pound them.

For the most expectant of guests, make a vanilla or rose-water flavoured cake, use microwave-roasted almonds as your nuts and then line the baking tins with rose-geranium leaves, which give a sensual smoky-rose flavour to the cake; it's a very old British trick that more than deserves rekindling. Serve with the leaves still added or make the flavour more mysterious by removing them.

COOKING IN LIQUIDS
Boiling/Braising/Poaching/
Simmering/Stewing

Boiling

Real boiling is the fast bubble and brouhaha of a kettle when water is boiling. It is loud and the liquid is lumpy. Yet if you speak of a New England boiled dinner – corned/salt beef and vegetables cooked together – the last thing you would want is boiled ingredients. The meat would not tenderise enough before it disintegrated and the vegetables would be mush.

A New Englander might speak of a boiled dinner but would never eat one that had been.

Green vegetables should *never* be boiled, as any kind of hot liquid heat extracts most of the goodness from them. Yes, the microwave *is* the answer. Root vegetables, potatoes particularly, must start in cold water. As the water slowly warms, so do the vegetables, which then cook through evenly. It is particularly important to use the cold-water technique when cooking floury potatoes, or they will be half-dissolved before they are cooked.

No problems like that in a microwave.

Thai Street-chicken and Rice

A last-minute boil makes all the difference to khao na kai, perhaps the most famous dish of Thailand's ebullient street vendors. Just as they do, you'll change an ingredient or two every time you make it until you develop your own version. But you must have hot rice ready before you start to cook the chicken. Press two or three cups of rice into a small bowl, so you can turn this out to make traditional moulded mountains over which the chicken is poured.

HOW TO DO IT:

1½ teaspoons dark soy sauce

2 teaspoons light soy sauce

1 teaspoon sesame oil

1 tablespoon cornflour

1–2 tablespoons Chinese oyster sauce

220–250g/8–9oz boneless, skinless chicken breast, cubed

4 tablespoons vegetable oil

About 150ml/¼ pint chicken stock

½ teaspoon palm or white sugar

Ground white pepper and salt to taste

Serves one or two

To serve

Sliced fresh red chillies

Sliced cucumber

Fresh coriander leaves

Mix together the soy sauces, sesame oil, cornflour and a tablespoon of the oyster sauce. Marinate the chicken in this for at least an hour at room temperature, four hours in a refrigerator.

Before starting, ensure the rice is cooked and being kept hot, or reheat it in the microwave. Quickly fry the chicken pieces at a high heat in the hot oil until they are cooked through. Stir in enough of the stock to make a thickish sauce, bring back to the boil very quickly and then season to personal taste, perhaps using more of the oyster sauce. Add then the sugar, salt and white pepper. The taste is usually predominated by the soy and oyster sauces. Turn out the rice onto a plate. Boil up the chicken once more and then pour directly over the rice. Garnish as you like with any or all of the suggestions.

Braising

A braise means meat (sometimes vegetables), cooked over vegetables and *minimal liquid* in a heavy closed container, on a cooker top or in the oven. It is also called a pot roast, though it is more accurate to call it a pot bake. Novice cooks are amazed a braise works at all because it looks as though everything will dry out and burn before it is cooked. It won't.

The best choice for a braise is meat cut through a number of muscles, or slices of meat from a multi-muscled source on an animal. Connective tissue, tendons, and gristle join the different muscles and such pieces cannot be cooked a fast way, by baking or grilling for instance, as the muscles would pull different ways and the connective tissues etc, would still be tough. Such complicated, cheaper cuts need long, slow stewing *in a liquid*, or to be braised.

The temperature must be kept low and eventually the once-tough connective tissues will melt and combine with the liquid and juices from the meat, and the build-up of heat caramelises and browns the meat, adding even more flavour. Meat for braising can also be browned before cooking: if you do this with thickly sliced braising meat the rewards are great, because there is even more to flavour the cooking juices. The pressure cooker is an excellent way to braise and takes only a third of the conventional time. But because the trapped pressurised steam keeps the outside of the meat wet, it's always best to brown the meat before cooking.

It is probably best to braise good thick slices but to avoid braising really big pieces of meat (say over 1.5kg/3lb) as the outside might begin to deteriorate before the centre is tender. Also braisable are tougher chops and the sort of steaks usually thought to be suitable for barbecues but which are always gristly and chewy; braising is the solution. Hearts are suitable for braising, too.

A Dutch oven – a large, heavy saucepan with a tight-fitting lid – is particularly suited to braising meats. Traditionally coals were put onto the lid if it was being used on coals or an open fire: better and more controllable base heat from a hob means nothing like that is needed these days. Still, I always braise in an oven.

Braised Beef

If you look in modern cookery books and 'bibles' and such you'd think braising no longer exists. You are richly rewarded for rediscovering it. Braising is very simple, so simple The Cookery Year, published by the Reader's Digest in 1973 (and still well worth owning), says it like this:

Coat the meat with seasoned flour and brown it evenly in hot fat. Place the meat on a bed of diced, lightly fried root vegetables in a casserole or heavy-bottomed saucepan. Pour in enough water or stock and tomato purée to cover the vegetables: add herbs and seasoning. Cover tightly and cook in the centre of a preheated oven 325F/160C or on the stove until tender after 2–3 hours.

HOW TO DO IT:
The only amplification needed is that the vegetables should include some onion and it really is worth taking the trouble to fry them all until quite brown before being added to the

casserole or saucepan: I'd say a bed of a good 3–4cm (1–2 inches) thickness is ideal for 1–1.5kg/2–3lb of sliced meat about 2cm thick and which has plenty of connective tissue etc, Adding tomato purée to the water or stock is an age-old custom and certainly helps the taste and colour. It's hardly worth adding herbs because their virtue will be lost in such long cooking: but a bay leaf and other fresh herbs added 20 minutes before serving will make a tremendous difference.

What rather magically happens is that liquids from both the meat and the vegetables are expressed, making enough to stew the meat. But because it stands very much out of the liquid some of the meat will be further browned by the heat, adding great extra savour. But sometimes the liquid will evaporate rather more than you expect, in which case you should add more.

The enthusiastic cook without recipes should now be racing ahead with their own ideas. Of course you can use wine or wine and water instead of stock. Of course you can add a couple of good squirts of Worcestershire sauce, indeed I think you invariably should. Choose carrots, swede, onion and parsnip and you have something resolutely British, but use onion, celery, fennel and celeriac and you have something deliciously different. Whatever the version I usually throw in six to eight cloves of garlic still in their skins, and these make wonderful talking points as you squash the creamy mess out and puddle it into the juices. Note that if you first flour the meat, this will slightly thicken the cooking juices into something like a gravy. But you can braise without the flour, when the juices will be rather thin, which I like very much.

I made the best and fastest version ever with no vegetables at all; instead I turned out a whole jar of a very good fruit chutney (it already has the onion and fruit/vegetables and spices, you see?), put the meat on top of that and then added red wine so it lapped well up the bottom layer of meat. Superb. Go on then – your turn now. Whatever you do, particularly smooth and creamy mashed potatoes are an absolute.

Poaching

This means to cook food gently in a liquid just covering it. The pan is generally left uncovered, although it might be covered if you are oven-poaching.

As usual in cooking nothing is clear cut. You poach a nice piece of smoked fish in milk or poach an egg or two in water and probably throw away the cooking liquid. Yet poach a peach in wine or poach a banana in coconut milk and the cooking liquid will be served.

Poaching liquid should never boil, but silently quiver as small bubbles gently burst onto the surface: it is a simmer and sometimes a bigger bubble will be seen in just one place. Poaching is commonly specified for delicate foods and the gentling of the heat is what keeps the food's special virtues intact.

You can poach in an oven, a very gentle way of cooking. It's often used for whole fish too big to fit pans sitting on the hob. Whatever you are poaching it is good to remember that your poaching liquid will inevitably extract flavour from the food. By cleverly flavouring the poaching liquid to be tastier than the fish, for instance, and/or serving some of it too, you balance that battle, yet there is still a gorgeously fishy stock looking for something wonderful to do. There was recently a fashion for oven-poaching fish in olive oil, but the reason is impenetrable: what do you then do with two or three litres of lukewarm, fishy, olive oil?

Poached Fish

There's a problem with cooking fish in water, no matter how slowly you do it; much of the flavour will leach out into the water. The answer is to steam the fish in a microwave instead or to cook portions between two plates over boiling water. If you insist on poaching, the secret is first to make a liquid that is measurably tastier than the fish – so it gives back as much if not more than it takes. This doubly repays you if you then use some of this delicious leftover fish stock (for that is what it is) in a sauce, or cool it to then freeze in cubes and use to make a seafood risotto or kedgeree or fish pie.

HOW TO DO IT:
Fill a suitable wide pan or frying pan with enough water, stock or white wine, or some mixture of any of them, so it will eventually cover the fish. To this add sliced onion, some carrot, some lemon peel, celery, lots of parsley stalk, a bay leaf or two and a dozen or so black peppercorns. Bring this to the boil very slowly indeed, to extract maximum flavour. If you like you can hoick out the flavourings now. Either way, lower in the fish and cook at a gentle simmer for about 10 minutes per 2.5cm (1 inch) depth of fish, but you really have to judge by appearances; it's done when it flakes easily. As long as the water is not boiling the fish ragged, you have quite a lot of leeway.

Whole fish like salmon are most often oven-poached, and to the other flavourings you should also add cucumber peel. In this case everything goes into the oven pan at the same time and goes into the oven at 180C/350F Keep your eyes on it and as soon as the liquid comes anywhere near the boil turn over the fish, turn off the heat, wrap the pan in foil and leave the fish until it's quite cold. It will be cooked through. (But see Steaming on pages 222–4 and Microwaving on pages 225–9, too.)

Simmering

This very important technique of cooking in a liquid is the key to success in many areas of cookery. The liquid must be hot enough to cook but gentle enough not to shred as it does.

Simmering is the right method to use for casseroles, stews, soups, beans and so on. When water is simmering properly, the French call it *'l'eau qui sourit'* – water that smiles. You should see small bubbles rising constantly and occasionally a bigger one, usually always in the same place. Even that bubble should be avoided if you are simmering in a thick liquid, because it might be a hot spot eventually burning the base. Simmering is pretty much the technique used for poaching, but uses more liquid.

Thus there are two sorts of simmering: if you have a thick liquid you must use a very low simmer and should avoid seeing a big bubble altogether, but if you are simmering thin water or wine or stock you can increase the heat a little and allow the big bubble and one or two others to break from time to time. Even so, for the sake of a half-hour, and in pursuit of the best possible texture and flavour, the lower simmer is always the best choice.

The Oriental's Green Chicken (or Prawn) Curry

This has always been one of the most popular dishes in the restaurants of the famed Oriental Hotel in Bangkok, my luxurious base when I was shooting my BBC-TV series Glynn Christian Tastes Royal Thailand. I was very flattered when they offered the recipe outline to me.

HOW TO DO IT:

8 tablespoons thick coconut cream

3 tablespoons green curry paste

450ml/16fl.oz coconut milk

2 Kaffir lime leaves, torn roughly

1 tablespoon nam pla (fish sauce)

1 teaspoon palm sugar

175g/6oz Thai aubergine in 2.5cm (1-inch) pieces

500g/1lb raw prawns, shelled and de-veined

12 large fresh Thai basil leaves

2 fresh red chillies, cut into thin strips

Serves four to six

Stir the coconut cream over a medium heat until it develops an oily sheen. Take out two tablespoons and reserve. Add the green curry paste and then stir for at least two minutes, when all its aromas will have developed. Stir in the coconut milk, lime leaves, nam pla and palm sugar and, once the mixture is boiling, stir in the aubergines. Simmer until the aubergine is soft but not mushy and then add the prawns and cook until they are just done. Stir in the basil and chillies, swirl on the reserved coconut cream and serve at once.

Recommended Detours
- Use cooked prawns, and add them at the very last minute, just to heat through.
- Take out the lime leaves and sprinkle the finished curry with fresh ones, this time cut as thinly as possible, so they can actually be eaten.
- Although usually served with a duck curry, the addition of six or more fresh or canned lychees is always a winner.
- Instead of the prawns, add strips of raw chicken breast and cook only for the few minutes these take to be done.

Finally, an important reminder: curries never taste fiery to those who have eaten them all their lives – if you and your friends are beginners, reduce the amount of paste to only a third or quarter of what is suggested and leave out the final chilli.

The Ultimate Tomato Sauce

There's nothing like a well-spiced but not too hot tomato-based sauce to liven up hot and cold meats – or to make your reputation as someone with a drop-dead store cupboard. The slow, gentle cooking keeps the virtue of the spices; boil it too fast and it won't taste as good. It will darken as it cooks, but shouldn't caramelise or burn. You'll soon learn!

Great with everything from barbecues or bold sausages to the delicacy of the tiniest spring lamb chops, this chutney-style sauce differs from the 'real thing' because it can be enjoyed as soon as it is made. Kept warm on the side of a barbecue it's even more fragrant and yummy, and because there's no onion there's no chance of upsetting a picky stomach. Once cool, the sauce should be kept refrigerated, where it will improve for up to six weeks.

Julie Biuso, food writer, editor and saucy *bon viveur* supreme of New Zealand, shared this recipe with me when her book *Sizzle – Sensational Barbecue Food* (New Holland) won her a Special Jury Award at the 2007 Gourmand World Cook Book Awards.

HOW TO DO IT:

Makes 325ml

1 teaspoon cumin seeds

1 teaspoon coriander seeds

1 teaspoon fennel seeds

2.5–5cm (1–2 inches) fresh ginger, peeled and sliced

3 cloves garlic, chopped

200g/7oz granulated sugar

250ml/8 fl.oz white-wine vinegar

1 teaspoon chilli powder

1 teaspoon garam masala

600g/20oz approx. canned Italian tomatoes, mashed

50g/2oz golden raisins

Salt to taste

Grind or pound together the cumin, coriander and fennel seeds with a pestle and mortar. Note all the spice amounts are only a guide, but the apparently small amounts add up to rather a lot of spices. Add the ginger and garlic and work into a paste. This can be done in a food processor. Set aside.

Put the sugar and vinegar into a saucepan over a gentle heat until the sugar is dissolved. Add all the other ingredients, including the juice of the tomatoes. Stir well and then bring to the boil. Turn the heat to low and cook gently for about 1? hours, stirring often, until the mixture is a shiny, thick pulp. You need to be especially vigilant during the last 15 minutes, stirring often with a long-handled wooden spoon. The objective is to have no excess liquid, just the shiny mass.

Ladle into a hot sterilised jar (pour in boiling water, leave a few minutes, and then drain and dry thoroughly) then run a clean knife through the sauce to knock out any air bubbles. Cover with a damp cellophane jam cover or a non-metallic lid and refrigerate when cool.

Recommended Detours

- Use chopped, canned tomatoes for an even smoother finish.
- Substitute stone fruit for up to half the tomato. Apples or red-fleshed plums make the best mixtures, but even exotic pineapple, tamarillo or feijoa can be used – chop them quite finely and add with the reduced amount of tomatoes.
- Roast the whole cumin or coriander seeds before you crush them.
- Use ordinary raisins, ideally seedless.
- Use cider vinegar rather than white-wine vinegar.
- Temper with more spice once this is cooked but still hot.

Stewing

Yes, this is just another word for simmering but it's such a delicious word, sadly underused these days, I couldn't resist. Let's call a stew a stew.

This is a long, slow way of cooking meats in a well-flavoured liquid until tender. As with poaching you ideally only simmer to make a stew. You can stew over heat or in an oven. There should barely be any movement of the liquid, yet if you do increase it the heat should bubble up quickly. If you don't have time to cook a stew slowly, put it into the pressure cooker or send out for takeaways.

It is usual to use cheaper cuts of meat with connective tissue, tendons, gristle and other contents. While making meat tough and inedible when raw or quickly cooked, these same bits and pieces slowly melt during stewing to give a unique special savour and silken texture. The French believe the best stews are made from a mixture of cheaper cuts, say chuck, brisket and shin, cooked together, and this would give the highest proportion of connective tissue. Only where flesh has a specially different flavour or texture, such as rabbit, oxtail or tripe, will it be cooked by itself.

Stewing expensive single muscles, like rump steak, is never rewarded by extra flavour and generally turns out to be tougher – that's because all lean, tender, expensive cuts of red meat are taken from a single muscle, which will have little or none of the important connective tissues. When you see rump steak specified for stewing, turn the page.

Asian curries or such long-cooked bean dishes as a cassoulet are other versions of a stew, and casseroles are all stews, too. The French daube is more of braise, because relatively little liquid, usually wine, is added.

Red meat for stews may be browned before stewing, and this will give a richer, deeper colour and flavour, but many do not think it essential. If the meat has been tossed in seasoned flour before browning, the sauce of the final result will be thickened, in proportion to the amount of flour used. The liquid added may be a stock, wine, water or some mixture of these, but if there are plenty of tasty root vegetables and herbs in the stew, water will do nicely enough and make a rich stock during the cooking.

Beer can also be used but this means you must be particularly certain to caramelise the onions so there is natural sweetness present; if such a stew is too bitter, the answer is to add a good vinegar (I'd use sherry vinegar) teaspoon by teaspoon until the bitterness has been ameliorated.

For maximum flavour impact it's very satisfactory to refresh or temper your base flavourings before serving. If you temper a stew by stirring in a glass of wine or stock and fresh herbs and spices no more than five minutes before serving, the difference is amazing. A simple mixture of parsley and black pepper stirred into a stew just before serving does very well.

All stews taste best when left to cool overnight – when the flavours exchange and blend in a quite magical way. And finally, a hard-learned serving tip: it's not always an idea to be Earth Father/Mother and serve directly from the casserole at the table.

Sometimes the meat in such dishes overcooks and shreds, at other times candle or other dull light might mean you are unable to distinguish quite what you're serving, so one guest gets pig's ear and trotter and nothing else. Far better to carefully dish out the best bits into a serving bowl and take that to the table – or to serve it up in the kitchen, away from critical eyes.

All round the world, hearty stews are based on economical beans of all colours and shapes. These are usually purchased dry and then rehydrated overnight; this can be speeded up if you put the beans into cold water, bring them up to the boil extremely slowly and then let the beans boil gently until hydrated – they won't be tender yet but will be close to their hydrated size and you will have saved hours. The soaking water or rehydrating water must then be thrown away because it now contains a high proportion of the ingredients causing intestinal wind. So, rinse the beans and then cook them on in fresh water.

Beans then cook with little or no extra flavouring at this stage; if you add salt or bacon you toughen the beans and no amount of stewing will ever tenderise them. Only after cooking and again being rinsed and drained should beans meet such as bacon and tomato, onion and garlic, molasses, olive oil or a hundred and one other possibilities. Stew everything together over a very low heat or on the edge of a fire or in a slow oven. Your patience and good technique will be richly rewarded. But you now understand why I always keep plenty of ready-cooked canned beans in my store cupboard.

If you would like a sauce with your beans, mash enough of the beans when cooked – anything up to a third – return them to the pot and cook on until nicely thickened.

Casseroles, like daubes, *estoufades* and cassoulets, as well as many other dishes, are all just stews even when bean rather than meat based. Their differing names are often found to be based on the locally made vessel in which they are traditionally cooked.

YOU CAN'T SEAL MEAT . . .

If meat really were sealed 'so all its lovely flavours stay there', how would the meat flavour the liquid in which it stews? How could the wine and herbs and onion and garlic and bacon and everything else delicious penetrate and flavour the meat? 'Sealing' meat is perhaps the best example – or worst – of a culinary misconception passed on as gospel truth for centuries, from generation to generation, but which is patently nonsense. When cubes of meat to be stewed are first cooked in fat or oil the outside goes brown, and this is almost universally called 'sealing'; but you are *searing* the meat, not sealing it. You can stew meat without first browning it, but frying meat before it stews makes it look nicer and the final dish tastes richer and is a better colour; these are the profits browning gives. If the meat really were sealed it would end up tasting only of meat, no matter how many delicious things you had added to the pot. Speak of searing the meat by all means, but don't mention sealing. There has never been such a thing.

Beef Stews

The basic British beef stew simmers in water or in stock and is always thickened to a greater or lesser degree. Some include carrots and other root vegetables but I think this encourages cooks not to pay attention – there is little worth tasting in vegetables after they have stewed for several hours, as their flavour has all been gifted to the liquor in the pot. But if you like stews with vegetables in them, put them in for the last 25 minutes or so (remembering the liquid in which they will cook is barely simmering) and cut them in big pieces, so they really can both give flavour and still retain plenty of their own. If you want something more sophisticated, cut the vegetables into neat matchsticks and rounds and barrels and add them for only 15 minutes or so.

HOW TO DO IT:

Makes four to six servings

1.5 kg/3lb stewing beef, preferably a mix of cuts,
    cut into 5cm (2-inch) pieces

A few tablespoons flour, salt and pepper

2 tablespoons oil or beef dripping

125g/4oz smoked bacon in rough pieces

250g/8oz onion, chopped

1 tablespoon flour

1 beef stock cube dissolved in 750ml pints water

  or

750ml/1 ¼ pints beef, vegetable or brown chicken stock

Bouquet garni of fresh herbs

1 tablespoon Worcestershire sauce

Heat the oil or dripping in a large frying pan and cook the bacon until it is well browned but not crisped, then put this into the bottom of a large flameproof or ovenproof casserole, keeping as much of the oil or fat in the frying pan as you can. Meanwhile, season the flour with the salt and pepper and quickly toss the meat in this; you want only the thinnest coating. Fry the beef in batches until nicely browned and add it to the bacon in the casserole. Turn the heat down under the frying pan and then fry the onion until really soft and sweet tasting, which might take twenty or more minutes. Turn up the heat to give it some colour and then stir in the flour and cook for two minutes. Pour in the stock, stirring continuously until evenly thickened; it won't be very thick. Pour this on to the meat and bacon, and then add what herbs you have – a bay leaf or two, some thyme and parsley tied with cotton long enough to tie one end to the saucepan handle. If you are feeling a bit Continental, add some garlic cloves, too. Bring the mixture slowly to the boil and the moment it bubbles cover and cook for at least two hours over a very low heat or in a 150C/300F oven. It's best made the day before and reheated gently.

Recommended Detours

Tempering this with black pepper shortly before serving gives excellent extra savouriness.

- Beef with wine: Make as above but use the equivalent of a bottle of wine or a mixture of wine and water. The wine should be a fresh, young and vibrant red rather than aged and mellow, because the expensive nuances will be lost. If you use a bright young Burgundy or other Pinot Noir you will have made boeuf bourguignon, traditionally finished with button mushrooms and small onions – but you don't have to do so.

- Beef with beer: For this you need more onions, so slowly cook and then brown 750g onions in 50g/2oz butter, stir in two tablespoons flour, cook a few minutes and then pour in 500ml/18fl.oz beer or stout (but not lager) while you whisk furiously. The meat is floured and browned the same way in butter or oil, and then added to the sauce with whatever herbs you have plus two tablespoons red wine or sherry vinegar. At the end of cooking you might like to add up to two tablespoons of brown sugar – but if you have properly sweetened your onion you will need none or very little.

Water Bath

The *bain-marie* is special friend of the refined chef of delicate tastes. By standing a container in a baking pan of hot water inside an oven, heat transferred directly from the water cooks the food in the container, and as water cannot get as hot as an oven, all is kept gentle. The outside of a paté does not get overcooked before the middle is cooked; it avoids egg custards becoming scrambled eggs. The most refined chefs actually put some folded newspaper or a folded tea cloth into the baking pan before adding the water, so the dish in which it is to be cooked gets no direct heat.

The water itself should come up to a finger's width of the top of ramekins or other small containers. Halfway up seems enough if you are cooking paté. Almost everything you cook in a *bain-marie* can also be cooked in low direct heat in the oven, but the results will never be as even and reliable as when cooked in a water bath.

Bain-marie is also the term used in catering and restaurants for the containers of hot water over which food is kept hot long enough to become indistinguishable and nutrition free.

COOKING IN FAT OR OIL
Deep-frying/Sauteeing/
Shallow-frying/Stir-frying

Deep-frying

Not the demon so many think. The modern digitally controlled deep-fryer is a marvel. If you take the trouble to ensure your oil or fat is at the correct temperature to deep-fry the food you have selected, this cookery method can be remarkably low-fat. For centuries it was often the only way of frying, as fat could be melted in a container suspended over fire. But, then and now, it's not for me.

It seems impossible to deep-fry food without always tasting the oil in which it was fried. That's great if you can afford to use olive oil – and you *will* taste it, because olive oil can't be heated high enough to seal food before it begins to seep in during the cooking. A peanut or groundnut oil can be taken up to a very high temperature before it starts to smoke and this very high heat means it will very quickly seal the outside of food. Yet you still taste the oil, or at least feel its sliminess on your palate.

Unlike the supposed sealing of meat in a hot pan, successful deep-frying in hot oil or fat at the right temperature *will* seal food.

The fatty-food problem comes only if the oil or fat is too cool (often because the fryer is overloaded), and so it's absorbed into the food or the batter. If you perfectly deep-fry a piece of fish in batter, and then take away the batter, you will find the fish steaming in its fat-free juices, and nothing is healthier or tastier than that. A pity that batter can sometimes taste so good.

Deep-frying is popular in many parts of the world. The Japanese excel at tempura, a light foamy batter with beaten egg white, wreathing in clouds rather than evenly wrapping seafood or vegetables. Yet no matter how fastidious the cook you always taste the oil, and often this is all you taste; this is because there is not enough of the batter for the hot oil to cook and make a seal – the oil penetrates the vegetable or prawn or whatever almost immediately. Just because it looks good doesn't mean it will taste good.

For centuries Italians have stuffed courgette flowers, put them into a light batter and then deep-fried them, and for centuries they have raved about them, just as food writers do now. Sure, they look great, but have you ever actually tasted the flower rather than the batter? I thought not.

Deep-frying courgette flowers is a prime example of why you should never accept the value of anything traditional just because it is what was done in the past. The time and effort taken to deep-fry courgette flowers is not repaid in the mouth. Traditions, like looks, are no guarantee of good flavour.

Once you start deep-frying calamari or prawns you lose me again, completely, just as completely as the flavours of those denizens are lost. Except once, on a beach in Corfu, I ate calamari that had been bullying one another with underwater ink-ball fights less than an hour before, which were in a mere spatter of batter and cooked in very good olive oil. They were superbly, astonishingly sweet, and because the residue of olive oil had its own remarkable flavour it contributed to the experience, rather than battering the food into meek submission.

Next time you think about deep-frying take some moments

to really assess the flavour of the outcome. Why should you use an outdated technique, still the easy retreat of the culinary illiterate even in the finest restaurants, when you have so many other options that will give lighter, cleaner and more gratifying results in your mouth? Deep-frying was resorted to in the past because most kitchens had no baking oven.

We no longer have that excuse.

Sautéeing

It is pretentious to say sautéing when you mean frying: to sauté, you fry and toss at the same time. Constant movement is what typifies sautéing. The word comes from the French *sauter* to jump. A true sauté pan is easily spotted. It is a cross between a frying pan and a saucepan, with a broad base like a frying pan with higher sides but that are still lower than those of saucepans.

Shallow-frying

Even today there are households where the frying pan is the default cooking equipment. Usually a signal of bad, repetitive diet, it is normally used with a finger-joint-deep thickness of fat or oil, which is often used again and again. For teenagers – particularly those who find themselves independent, whether they've chosen to be or not – the frying pan quickly gratifies their raging hungers and equates with their stubborn disinterest in diet or cooking. Unfortunately such dependence can continue when they too are parents.

There is nothing intrinsically wrong with shallow-frying; it's just that it is too easily the fast track to eating too much fat. The greatest answer to this is the nonstick pan, which needs little or no added grease to perform quickly and deliciously. When I first introduced one on *Breakfast Time* in the early 80s, professional chefs sniggered. Yet within a year, these pans were the professional chef's darling and the doorway to much that was wrong with *nouvelle cuisine*; today you'd be hard-pressed to find a top-line chef who could cook without them.

So, shallow-frying these days should mean frying with only enough lard, dripping, butter or oil to help the formation of a tastier, browner crust, and not to shield the food from the pan to stop it sticking. Many foods previously fried in something oleaginous need none at all in a modern nonstick frying pan. But a fried egg without olive oil, bacon fat or butter isn't quite the same thing – so don't be dogmatic.

The Tortilla

There is nothing, nothing, more delicious than this carefully fried Spanish combination of just three ingredients: good olive oil, good potatoes and good eggs. The British inclination is to add onion, huge amounts of it, but then it doesn't taste like the tortilla you get 99 times out of 100 in Spain. Neither do these three regal ingredients need the company of whatever else is left over in your household.

Old recipes for tortilla demand you exchange the initial oil for fresh once you've cooked the potato and before you add the eggs, but those were the days when there was so little extra-virgin oil, and so you generally cooked with virgin olive oil (or even lower-quality) and used extra-virgin only for the last touches or as a dressing. These days there is so much EVO about at a good price you can afford to cook with it, even though you still lose a lot of the finesse for which you were charged.

A tortilla this size can feed only one person in dire need of comforting on a wet and windy winter night, but with salad and other entertainments it stretches to two. For more people it needs a bigger pan, and this is the easiest recipe in the world to multiply. But be patient or you will burn the base before the top is set.

FLAVOUR TRAIL

HOW TO DO IT:
Start with a nonstick pan about 20cm (8 inches) diameter. Into that pour three or four tablespoons of good olive oil to make a shallow frying depth. Then load the pan with starchy or waxy

potatoes you have peeled and cut into chunks 2–3cm (1 inch) square, probably about 750g before peeling. Salt them quite well and then, using low to medium heat only, cook the potatoes with a lid covering the pan – this is important as the retained moisture slows down any potential browning and ideally the potatoes shouldn't brown. With patience and an understanding of how good the result will taste you soon learn the best temperature for this on your hob. Occasionally, move and turn the potatoes in the oil and, as you do, break the bigger pieces up so the effect is less regimented. Once the potatoes are cooked, leave off the lid for a while so any excess water can steam off. Beat up some eggs, enough to cover the potatoes – four to six usually, depending on their size – and then add them to the pan.

Cover the pan again and cook on ever-gentler heat, from time to time breaking in to the egg so it runs down to the pan's base and sets, rather as you would for an ordinary omelette. When the egg is almost cooked through, remove the lid altogether and continue to cook until you can shimmy the omelette on the nonstick surface. It doesn't matter if there is a little unset egg here and there on the top because this will set in the retained warmth after the tortilla has been turned out.

Now, normally you are instructed to brown the top of the tortilla, by messily turning it onto a plate and then adding more olive oil to the pan and then putting the thing back into it and then . . . but do you really need to? The egg is cooked and the top will become the bottom, so who cares?

Turn the tortilla out onto a large plate, where it will sit domed and golden and keeping its creamy bottom to itself, as should we all. Let it cool to a homely warmth before eating. It is even better cold the next day, and stuffed into decent bread makes a sandwich to solve the worst domestics.

Recommended Detours

Of course, you can add other things, as long as it is not onion, well, not much anyway.

- The best is rather thickly sliced smoked salmon, in turn cut into fingers. Put this onto the cooking mixture when the top of the egg is almost set and mess it up to cover most of the salmon. A few added green peas or bright, podded broad beans make this seem you have made an effort.
- Excellent chorizo keeps up the Spanish theme, although I prefer it served separately.
- Almost any sort of cheese can be added, starting with Spain's sheep's milk Manchego, of course. Chunk it in rather than grating.
- If you are entertaining someone youthful and golden, or simply fancy giving yourself a good time, soak a good couple of pinches of saffron stigma in a little boiling water for twenty minutes and add the fluid and the saffron to the beaten eggs. Served with bountiful amounts of prawns and other seafood, this redefines pleasure.
- And then there is chilli. A temperate amount of fresh chilli makes a good addition, particularly if you are sharing a tortilla outdoors. Use no more than two medium hot chillies (see chart on page 76), relieve them of both seeds and inner ribs, chop very finely and add with the eggs. Or swirl some sweet chilli sauce into the eggs when beating them.

Stir-frying

Is this really the way China and Southeast Asia cook? Not the way we stir-fry in the West.

If you put a circle of a suitable sheet metal over an even heat, say flames, it would bend itself pretty much into a wok shape: it is the optimal shape for even heat distribution over the metal. So why was this thought the best way to cook over the small flames of domestic gas cookers in Watford?

Traditional Chinese wok cooking is done over an open fire around which a solid frame of bricks or earth is built. On top is a hole and into this a wok slips nicely, with only a small part of the rim remaining exposed. Metal of the right shape is now immersed evenly in long, licking flames. The wok is the right shape not to warp, and everything conspires to make its entire surface a high temperature.

I reckon you can't properly stir-fry for more than two in a wok in a Western kitchen, because the wok can't possibly collect and distribute enough heat for real stir-frying; the food merely stews in its own juices. It can be delicious but it is not real stir-frying. Unless you use the microwave-wok method outlined below, you are simply cooking another rather wet fry-up in a funny-shaped frying pan. Perhaps this is why more and more woks sold in the West have a flat bottom . . . like frying pans?

There are two important techniques in wok cooking.

First, the wok must be brought up to maximum temperature with no oil in it: if you heat a wok with oil in it you are more likely to get sticking.

Second, when adding oil or any other liquid flavouring, you should pour it in a circle around the wok's upper sides, well above any food: by the time it has run down it has been heated. If you pour the oil or flavourings into just one place they will cool either the wok or the food, or both, and you will be stewing rather than stir-frying.

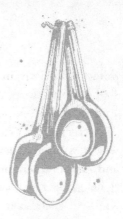

MICROWAVING THE WOK

The most extraordinary use of a microwave is to help kitchens achieve something like genuine wok cooking; it's a technique that seems to have originated among Southeast Asians in London because the hobs of Western gas cookers create nothing like the heat of the air-forced hobs built specifically for woks in Asia. Food for more than two is more likely to stew in liquid – liquid that the high heat of a proper wok would evaporate.

For the flavour of wok-burn, that slight scorch signalling authenticity, you should microwave everything first. Once it is *almost* cooked – heated all through by the microwave – immediately tip your 'stir-fry' into a fiercely hot wok, which has been preheating for some time at maximum temperature. Stir, shake and tilt. In a few minutes the food will have absorbed the excess heat of the wok and no matter how much more you heat it, it will not get that hot again.

The fierce heat of the wok on the piping-hot microwaved food should have given it the special savour you are seeking. This is the only way to get something like real wok-cooked food and taste if you don't have forced-air gas flames. The bigger burners now available on some cookers make woks hotter than before, and mean you can cook dishes that are not too bulky for up to four.

For all the fuss about stir-fry and health, most people are still just frying. More often they are stewing without a lid and could be doing this in the old frying pan from the back of the cupboard. Cue microwaves to the rescue. Again.

The Microwave Vegetable Stir-fry

When you microwave frozen or fresh vegetables without added water, they steam in their own liquids. Anything that evaporates is just water, leaving behind all the nutrients that are not heat-sensitive, and this concentrates both the flavour and the goodness. Many people find they do not need to add salt to microwaved vegetables.

Don't bother with the silly nonsense of using clingfilm to cover vegetables in the microwave. Instead cover a shallow bowl or dish of vegetables with a plate, and when the vegetables are cooked you'll also have a warm plate.

Dense root vegetables like potatoes or carrots need a little extra water when you cook a big amount, or the outsides of the vegetables can begin to dry. Try to use any water left over in the food you are serving. When you microwave potatoes to crush or to mash, they will have already lost excess moisture while cooking and so can be mashed or crushed straight away, and what excess water there is can be incorporated with the milk and butter.

Doing a mixed-vegetable stir-fry in a wok has never been high on my list of things to master. The vegetables don't seem to cook evenly, and anyway, as mentioned above, woks are meant to cook over the far hotter forced-air gas flame. Indeed, you might as well use a frying pan. (And then you are frying rather than doing a real stir-fry.)

There is only one rule to make a microwave mixed-veg stir-fry successful and that is exactly the same as cooking successfully in the wok:

Vegetables should be cut so their density and bulk are all equal.

A very wet vegetable, like celery, can be cut into much bigger pieces than a dense carrot. The small piece of carrot will then cook in about the same time as the bigger piece of wet celery. Once you have that right you'll do the microwave stir-fry with barely a thought. Actually, the vegetables have been steamed, but they look stir-fried.

Micro-braised Mediterranean Vegetable Medley

Provided each vegetable is prepared to about the same size and density you can use almost any that you like, but go for some of the more exotic ones for the best effect, and the best effect definitely comes from cutting them into big, bold chunks.

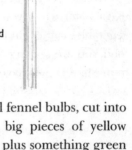

HOW TO DO IT:

1kg/2lb mixed Mediterranean vegetables – see method

Extra-virgin or virgin olive oil

Sliced garlic

50g–100g/2–4oz Parmesan/Grana Padano cheese, cubed

25g/1oz or more flat-leaf parsley, roughly chopped

Serves four to six

The vegetables I most enjoy using are small fennel bulbs, cut into quarters, chunks of butternut pumpkin, big pieces of yellow capsicum, quartered fresh baby artichokes, plus something green like shelled and podded broad beans, which go in towards the end of the cooking. Mix all the vegetables except the green one with plenty of olive oil and as much sliced garlic as you dare.

Arrange evenly in a flat-bottomed microwave-safe dish, cover with a plate and microwave on High for fifteen minutes, perhaps stirring once. Add the green vegetable, cook for another two or three minutes, ensuring you keep the earthy greenness of their flavour; it won't matter if they are a bit raw if they are really fresh. Tip in the Parmesan or Grana Padano cubes and the flat-leaf parsley, toss and serve. Some grated lemon zest over the top, also *very* Provencal, and more extra-virgin olive oil makes this a wonderful main course. It's excellent cold, too.

TEA-SMOKING IN A WOK

Tea-smoking – smoking over smouldering tea leaves in a wok – is especially associated with the southeast of China. It is used there mainly as an intermediary process, such as to flavour a poached duck before it is then roasted. Traditionally, scented wood shavings were also included, particularly shavings of camphor wood.

The tea and grain used as the basic smoking mixture need not be special, as none of their intrinsic flavour will be carried with the smoke. Equally, most herbs and many spices will make no contribution other than more smoke if added to the smoking mixture, but any with a fragrant oil component, like fresh rosemary, might add extra aroma, just as chips of fragrant hickory wood can be added. Everything else you might see added is mere swank and will make no discernible difference to the smoking process or the flavour of its outcome. It's as bad as expecting ingredients put into steaming water to flavour food sitting above it.

Smoking leaves an inherent bitterness and thus it is best not to smoke food too heavily as this will ambush the food's tastes and flavours. It will also require so much acidity as a taste balancer the result will be unpalatable to anyone with a palate.

Smoking over tea leaves in a wok can be used two ways: briefly, to add smoke flavour and colour to cooked food, or longer, to hot-smoke, that is to cook and smoke at the same time.

Basic Smoking Mixture

HOW TO DO IT:

4oz/125g rice, barley or wheat grains

2–3oz/60g–100g black tea leaves

Before starting, line both the base and the lid of a wok with aluminium foil, with the shiny side up. For best results, use a wok in a wok stand over gas: on electricity a flat-bottomed wok is required or there will not be a high enough heat.

Mix the grains and the tea leaves evenly, using the larger amount of leaves when smoking bigger amounts of food or wanting a stronger smple flavour. The grain plays its part by keeping the tea leaves separated, aerated and evenly spread.

As ever, you will need to experiment to find what's just right for you, by varying the amount of tea, and by varying the degree of heat you apply and for how long.

Note: many recipes, including earlier ones of mine, include sugar and/or alcohol, but these are unnecessary – the burned sugar makes a darker smoke but it is particularly bitter.

Smoking for Flavour

This can be used to add more or less flavour to all kinds of cooked food: but those with a fat content are the most successful. Hard-boiled and shelled eggs, poached sausages, poached salmon, and grilled, steamed or microwaved poultry, even whole birds, are all suited.

Put the smoking mixture in the base of a foil-lined wok and over this put a round or square cake rack. *In extremis* you could follow Jamie Oliver's suggestion and scrunch up some chicken wire. Arrange the food evenly on the rack, covering no more than two-thirds of the area. Put on the foil-lined lid. Then lightly twist two or three damp tea towels and use these to make a secure seal – although the smoke tastes good it is particularly invasive and if it escapes is hell to get rid of from the house.

Put the wok onto high heat for five minutes and then reduce to low for another ten minutes. Turn off the heat and leave the wok covered for five more minutes, which allows the smoke to subside.

For a stronger smoke flavour, or when smoking food that is already highly flavoured, only reduce the heat to medium and keep it there for ten minutes: allow a full five minutes, perhaps more, for the smoke to subside.

Hot Smoking – to Cook and Smoke at the Same Time

This technique differs from the previous one by (a) allowing more time and (b) requiring you to be aware of how much moisture might drip from the food. You will cook and smoke such oily fish as mackerel and salmon superbly. But the extra heat will mean moisture drips from the food and so no more than half the entire surface of the wire rack should be covered by the fish or the smoking will be too inhibited.

Turn the heat to medium only and keep at a steady heat for ten minutes and then to low for another five minutes. Turn off the heat and then wait ten minutes before opening the wok.

A layer of fresh rosemary over the smoking mixture will give a slight extra flavour – but don't use dried rosemary as this will burn too quickly and leave no noticeable added flavour. Hickory chips can also be used. But frankly, if you want more than simply smoke flavour you are better to marinate the fish, sausage or whatever before smoking. A Chinese-style marinade of soy sauce, hoisin sauce, five-spice powder, grated orange zest and grated fresh ginger works specially well on chicken to be hot wok-smoked and then eaten cold outdoors.

If the wok is kept sealed the food within will remain hot and moist for up to an hour.

In the following recipe, I created a special way of handling the fillets, which helps keep in their moisture.

Tea-smoked Fillets of Trout

HOW TO DO IT:

6 x 6oz/175g trout fillets

2–3 teaspoons horseradish sauce

2–3 teaspoons roughly chopped, flat-leaf parsley

1 generous smoking mixture

3 tablespoons soured cream

Freshly grated lime zest

First remove as many bones as you can from the fillets. Then slide a knife between the skin and the flesh at the tail end of a fillet and, by slowly working the knife back and forth while keeping tension on the skin, detach the skin from the flesh until about 5cm (2 inches) from the wider shoulder end of the fillet. Leave the skin attached.

Spread the horseradish and parsley evenly onto all the prepared trout fillets. Roll firmly from the tail end, and then wrap the free skin around the fish: this is what keeps maximum moisture in each fillet and also prevents over-smoking.

Arrange the prepared fish evenly on the rack, put on the foil-lined lid and seal with twisted, damp tea towels.

To serve, unroll each fillet to expose the cooked flesh, which will be golden brown at both exposed ends. Then fold back the skin to show the beautiful smoked effect. Add a spoonful of chilled soured cream to each plate and then grate lime zest directly over each plate. Serve warm rather than hot.

COOKING IN STEAM
Classic Eastern steaming/
Western steaming

There are two types of steaming, one originating in the West and another from the East. The West's classic reason for wanting to steam is for higher nutrition, yet this is something rarely achieved. A third more radical way is to steam in a microwave and for most of us in the West this is the easiest to do – and it guarantees up to 85 per cent higher nutrition than boiling in water or steaming in metal.

The particular advantage of steaming is flavours don't exchange, because steam and vapour do not carry them. Steaming in bamboo containers developed in the East because you can steam over dirty water, even filthy water, yet none of its smell and taste transfers to the food. Cook garlic, custard and apple side by side in a bamboo steamer and they won't flavour one another unless they are touching. Any book or any recipe suggesting you salt or otherwise flavour steaming water is ludicrous. Food sitting directly above (rather than on a plate) will flavour the water, not the other way around.

However you steam, your food pieces should have equal density. This means a firmly textured piece of carrot should be half the size of something soft and moist, like broccoli. This is so they cook at the same rate and are ready at the same time. It is very irresponsible but commonly seen for steaming (or stir-fry) mixtures to be suggested, but with no guidance on the best size for individual vegetables. The result is a mix that's part overcooked and part still raw.

If the food to be steamed is entirely protected from the steam, then it might successfully be steamed in a colander – fish wrapped in greaseproof paper or in foil, perhaps.

Steamed puddings are protected from the steam and water vapour, but as they actually sit in the water, they are really boiled puddings. A lighter and incredibly much faster result can be achieved in the microwave cooker, also by far the best way to steam vegetables and fish.

Classic Eastern Steaming

Chinese and other food in Southeast Asia is cooked in a bamboo steamer. The food sits on a plate in the bamboo base, this is put into the steamer and a woven bamboo lid placed on top. As the bamboo steamer sits over boiling or simmering water, steam and water vapour travel up through the steamer's bottom slats and their heat cooks the food. It is vital to understand that excess water vapour or steam escape through the lid or *are absorbed by all parts of the bamboo steamer.* There is no condensation to fall back on to the food, which would dissolve out goodness and flavour and drip back into the water.

Western Steaming

Don't bother. Western steaming puts such food as a cauliflower directly onto a pierced colander or other punched container, puts this over simmering or boiling water and seals the container with a metal lid. The water vapour and steam rise to the food and cook it with their heat, but then have nowhere to go. They condense on the metal lid and fall onto the food. There they dissolve vitamins and flavour from the food and drip back whence they came, into the steaming water. That's where the nutrition and much of the flavour goes, into the steaming water, usually thrown away but which could be used as stock.

You might get a firmer texture but food steamed Western-style is little better nutritionally than food boiled in water. The folding-petal steamers made to fit into the bottom of a saucepan are no better, even if they are French.

Of course, if you are going to make a cauliflower cheese, steaming this way and then using the liquid to make your sauce guarantees all the flavour and nutrition you can expect. But (yes, here I go again) the flavour of cauliflower microwaved without added water and then added to a good sauce is very much better – bigger, more accurate and more gratifying. Better nutrition, too.

DYNAMIC PARTNERS – THE PRESSURE COOKER AND MICROWAVE

Everyone who wants healthier, more nutritious food that's also cooked quickly by a method that dramatically cuts energy costs should have a pressure cooker and a microwave. You will cook traditional, comforting food again, yep, just like grandma, yet do it in a third of the time.

This is fast food with not a stir-fry, deep-fry, chopstick, fish stick, soy-sauce dip or coriander leaf in sight. Or chilli, in any form. In fact, if the Mediterranean diet is the healthiest in the world, these two combine to cook it the fastest, healthiest way. The Mediterranean Microwave is the future.

COOKING BY MICROWAVE

Not to use a microwave is plain dumb, or eccentric. Probably both. There is more misplaced ignorance about microwaves than there is about pixies, fairies, gnomes and goblins. The microwave is the fastest, safest and cheapest way to cook the world's healthiest diet, the Mediterranean diet. To that you can add much of the fish and vegetable diets of India, Southeast Asia, China and Japan.

You can't argue with the science. The most nutritious vegetables by far are those cooked in a microwave without added water – the difference can be up to an 85 per cent gain in nutrition. And that's an official British Government figure. Frozen vegetables are often even better than those you have bought as 'fresh', because their goodness was locked in within hours of being picked. 'Fresh' vegetables in shops have been losing nutrition every hour they are in sunlight or at ambient temperature – and refrigeration only slows rather than stops this.

In this day and age, where healthier food produced faster and using less energy is the cry, the microwave should be everyone's best mate. And while it's producing that food faster and more cheaply it's also saving on washing up, virtually eliminates excess steam and moisture problems and so markedly reduces kitchen heat. The microwave has been in countless millions of kitchens for over forty years now. Ask a microwave doubter to show published, scientific evidence of a problem and . . . there isn't any, anywhere.

Food writer Clare Ferguson got it right when she said the microwave cooker is an obedient cooker, because it turns itself off when it should. This safety aspect, plus the fact it can be positioned on a kitchen bench and because foods cooked this way offer maximum nutrition all make the microwave a great and a safe friend of the elderly. If only someone would tell that to them or to those who care for them. And then knock it into the heads of everyone else. Yes, I do know St Delia once said she thought the microwave took the soul out of food – she was wrong; it must have been overcooked.

How microwaves work is simple. Imagine the steam if you were to jiggle against your partner two billion times a second. That's how fast microwaves make the molecules of food and drink jiggle. This friction causes tremendous heat, but this jiggling is not unique to the microwave. All food jiggles this way when it is heated and however it is heated; it's the natural state of hot substances. That heat cooks the food as it converts the internal liquid in food into steam, concentrating the nutrition and flavour as it goes because only water as steam has been lost, and this cannot take goodness or flavour with it. In fact many people find they need far less salt to enjoy microwaved vegetables, because the natural salts in them are so much tastier.

Microwaves work wherever there is water, oil, fat and sugar, and so the more of any you have present, the faster food will cook. It's simply not true that microwaves cook from the inside out. A microwave cooks so speedily because its waves penetrate and work as far as four centimetres (almost two inches) into the food and does that from all sides. They don't start on the outside and work in like an oven or grill; they are cooking deeper immediately rather than relying on radiant heat to penetrate from the outside.

Arranged properly, food gets microwaves from all sides. If the food were 4cm square cubes, then all of each piece would be cooking at the same time. However, because the centre of the piece is getting rays from all sides, it is likely to overheat or at least be hotter: reheat a scone for ten to fifteen seconds and the outside seems barely warm, yet the centre will be steaming hot. You soon learn.

All food should be rested when taken from any heat source, as all food is unevenly hot and it's important to let it even itself out. With microwaved food it is marginally more important as the differences between inside and outside temperature can be greater than with other cookery methods. In another fifteen or twenty seconds your scone will be evenly warm.

Microwave cooking should always be done on a microwave-safe trivet or on an upturned saucer or bowl, so microwaves can bounce off the floor of the cooker and up through the food. If you don't do this you risk overcooking the top while undercooking the bottom. If you buy one of those devices that stack two plates at a time for microwave cooking, use the upper level if you are cooking just for one.

Vegetables are top microwave performers, sliced or cut into pieces of even bulk, as you would for a stir-fry, and put onto a plate or a bowl: the flatter they lie the better, so it is best to put them on a flattish plate and to cover that with a bowl, rather than the other way around. An excellent compromise is to use a broad shallow bowl covered with a plate, and it's also an advantage to arrange food in a ring with a hole in the centre: food in the centre easily overcooks because it is receiving microwaves from every direction.

Vegetables, including frozen ones, should cook *without* additional water. If you add water this will leach goodness out of the vegetables, as happens with boiling and with bad steaming. Only bamboo steamers come close to microwave-level nutrition. The only vegetables to benefit from having a little water added are dense ones that will take a while to cook – celeriac, or a big bowl of potatoes: ideally this liquid will then be mashed back into the vegetable.

The fiddle-faddle of covering food to be microwaved with clingfilm quickly outweighs any speed benefits, so forget it. If you have to use it, forget any nonsense about piercing it, simply turn back a small portion so excess steam can escape. Much simpler is to microwave with plates as covers, and then you always have warm plates, too.

The principle of cooking food in its own steam applies to fish too, including fish flavoured and exotically wrapped in cartridge paper, banana leaf or vine leaves. Much more flavour and nutrition, much less fuss and not a lot different from the way one of my grandmothers would cook fish between two plates over boiling water: 'I didn't pay all this money for John Dory to flavour a pan of water,' she would say. Microwave John Dory or other fish between two plates with a dot of butter and no added water and you'll really taste the fish, far more than any other way.

In bowls or Pyrex measuring jugs, a microwave will cook sauces and custards for you without fuss, tears, burns or lumps. It will infuse and hydrate like anything, too. You'll rehydrate porcini or dried apricots much faster, effortlessly infuse saffron into oil or herbs, and spices into milk for a béchamel. Once you have toasted nuts in a microwave, or roasted black peppercorns or cumin and coriander seeds, you'll never do it another way; you'll find instructions on www.glynnchristian.com. No fat is needed, which would dilute the flavour, and the process toasts them all the way through because it uses the natural oils in the nuts or spices. Nothing is more disappointing than an almond that looks toasted but is soft inside (because only the outside has been coloured) and anyway tastes of oil. Do such things in a flat plate, arrange the spices or nuts in a circle and cook them in short bursts, mixing them up and rearranging each time you do.

Rice cooks superbly, porridge is done in minutes while you are in the shower, couscous or burghul take less. Cakes cook very well, but because they steam rather than bake they can overcook easily, becoming tough or dry; you soon learn how to get the best results. They also don't brown, which doesn't matter if it is an upside-down cake or a chocolate one. Your microwave will cook wonderful steamed puddings, not least because they usually contain everything possible to microwave faster – fat or oil, sugar and water. Three hours, two hours? No, as little as 10 minutes sometimes, 25 minutes tops. While your pudding is resting you make the sauce or a custard in the microwave too. No mess, no fuss and it's faster.

Internationally, power levels for microwaves are being standardised, but so far it has proven difficult to know what these standards are. Most people go for a powerful machine, because this means speed. New microwave cookers seem to hover around 1000W.

Most writers give very explicit instructions about temperatures and temperature changes, but don't do so for the microwave. Everything is usually attacked with maximum power. This universal blasting at full power leads to much disappointment and is why more than 90 per cent of microwaves sit idle until it's time to heat up milk or defrost meat for the dog.

For instance, when melting chocolate or butter you should use less power, as you would on a hob. Fish or chicken always come out deliciously moist if cooked on a medium power, simmered rather than boiled, just as you would with conventional cooking.

But whatever anyone thinks, the facts speak for themselves and cannot be denied. The microwave is faster, very energy-efficient and delivers food with higher nutrition: isn't that what every sane person wants?

COOKING WITH PRESSURE

Mention a pressure cooker and most people under forty won't know what you are talking about: but everyone over forty remembers the night dinner was on the ceiling instead of the table. For all their advantages, the old pressure cooker had a serious disadvantage. Sure, they could reduce cooking times by two-thirds, but they could also explode. Not any more, and so the faster you lead your life the more you need this icon from the past.

It is curiously gratifying to discover that today's improved state-of-the-art pressure cooker is so well suited to giving us back the comforting foods of the past: beans and barley in soups, invigorating stews and strident curries, rich meat sauces and deep stocks, and the voluptuous textures of pigs' trotters and lamb shanks. You can again play master or mistress of bountiful eating, actually be eating better while spending less on energy and ingredients – and taking less time about it. The renaissance is as much to do with modern pressure cookers being constructed differently and from different materials, as them now having fail-safe, sometimes triple fail-safe, safety systems. It was never the whole pressure cooker that exploded, but a failure of the pressure system that went wrong. Suddenly the pressure had somewhere to go, usually through an upward-pointing valve, and with such force food particles buried themselves in the ceiling paint. Such were the heights of childhood excitement before television.

The theory behind pressure-cooking is simple. The higher the air pressure, the higher cooking temperatures can go: the pressure created in a pressure cooker allows them usually to cook at 250C rather than 100C, hence the speed. The pressure also speeds up the transference of flavour. The perfect example is a curry of chicken thighs, which will be pressure-cooked in fifteen minutes. In that time the flavours of the spices have actually penetrated the flesh and the curry tastes as though cooked conventionally for hours. Even so, like all curries it will be better for hanging around a bit and being reheated. What I tend to do is to cook something like this in the morning, giving it the day to relax and fraternise: the brief cooking time means those who leave early and get home late can still eat properly and interestingly. While the meat is reheating, vegetables cook to super-nutrition in the microwave. You cook and serve gratifying, nutritious meals in the same time or less that might be spent fiddling with a combination of a takeaway and a guilty salad.

The flavour advantages of a pressure cooker can be spread further, by making stock in them. Instead of hours of steamy kitchen it's ten minutes for a vegetable stock, five minutes for a fish stock, and –twenty to thirty for a chicken or meat stock. It's just so easy and fast, and then you have something to add even more flavour to what comes next, that curry perhaps, or a soup. Soup makers will see the sense of pressure cooking a hambone, or doing the initial tenderising and plumping of barley and other grains, pulses and legumes. It's all done so much faster and without sacrificing a jot of flavour.

Pressure cooking puts wonderful soups, stews, curries, sauces and so much more back on the menu for people who love traditional food but who don't have as much time as they would like. You can have chicken stew or curry in under half an hour. Meanwhile, cook basmati rice in the microwave and while this steams and fluffs up, microwave a vegetable or two; both can go to the table in the same containers. Everything will be ready at the same time, there's little washing up, no kitchen full of steam, no rice pot to rinse, no vegetable saucepan to scour.

It would take longer to order takeaway. And you've lessened your carbon footprint.

Pressured to Convert

Many people won't buy a pressure cooker because they reckon they'll have to learn brand-new recipes. But you don't. You can still cook your favourites. Yet pressure-cooker manufacturers curiously don't support their cause and tell you how to convert your favourite recipe into a pressure-cooker recipe. There are just two steps:

1: Divide the recipe's standard cooking time by three: the answer is the pressure-cooking time. If it would take an hour on the hob, it will take twenty minutes in a pressure cooker.

2: Divide the pressure-cooking time by ten: for every ten minutes of pressure-cooking time there should be at least half a cup (4–5 fluid ounces) of liquid in the pressure cooker; if the recipe takes twenty minutes in a pressure cooker you will need a minimum one cup of liquid in the cooker.

That's all you need to know. If possible the liquid should be boiling hot when added, which means the cooker and its contents heat up faster. The simplest way to do this is first to pour the correct amount into a microwave-safe measuring jug and to heat this in the microwave.

TEMPER, TEMPER

The only things that should 'pop' in a kitchen are corn, bubble wrap and weasels. Yet how often are we told to 'sprinkle with cheese and pop under a grill until, etc., etc., etc.'. What's really happening here is the dish is bland, and 'popping' is the only way the writer can think of making something tasty out of it. What you do when a dish is cooked, or almost cooked, is as important as the way it was started. Of course there are times when the process is quite right, adding the savoury comfort of the cheese's flavours and umami taste as a final touch to a well-balanced tasty dish.

The ideal finishing process is called tempering and is a way of refreshing, of brightening up flavours and adding extra depths of savour or of texture to both complement and extend what is there already. Sometimes the tempering ingredients are simply scattered on, sometimes they are stirred in, and sometimes they are stirred in and then cooked for a few minutes. Almost always, tempering is done with ingredients already in the dish, and so the best tempering is one or more Solo Flavour Trail – see page XXX.

Tempering is a fact of life in many Asian and Oriental cuisines. Sri Lankan tempering mixtures begin with the beguiling sweetness of slow-cooked, well-browned onion rings, to which are added quantities of any herb that has also been used in the cooking: lemon grass, curry leaves and pandanus are fairly common. The objective is easily understood: the flavours with which the dish began are reintroduced in their original, fresh form, thus giving a greater spectrum of flavour to the final dish without introducing yet another.

Anyone who has ever thought deeply about their cookery must have questioned the sense of putting herbs and spices into any dish that will then cook for hours. Whatever goodness and flavour the herbs first contributed is largely lost by the time the dish is ready: the freshness and elegance certainly disappear. Yet we still do it because it is Gospel and it's what the recipe tells us to do. You do it and I do too, but now I temper as well, knowing the dish will then positively zing with recently released flavour. So, my red wine stew has a sprig of thyme and a little garlic and some orange zest stirred through not long before serving, a meaty sauce for pasta will have a splash of white or red wine and some oregano or parsley, which are added just long enough to lull away the sharper edges of their freshness and then taken out. Roasting juices from chicken stuffed with tarragon should be simmered with a quick addition of fresh tarragon and black pepper to revitalise what is otherwise merely lurking in the background. Flavours that lurk give little pleasure.

Black pepper is the ideal way to prove how much we are missing by only long–cooking our herbs and spices and to discover the potency of tempering. To any cooked or almost-cooked dish – whether it began with pepper or not – add freshly ground black pepper and then continue cooking for at least three minutes but absolutely no longer than five minutes. Voila! The fascinating flavour of hot black pepper will have been released yet still be vital, the volatile flavour oils will have been excited by heat into their full exuberance, their dramatic, multidimensional aromas will have become pungent yet perfumed, voluptuous yet aristocratic . . . and taste bloody good too! Adopting this simple technique with only black pepper would transform the food coming from most kitchens.

Garam masala is an Indian spice mixture designed specifically for tempering, a medley only of sweet and fragrant spices: sometimes the mixture is simple and sweet, sometimes there are fifteen or more ingredients, but don't look for chilli as chilli is rarely appropriate in a garam masala. When you add garam masala shortly before serving, the finer flavours and perfumes created perfectly balance the enervated flavours of long-cooked spices with the fresh tastes of the same – or broadly similar – spices.

Although I think tempering works best when it is refreshing flavours already there, you can mix and match. For instance, a European-style poached chicken flavoured only with herbs and vegetables could well be helped several steps closer to heaven by serving it tempered with the spices of garam masala, and perhaps some of those caramelised onion rings too.

In summer kitchens, tempering means you can cook simply but with better results guaranteed – not more flavours, but the same flavours experienced more intensely. It can be as simple as beginning with olive oil and finishing by chucking on some olives. Even a sprinkle of the same or a better olive oil, unaffected by heat, adds dimension. Flavour a fresh tomato sauce with ground cumin and temper it with roasted cumin seeds. Add fresh cherry tomatoes and some sprigs of flat-leaf parsley to a tomato sauce and then serve with the parsley hoicked out but with the barely exploded cherry tomatoes reminding you of what has gone before. If you are using a bought sauce, any bought sauce, simply read the (recognisable) ingredients to see what you might use as a tempering device.

If you temper too long, long enough for what you have added to taste cooked rather than fresh, you have wasted your time and money. Bad temper time, all round.

Adopting this simple technique would transform the food coming from most kitchens.

CHAPTER SIX

THE PONCING ABOUT FACTOR

THE PONCING ABOUT FACTOR

Recognising pointless ingredients, useless techniques and bad writing.

A very important step towards cooking without recipes is being able to spot the level of Poncing About Factor in other people's recipes – pointless ingredients, useless techniques or bad writing – and then knowing how you can do better.

The Poncing About Factor or PAF

This is what I call it when the men or women in white coats, professional chefs you probably call them, write recipes that demand a huge staff or cost a fortune to cook. Like browning something in a pan and then finishing it in an oven. Yes, it does give great results, but who puts on a domestic oven for just ten minutes to finish something for one or two people? It's specifying a litre of chicken stock to make a cottage pie when we all know Worcestershire sauce is quite as tasty and doesn't inter-mix species; or trimming roast potatoes to be the same size, or 'refreshing' vegetables, or expecting us to get our hands on ten varieties of tomato. None of these should be in a book aimed at domestic cooks and cookery. It's just Poncing About.

With more and more of the biggest-selling books being written by professional chefs (actually, most are written *for* them) who cook in large, professional kitchens, there is more and more Poncing About, with too many recipes written by chefs for the approbation of their peers rather than being suited to the home kitchen.

First, some reminders of what it is reasonable to expect from any recipe meant for the home cook:

- It will taste good
- Its title accurately reflects the ingredients
- It does not contain pointless ingredients
- Flavour Trails can be followed between the ingredients
- It does not require techniques more suited to a professional kitchen
- It does not include pointless preparation steps
- The portion outcome is adequate and practical
- It makes no false claims about authenticity
- It will look good
- Overall, it generously fulfils the promise it makes
- A published photograph shows what result you can reasonably expect

Using that list as a guide while reading cookery books, magazines and articles is a revelation. Here are the common Poncing About Factors to look for before cooking a recipe new to you.

PAF One: Poncing About with Recipe Names

It's reasonable to expect a recipe to be defined by its leading and strongest flavours. This is not always the case. Often a title has been changed to fit a line length or because someone thinks it 'sounds better'.

Example: I recently encountered this recipe title: Warm salad of wild rice, green beans and pecans. The reasonable expectation was of rather a lot of expensive wild rice with a few green beans and pecans to perk up the interest, look and flavour. Nice. The reality was that the major ingredient, by both bulk and flavour, was raw onion. It beats me how anyone considered good enough to write a book would contemplate serving so much corrosive raw onion with delicate and expensive wild rice. Thus the recipe title was comprehensively misleading about the recipe's actual ingredients, its expected taste and the balance of its ingredients. When I saw the made-up dish it was actually: Warm salad of raw onion, green beans, pecans and wild rice. How could a responsible food writer or cookery editor allow such deliberate dissembling? Why aren't recipe writers forced to follow the same rules as food labelling, where ingredients must be listed in order of quantity used? Not to do so is wilfully to lie and that's something worse than mere Poncing About.

PAF Two: Poncing About with Imprecise or Silly Ingredient Amounts

Example 1: With a quick glance at a recipe for a Thai-style sauce you'll quickly assess if your store cupboard is up to it. But what if you suddenly find this in an ingredient list: '17 garlic cloves'. Not 16 or 18 but 17. Honestly! Would you ruin the recipe if you only had 15? And how big is each clove supposed to be anyway? Like the tiny Thai ones, like elephant garlic – anything in between? This was published in November 2007 by a nationally known chef/restaurateur.

Example 2: In another famous chef's recipe published (actually republished) at the same time, bulb fennel was teamed with chocolate, very daring and potentially rather wondrous, exciting even. Except, the recipe asked for one fennel bulb and then for another half-bulb. On any market stall fennel bulbs vary from the size of a baby's fist to the size of a baby's head during the season; even in supermarkets they do. When a combination is as edgy as fennel and chocolate, and which could thus be horrid, I expect much better guidance than this. Why not a weight of fennel, or a specific number of slices? Had it ever been cooked before it was published?

PAF Three: Poncing About with Totally Useless Ingredients

Sometimes, ingredients are specified only because they tick certain fashionable boxes. So, this Poncing About Factor is a sign of recipe writing in a hurry, or of someone with no fresh ideas. There are two pointers to this. One is the balance of the flavour, the intensity of each ingredient compared to the overall bulk of the recipe. The other is the amount of time it will cook; for instance, the longer a herb or spice cooks the less flavour it will contribute to the finished product.

Example 1: Herbs and spices are the ingredients most ponced about with. A pinch of cinnamon in a Christmas pudding mix that will boil for four hours is less than useless. Even a half-teaspoon is likely to disappear in a pudding for six people.

Example 2: Another very common PAF is the use of sugar with tomatoes. Nothing wrong with that, of course, but how can a pinch or a teaspoon of sugar help a sauce for four or six people? You see it often, but the pinch is there because the author doesn't dare leave it out, in case another writer mocks them. I mock them for putting it in!

Example 3: Some of the worst misuses of an ingredient come at Christmas time, when thousands of people buy a black truffle for the first time. Forget every recipe that tells you to add truffle and then to cook, or to strew truffle and then serve. You will get little or no flavour. For the magic of black truffle is to taste of little itself but somehow to make other ingredients taste of what you thought the truffle might, and this really works only if the truffle is still raw. Like other heights of human pleasure, you need to give it time. When truffles were much more common, a truffled turkey meant a turkey stuffed with several pounds' weight of uncooked truffle, and then buried in the garden, back in their natural habitat, for a week or so, wrapped in sacking. Then you got a truffled turkey. One ready-cooked black truffle sliced and put beneath the skin of a turkey or even a chicken does nothing but devour budget. I know some sneer at black-truffle oil as the ketchup of the middle classes, and that much of it is totally artificially flavoured, but the flavour is accurate and you get rather more of it for considerably less outlay. Works for me.

White truffles are very different – they are naturally highly fragrant, should never be cooked and only be sliced thinly over food just before it is eaten.

Example 4: It's onions again, I know, but I've just found a recipe for onion soup suggesting you use five strong white and a couple of sweeter red ones. That's fair enough, at least you are told properly to cook them slowly and for a very long time so they become beguilingly sweet. But it also specifies two banana shallots (something suddenly very fashionable, darling). Two? What if you have or can grow only very little ones? Or very big ones? It's a thoughtless specification, not just because of that but because even two really big banana shallots could make no discernible difference to so many stronger onions.

PAF Four: Poncing About with Historical Accuracy

The very greatest sin of cookery writing is to publish your own version of a classic recipe – but not say so. This is how great dishes become bland or chilli-flamed yet still claim authenticity, and how the real thing gets forgotten or sent back to the kitchen.

Example 1: I'm sure Gordon Ramsay, who rethinks many classic ideas superbly creatively, must squirm with embarrassment at letting one of his books publish a 'Classic Bouillabaisse' recipe, which has as little classic about it as Wuthering Heights performed as an East End musical by Pearly Kings and Queens of mixed Ugandan and Balkan ancestry. The special bridging flavours of bouillabaisse are given by fennel and saffron and by the technique of letting the mixed fish first sit at ambient temperature with olive oil, saffron, fennel, herbs, orange zest and a little onion. This way the fish is well flavoured before it goes into water and heated only until the lot boils up, when the heat should be discontinued. Hence the name – *bouill* (boil) and *abaisse* (fall). There's precious little chance for flavour to develop if the fish have not been marinating.

In Gordon's recipe for rather a large amount of bouillabaisse, three large onions were included (very British, that), only a pointless single pinch of saffron was suggested and there was no fennel at all. A powerful clue to the recipe not working was the colour illustration, which showed heaps more saffron threads than a pinch. Then, rather than serving bouillabaisse the classic way, with the soup poured over slices of baguette in one plate and the fish served separately, both are served in the same plate – with garlic mayonnaise and croutons. The shame here is that the Ramsay name will convince people this really is the classic way, and so when the real thing is served a customer will reject it or criticise it unjustly. If he had simply called it 'Gordon's Bouillabaisse' there would still have been a severe Poncing About Factor, but to call it classic was wicked. Get it *@?!ing right, Gordon!

Example 2: The same applies when you see a foreign term used. Gremolata is a very useful combination of finely chopped lemon zest, raw garlic and parsley, the proper accompaniment to osso bucco, not made from plate-sized slabs of dark shin meat but with small, delicate slices through veal shank; the clue is the correct use of white rather than red wine. Yet November 2007 (a bad month for bad recipe writing) saw a recipe printed incorporating gremolata of only lemon zest and parsley. This is confusing to the newcomer and infuriating to the majority who know what it should be; if this lemon/parsley combination is a little-known but still traditional version, that should be said and we'd all then be grateful to learn something new. Bet it's not.

Example 3: Until a BBC TV series about Mediterranean food in the late 1980s, taramasalata was a whizzed-up dip based on fish roe and olive oil, which never, or very rarely, included onion. Millions of deliciously sweet, gentle portions were eaten in Greek/Cypriot restaurants throughout the UK with fresh pitta. But once the episode had been aired, having found perhaps the only family in Greece that used onion, previously acceptable taramasalata was sent back to authentic kitchens because it 'wasn't right'. No wonder it has almost disappeared in the UK.

More Examples: In a recent prize-winning book, mistake after mistake is made with traditional ingredients and techniques while purporting to explore flavours and tastes. Fish is salted for only an hour, but then held under running water for five minutes, soaked for ten minutes and then under running water for another five. It can only be flabby and tasteless. The traditional point of salting fish is to make it firmer because it will contain less moisture, and tastier because salt has penetrated the flesh. If it is soaked and rinsed after only an hour in salt it will be rehydrated and flavour will be dissolved away; pointless Poncing About. The young author also says pickled salmon or gravadlax salted for more than an hour goes rock hard. That's not the experience of millions of Scandinavians over countless centuries who cure it for several days; but then they know the correct proportions of sugar to salt and certainly never exposed the cured salmon to running water as he does. And then he rolls slices thin between clingfilm, when gravadlax is never served sliced thinly. Even if what he makes is tasty, it's definitely not gravadlax.

He also makes North Africa's salted lemons by boiling them in brine: this is actually a brilliant advance in thinking and works very well, but it is not the classic Moroccan way to pickle lemons, and because this difference wasn't acknowledged it is confusing. A tea-smoking mixture was packed with ingredients whose flavours could not possibly transfer to the food being smoked. And so on . . .

As well as the author being woefully underinformed about the world in which he is working, none of the salubrious names who recommend the book, nor the judges of his award, appear to know the very basics of traditional or authentic cookery . . . scary.

PAF Five: Poncing About Like Professionals

Remember you are a domestic cook, cooking in a domestic kitchen. The techniques of restaurants, where each chef is cooking only a few elements of a dish or for one or two guests at a time no matter how busy they are, have nothing to do with entertaining at home, feeding kids the moment they deign to come home, or making you feel good.

Example 1: Most chef-auteurs live in a world completely removed from domestic reality; they cook in kitchens where ovens are roaring hot all the time. It's certainly true a blast in an evenly hot oven cooks such food as fish and meat superbly. But on the domestic scene, how many can justify heating up an oven space and then using it for just ten minutes? Yet many cookery editors are in such thrall to the 'celebrity' status of their authors they don't or won't dare ask the questions they should. We get a combination of Poncing About and pussy-footing and thus a great deal of silliness from recipes cobbled together in a chef's spare time. Unless you are cooking for a crowd, avoid recipes where something is put into the oven for just ten or so minutes. That's what professionals do in professional kitchens. Otherwise it is Poncing About, big time.

Example 2: It's extraordinary in these nutrition-aware days still to see vegetables being 'refreshed' when the opposite is the outcome. In professional kitchens vegetables that have been boiled in water so they lose most of their goodness and flavour are then plunged into cold water. This certainly stops overcooking and keeps their colour – but the two lots of water guarantee most nutrition and much of the flavour has gone. And they still have to be reheated prior to serving – sometimes being put back into yet more boiling water. That's a technique only for busy professional kitchens, so the vegetables they serve are quickly reheated rather than carefully cooked to order. It's for their convenience, not because it in any way enhances your pleasure.

Example 3: I recently saw a magazine recipe where courgettes were sliced finely, boiled, refreshed, patted dry and then fried. A ludicrous waste of time and busybody cooking just for the sake of it. The courgettes could easily have been fried from the start with a little more care or, best of all, microwaved and then fried, when they would be just as crisp and bright green. All that patting dry and refreshing is old-fashioned humbug, developed before anyone knew much about nutrition and looks were everything. Putting such outdated and nutritionally bare techniques into recipes meant for home cookery is either misdirected showing off or fear of progress. Poncy, either way.

Example 4: A very favourite TV chef of us all suggests you cut potatoes for roasting in half lengthwise and then trim them so each half is exactly the same shape and size. That's exactly what home cooking doesn't want. Another shows you how to smoke over wood chips in a biscuit tin with a pierced lid. The result? A house filled with smoke and grossly oversmoked food, bitter and unbalanced in flavour.

PAF Six: Poncing About with Old-fashioned, Outdated Habits

Bad recipe writing is packed with other ideas quite as bad or pointless as refreshing vegetables.

Examples

- There's no need to add oil to cooking pasta; pasta won't stick if you cook it in enough water – ideally at least half a litre per serving.
- Sugar should not be mixed directly with fresh yeast, only with dried yeast.
- Salt should never be mixed with yeast but mixed into the flour for baking, otherwise salt inhibits the yeast's growth.
- Flavouring steaming water can't possibly flavour the food being cooked in the steamer above.
- Marinating something in a refrigerator for less than an hour is pointless, as the refrigerator inhibits and slows the process by a factor of four: so an hour in a refrigerator is the equivalent of only fifteen minutes at ambient temperature. Does marinating for fifteen minutes really make a difference? Would food in marinating oils and acids really go off if left to marinate for one hour at ambient temperature? Of course not.

MENUS TO THE MAX

A sad but comforting truth . . . if the pudding is delicious, that's what people most remember.

If variety is the key to good, balanced nutrition it's also the word to remember when planning a menu. Whatever you serve in the first course should never be seen or tasted in the second course – or the third. Simple really. No matter how great that clever dessert of pineapple and mint, you simply can't serve it if there was pineapple with the pork or mint with the first-course prawns.

Even if the mint in the first course was only a garnish, it should never appear again. Remember how easily the palate gets tired of something? This used to be drilled into chefs from day one of their training, but you see it ignored on television and it's sometimes impossible to avoid in restaurant menus. I remember when a waiter would have pointed out that a first and a main course someone ordered both had wild mushrooms or fried parsley or a lemon-flavoured sauce. Not now. They universally murmur, 'Good choice, Sir,' while wondering what will be happening on *Big Brother* when they get home.

Colour can be a repeated theme, say for a Valentine supper or wedding anniversary or girls' night in. But if you serve, say, a pink menu, refresh the eye by using a different-coloured plate or glass for each course and by changing the contrast of other ingredients. So, pink and green for the first, pink and white for the main, pink and other pinks with a touch of white for the dessert.

Then there is shape. I once saw a very well-known TV chef help a woman do a very chichi dinner party at home, where every course was a round tower, each of them very fiddly to make. Surely one such phallic triumph would have been enough? The shape should be different for each course – as should textures. It's horrid to get a meal that is all moussey and squishy, no matter how good it tastes. This happened to me in Sydney at a Japanese chef's famous restaurant where there was no choice, only a procession of small dishes, each more intricate than the last. But the portions were small and so there was never anything really to get the teeth or the taste buds working. After three hours we got up having overeaten but feeling monu-mentally unsatisfied – we went to the nearest store, bought an apple each and thoroughly enjoyed its mouth-filling crispness, and having a palate packed with flavour rather than teased with flavours, exquisite though they might have been. It had been astonishing food, but food planned in the mind to astonish and not as a menu to gratify. More emphasis on the palate rather than on the plate, please.

Thus, use every means possible to provide a well-contrasted menu, and this means not repeating a method of cookery, not serving three deep-fried or roasted or boiled courses. That might seem very obvious but it wasn't until after I made my TV series in Thailand that I adopted this consciously. In Thailand the typical full menu of seven dishes is like this because each of them is cooked a different way; sizzled on grills, steamed, poached, stewed, etc. This is because using different techniques is the best way to operate a small kitchen with limited facilities. What a good cook will do at home is plan a menu so no two dishes are cooked the same way unless the facility needed can do it without usurping the time or space needed for another. Yes, you can sometimes bake a pudding in an oven when you are also roasting and sometimes also bake something after the roast is out and while you are eating. But what about space in the oven for keeping food warm, or heating plates; even if you have the space, opening and closing the door will mess up your cooking times. A double oven avoids this problem, of course.

Most meals go wrong with the vegetables. Juggling the different saucepans on the hob at the same time while trying to make a sauce or a gravy is the last thing a cook needs; that's why most of my veg are always made in advance and suited to being kept warm (like mashed potatoes or braised fennel), or else are cooked in the microwave, not only then having maximum flavour and nutrition but, incidentally, adding no more heat or steam to the kitchen. They can often be served in the same dish, too.

A sad but comforting truth is that however good or bad your first courses, if the pudding is delicious, that's what people most remember. So it's no bad scheme to start planning a menu with the pudding. Get clear what it is going to taste like and whether or not it needs much last-minute attention. The more attention it needs, the less the previous courses should demand.

I used to think it a bit wussy, but now I always write down a menu with the proposed garnishes. It helps me see where there are clashes of flavour, colour or oven space. It's hard to know who expects or appreciates such rules these days and all too easy to dismiss them as not being important any more. But if you *do* know you are at a great advantage. Not only will you be above criticism, you are in that most gratifying position of knowing when others are wrong. Delicious.

The simplest things in life can be triumphant if you bother to understand how they work. Very little is casually perfect. So even the way you put food on to a plate affects the way it's appreciated. This doesn't matter if you are plonking bowls in the middle of the table and expecting friends or family to help themselves. But if you are plating the meal (twenty years ago this was unthinkable and spoken of as doing dogs' dinners) make it look special by:

- Serving each plate with the main part of the meal closest to the diner, i.e. the meat or the fish or whatever.
- Serving sauce, gravy, etc. under or around food rather than all over it.
- Looking for an opportunity to get some height into one or more of the ingredients, even if not centrally – this is especially important with desserts.
- Not serving your pudding course in bowls unless this really is all you have; flat plates always look better, are easier to eat from and stop everyone dolloping custard all over everything because there is no surrounding space on which to serve it. It's one of the most hateful sights I can imagine at a table.

To stop guests ruining your perfectly plated desserts, you should serve the custard or any other sauce yourself, putting it onto the plate first ideally. And look for height. If you were serving poached saffron pears with some iced rose-water rice pudding, you would pile the rice pudding as high as you could in the middle of the plate, lean the pears against that and then add extra height with your garnish of, what? Sliced pistachio nut, a small scoop of ice cream? Putting each of these all beside one another on the plate make them look like yet another graveyard of memorials to previous meals, which is what fancy restaurants tend more and more to do.

And the final point on serving your wonderfully composed Flavour Trail menus. Don't do it on white plates, unless they are huge. White drains the colour from most food, just as white gold drains the colour from rubies, emeralds, sapphires, opals and pearls. Yes, it does! Huge white plates can work because they isolate food from their surroundings. But you are generally better with a plate with a strong colour (black is actually best of all) or those with a white centre and a strong border. Dark colour on plates and plates with a strong border both frame the food well.

The worst choice is plates with overall patterns, works of art though they are claimed to be. When filled with food the rims make a sort of frame, I suppose, but once you have tucked in and slowly expose the rest of the pattern the plate looks nastier and messier than could ever have been imagined.

The setting is important too. Turn off the bright top light and use sidelights or candles or both. *Don't* use scented candles or put scented flowers on the table. Don't come to table reeking of scent or deodorant, and sit yourself as far as possible from anyone who does. Don't put the spoon and fork for dessert above the plate – this is done only by harassed caterers in town halls or in palaces; you should bring out that cutlery just before serving dessert.

But most of all – never apologise until you are accused. No one will know what the food *should* have tasted like, that you have left out an ingredient, that it is too hot or too cold. So why tell them? If there is someone who both knows and points out your errors and omissions you must graciously agree, perhaps murmuring, 'Oh, but this is the version we found when we were on the Karakoram.' Or: 'I know, but Her Highness the Rajmata likes it best this way and I thought you might be interested.'

TAKING AN AUTHOR
TO BED

. . . the greatest compliment.

Even the staunchest bloke can be heard saying he reads cookery books in bed. Indeed, I think the greatest compliment to this book or to my REAL FLAVOURS is for someone to have them beside the bed rather more than in the kitchen. Women of all ages take cookery books to bed, too. So cookery and food books are clearly a great source of pleasure to other parts of the body than the palate. But wherever there is personal pleasure there can be personal pain, too. I hope the following will help you avoid the pain.

My current favourite recipes are not chosen from each writer's complete works but from books I own or have borrowed.

Harriott, Ainsley

What is he like? Well, like no-one else on the planet and that's a fact. I remember watching his first BBC Pebble Mill appearance and there was at first complete silence from the audience. Was he a cook or a comedian? Who had ever seen a very tall, black, joke-telling, laughing, dancing TV cook before? Then they caught on.

This was comedy and culinary talent combined and he's been just as loud, showy and in-your-face ever since. And what you get on screen is a fraction of what you get in real life; I'd be arrested if I told you just one of the jokes he's told me!

But there's more than racket to Ainsley, and that's very clear from his books. There's no way such an extreme personality would have survived if it wasn't entirely spontaneous and if his food wasn't acceptable. It is; because he's not from a professional food background Ainsley's books and his recipes have a very reliable focus on the domestic kitchen, while always adding twists and turns based on good flavour and taste which get thousands rushing for the kitchen, including me.

Sexy read? Very vanilla compared to his TV persona
Sexy food? Guaranteed satisfaction from something different, without any need to purchase special gear
Take home to bed? Yep, knowing whatever takes your fancy is achievable
My current three favourites: Roquefort and Walnut Souffles: Mustard and Salmon Burgers: Orange-flower, Yoghurt and Pistachio Pudding (Ainsley Harriot's All New Meals in Minutes: BBC Books)

Lawson, Nigella

I won't hear a word said against Nigella's books. Here's a woman with intellect, a terrific vocabulary and a magical way of enveloping you in the enjoyment of what she enjoys. I did resist her appeal at first but how can you dislike a woman who enjoys food so disarmingly and who tells you how to cook ham in Coca Cola? No girlie shuddering of the insecure or organically-correct food writer: if it tastes good, she tells you about it.

Yet I am not blind or unthinking. There are moments I am put off by the gratuitous greediness Nigella espoused for her TV series Express. Then there's that Christmas debacle. Everyone else in the world knew soaking a turkey in a barrel of cold water would give results like a water-retaining, factory-raised animal and that none of the added flavourings would make an iota of difference unless they and the water had all been heated together. Anyway, who else has space for a bucket the size of a space shuttle at Christmas time? Very silly. And so was not telling us to rest it well before carving. Yet I specially noted the guests she invited for Christmas looked like real friends whom she genuinely wanted to give a good time, which they got in, well, in buckets. And then she crept back to the fridge in the middle of the night to entertain herself. Which harassed host or hostess can't relate to that . . . and if some of her recipes don't work, then I say it must have been the oven or the ingredients which did you wrong.

Sexy read? There's a moment on every page, unless you are dead

Sexy food? Yes, unless you are dead

Take home to bed? Do whatever you must to own a copy of every one, slide between the sheets and be happy ever after

My current three favourites: Party Popcorn: Scallops with Chorizo: Ginger Passionfruit Trifle (Nigella Express: Chatto & Windus)

Martin, James

Who's a busy boy? James's commanding, sculpted profile but down-home accent have jet-propelled him deep into the public consciousness, until there hardly seems an event or television happening without a word from James, like a culinary Titchmarsh. He does it all well but sometimes awkwardly, which I think is actually modesty. But it's not always good to be modest and unassuming, for surely only such malleability persuaded him to make a TV series on puddings and desserts called Sweet Baby James, and then to present it to some unseen no-body off camera. Grisly.

His huge output of books is interesting. He does ponce about with classic names and procedures (traditional Scottish Bridies with olive oil and balsamic vinegar?) without always saying so and his was the recipe with the chocolate-fennel problem. Now he's the face of BBC cookery on Saturday mornings expect many more books from him. *The Great British Village Show Cookbook* is excellent and includes many recipes from winners of the eponymous TV series, great tips and useful addresses.

Sexy read? Ideal for gerontophiles – there are an awful lot of Gran and auntie stories . . .

Sexy food? Choose the time and place carefully to ensure satisfaction

Take home to bed? A clean-cut, middle-of-the-road partner, but perhaps more handsomely rewarding as a bit on the side

My current three favourites: Tomatoes in Tea: Seared Tuna with Grape and Dandelion Salad: Chocolate Stout cake (James Martin's Great British Village Show Cookbook: Dorling Kindersley)

Oliver, Jamie

Jamie would be a great mate to have living close, except, I mightn't be good-looking enough to borrow a cup of flour. It always seemed so incongruous to be cooking in a shonky district of lesser London but to have only friends who look like a modelling agency's Christmas party. Doesn't he have any ugly friends? Now he's enthusing over the produce of the walled garden of his Essex mansion he's moved into an even less believeable world. I mean, we can all grow or buy 10 types of tomato, can't we? Be really nice to see you cooking in a street market, Jamie mate. Or a supermarket.

Still, you can't beat his enthusiasm and he gets great credit up and down the country for giving people the confidence to plonk a dish or bowl of something in the middle of a table, for getting families and friends back around tables. But some of his recipes are juvenile and over-flavoured with too many ingredients, he does over use lemon juice, and smoking in a biscuit tin is just plain silly. Yet these are increasingly minor blips. His last two books,

Cook with Jamie and *At Home with Jamie* are huge, generously packed with advice telling you what things should look like when you've done what he's told you to do. Invaluable technique teachings, and huge amounts of ingredient information are part of his natural instinct to share and to make others feel good through food. There's more proof in the Fifteen restaurants he set up to give the less-fortunate opportunities to cook professionally.

Sexy read? Lots of patter and cheekiness, if that turns you on. Latterly first-class technique teaching adds maturity to sometimes wayward ideas

Sexy Food? Plenty of come-on, but not always a guaranteed pop-shot

Take home to bed? To have and to hold, but you must be patient and both expect and forgive the over-excitements of youth

My current three favourites: Pear and Apple Salad with Chicory and Blue Cheese Creamy Dressing: Pizza Fritta (Jamie at Home; Penguin Michael Joseph): Slow Roasted Pork Belly with Braised Fennel (Cook with Jamie: Penguin Michael Joseph)

Patten, Marguerite OBE.

There is nothing like a dame and it's a national disgrace Marguerite Patten is still nothing like a Dame. Now over ninety, Marguerite Patten really was Britain's first television cook – before the Second World War - and filled the Royal Albert Hall with cookery demonstrations before most people in today's Britain were even born. It was she who worked tirelessly throughout the war to give people recipes, the sort of recipes which made Britain healthier than ever before or since, in spite of vicious rationing.

I sigh when I pick up one of Marguerite's books, and any tension between my shoulders swirls away; it's like being home again after a long journey. And you are safely at home here, with recipes tested or based on more than six decades of hands-on experience. There's comfort, reliability, good sense and no nonsense. It's always straightforward food that's also very up to date where that's relevant and good to eat too, all from hands which have cooked everything often enough to have absolute confidence what she prints is fit for purpose. When Marguerite Patten told 21st century Britain to cook their Christmas pudding in the microwave, because it was just as good, so much faster and keeps steam out of the kitchen, Britain took note. As it has been doing for most of a century.

Sexy read? Very satisfying, without the risk of undue excitement
Sexy food? Satisfaction guaranteed in the safe hands of an older woman
Take home to bed? Neither kitchen nor bedroom of any real lady or gentleman is complete without one or two, to put culinary matters properly to bed
My current three favourites: Eccles Cakes: Chicken and Leek Pie: (Classic British Dishes: Bloomsbury). Microwave Christmas Pudding: (www.microwaveassociation.org.uk and www.glynnchristian.com)

Ramsay, Gordon

Bless him! He's so butch and dirty-mouthed on television but I bet he's privately one of the best, most caring and careful teachers imaginable. He'd have to be to serve such prize-winning dishes in his multi-starred restaurants so consistently. For the sake of a reported £60—70 million fortune he's allowed himself to be portrayed as a monster for the sake of ratings and book sales. It's a life I suppose, and I might have done the same, except when I was on BBC-TV I was twice threatened with being fired if I once mentioned there was a book of what I was doing. How times change.

The care Gordon expects from others hasn't always been given to his books. In *Kitchen Heaven* you'll read Desiree potatoes are waxy when they are starchy. Pizza on a puff pastry base suggests using 'that nice black ham pata negra'. But pata negra means black feet not black ham. It indicates a particular breed of pig, which makes a very superior type of ham, but which is not black. There's much more like this, including the non-classic Bouillabaisse.

Yet I'd now forgive Gordon anything. His new book, Gordon Ramsay *** Chef is the most aristocratic, the most elegant, generous and, there is no other word, sensuous thing I've taken to bed since, well, that's my business. It's huge and glossy and demonstrates the haute cuisine with which he made and keeps his reputation has nothing to do with grubby reality shows. It all seems achievable by anyone with care and an equivalent love of ingredients which contribute more to a plate than novelty and decoration. It's truly iconic for domestic cooks and professional chefs.

Sexy read? Older recipes sometimes suffer from Poncing About Factors: his latest book is the sexiest possible result for 40 quid.

Sexy food? Choose carefully and you won't care if you have to sleep alone.

Take home to bed? Flirt with others in the bookshop but go home with: Gordon Ramsay *** Chef

My current three favourites: anything from Gordon Ramsay *** Chef. Honest!

Rhodes, Gary

As his extraordinary hair spikes have become shorter, I think Gary's food, books and restaurants have got better. Gary has kept to the straight sometimes confining path of specialising in British ingredients and recipes, to the advantage of us all. To keep up interest over the years it has thus been too easy for him to veer towards PAFs, the professional chef intruding into what we really want at home. Twenty years ago Gary did his first-ever cookery demonstration in my Kitchenclass TV theatre of cookery, and even then he adamantly, sometimes ferociously, insisted we recognised the flavourful results of everything he did: 'I'm adding flavour onto flavour onto flavour!' And he was, and generously revealing how we could do it too.

It was Gary who suggested roast potatoes be trimmed to the same size. Yet the tone of his books makes me think he really does write them, for there is an intimate warmth and hospitable interest in you doing quite as well as he is able, and an excitement that's discreet and thus entirely convincing. His latest book The Cookery Year is totally inspirational with many wondrous and inventive Flavour Trails.

Sexy read? Not the heat of a Latin lover, but if you relax and let him work his restrained magic. . .

Sexy food? Absolutely, and never quite as weird as his past hair suggested

Take home to bed? Prepare to be surprised and stimulated where you least expect it

My current three favourites: Steamed oysters with rhubarb and oyster cream: Beer braised pheasants with leeks, potato and prunes: Clementine dumplings with passion-fruit syrup (The Cookery Year: BBC Books)

Slater, Nigel

Nigel Slater once said his favourite thing was the light from a refrigerator door in a dark kitchen. What a guy. No poncing about confusing professional and domestic techniques in his books but determined, independent and able to say something useful in a few pithy words. Not everyone has a kitchen garden or his apparently easy access to markets and great shops but this doesn't matter when there are just so many good ideas on every page of his books.

All his books are brave and direct, from *Real Fast Food* and *Real Fast Puddings* via *Appetite* and *Toast* to *The Kitchen Diaries*, in which he also fearlessly records his failures: '*What was I thinking?*'

Now he's given us the insightful, spiky and hilarious paragraphs of *Eating for England*. Nigel's books have given hundreds of thousands of cooks the confidence to serve something simple. That's a real contribution.

Sexy read? If you speak his direct sort of talk, it's hot
Sexy food? Irresistible, and you'll want to do it again
Take home to bed? Absolutely, even if it means becoming bi-culinary and sharing the duvet with Nigella or Delia
My current three favourites: Bramley Apple Shortcake (with lightly caramellised apples): Roast Pork sandwiches: A Tomato Curry (The Kitchen Diaries: Harper Collins)

Smith, Delia

I adore Delia, but am starting to wonder what happens when you criticise a living saint; I guess I'll soon find out. When I first appeared on BBC-TV Breakfast Time Delia, who at the time had almost no competition on television, took the trouble to cross a very crowded Great Room at Grosvenor House Hotel to tell me she liked what I was doing. Then and there I decided she was the woman I'd most like to have living next door. I've never changed my mind.

Delia's recipes work and she does give very good detailed instructions to help you get things right. Yet often there's not a basic recipe in her *How to Cook* series but only something fancy and so you still don't know how to do it yourself. Many instructions seem to be stream of consciousness, perhaps even taken down from TV performances. Sentence after sentence imperiously starts with Now, or Then or Next and then Now, again and again; exhausting.

Deep testing by a dedicated team is the promise and it's delivered with very few challenges to received knowledge. Except for reserving and then using again some of the water in which dried beans have been rehydrated, when this is where you find most of the chemicals which cause farting. Perhaps saints don't?

Sexy reading? Saintly and thus busy but very, very cool

Sexy food? Disguised as missionary position but actually Karma Sutric

Take home to bed? Guaranteed answers to most culinary prayers

My current three favourites: Luxury Smoked Fish Pie: Marmalade Soufflés: Summer-Fruit Brulee (Delia's How to Cook: BBC Books)

Stein, Rick

Before Rick made his first television series he asked me if there was any advice I could give. 'Make the food the star, not yourself', I told him, still the best advice for cooking on TV. Yet when you are genuinely as hospitable, think as deeply, and care as much about getting something good into other people's mouths there's no doubt a persona like Rick's just had to become as important as the food he shows us. You can't dissemble for long on television without being uncovered and Rick has always been great at making us think as well as cook.

Rick's initial focus on fish moved on to hunting down specialist growers and makers each of whom he generously allowed to star, and who were then more than happy to pass on their secrets to him – and to us. Then he sailed the canals of France before finding more entertaining characters and some great recipes in his round-the-Med series, which comes with a gorgeous book that shares more of his thoughts.

Sexy read? Don't you want to know what to do with rascasse, or where to find a pullet's egg or molasses-cured ham?

Sexy food? It's difficult not to fall completely for the simply obtained textures and flavours he hooks

Take home to bed? Whether you fancy hot and spicy, saucy, fashionable or traditional, Rick will always satisfy

My current three favourites: Pastitsio (beef and macaroni pie with cinnamon), Almond cake with dairy-free almond ice cream (Mediterranean Escapes: BBC Books): Magret de canard with red wine, prunes and chocolate (French Odyssey: BBC Books)

Worrall Thompson, Anthony

With the power of several hours of television each week for much of the year behind him, Anthony can guarantee big sales of any books he puts his name to – and others do write them. But at least there is no attempt to disguise this with clever-dick writing or endless references to childhood memories. Like the writing, his food is approachable, with plenty of it suited to weekday family dinners.

Anthony first came to attention with his Ménage a Trois restaurant in a Beauchamp Place basement, which served only starter portions and was a great favourite of Diana, Princess of Wales. He gave Bob Holness, Doug Cameron and me from LBC's AM programme a fantastic menu. But each complicated dish had as many as 15 ingredients and the gloss went when one of the wives looked down resignedly and said: Think of the fingers! AWT has relentlessly moved on, keeping up if not helping create culinary fashion and with a bigger and bigger organisation behind him. His website is said to be one of the biggest earners in the UK.

Sexy read? He's honest about not doing most writing, and it shows in its sparse, unromanticised style; that's not a bad thing

Sexy food? Not when the family's at table, but plenty else to excite palates

Take home to bed? There's no real need for take-away when so much of his recipes and advice are available on websites or when he's on telly

My current three favourites: Artichoke 'Sin' with Tortilla Chips: Honeyed duck confit with mash and crisp seaweed; Apple and marscapone rice pudding (Real Family Food: Dorling Kindersley)

For more guaranteed inspiration old and new, look for anything by: Lindsey Bareham, Antonio Carluccio, Elizabeth David, Jane Grigson, Fergus Henderson, Mark Hix, Simon Hopkinson, Madhur Jaffrey, Elizabeth Luard, Claudia Roden, Hugh Fearnley-Whittingstall. Plus any book from *Good Housekeeping* or Leith's and both *The Curious Cook* and *On Food & Cooking* by US author Harold McGee.

. . . AND THERE'S MORE

I felt it important not to overload you at first. There's more than enough to set you thinking and cooking and blazing Flavour Trails in this small book.

When you do want to know more, there's much more on my website: *www.glynnchristian.com*

It's free of charge, and as well as many more Flavour Trail recipes and countless Recommended Detours, there are also guides to:

- Getting the Balance Right – putting variety into your diet.
- Ingredient Substitutions – why eat an unnatural product?
- Organic Ingredients – taste is not related to the way something grows.
- Cooking for Vegetarians – a guaranteed route to ill-health?
- Is it Good for Me? – no food is either good or bad for you.
- Allergies and Intolerances – don't believe all food scares.
- Farmers' Markets – three generations with no continuous heritage.
- The Piano in Your Kitchen – tastes and flavours for store cupboards.
- Making Your Own Ingredients – oils, vinegars, salts.
- Buying the Small Stuff – simple tools for kitchen success.

ENJOY EATING MY WORDS . . .

INDEX

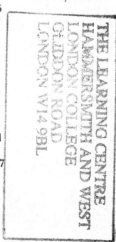